ONE NATION, UNDER DRONES

ONE NATION, UNDER DRONES

Legality, Morality, and Utility of
Unmanned Combat Systems

CAPT John E. Jackson, USN (Ret.)

Naval Institute Press
Annapolis, Maryland

Naval Institute Press
291 Wood Road
Annapolis, MD 21402

Library of Congress Cataloging-in-Publication Data

Names: Jackson, John E., Captain, editor.
Title: One nation under drones : legality, morality, and utility of unmanned
    combat systems / edited by John E. Jackson.
Description: Annapolis, Maryland : Naval Institute Press, 2018. | Includes
    bibliographical references and index.
Identifiers: LCCN 2018046312 (print) | LCCN 2018047145 (ebook) | ISBN
    9781682473801 (ePDF) | ISBN 9781682473801 (epub) | ISBN 9781682472385
    (hardback) | ISBN 9781682473801 (ebook)
Subjects: LCSH: Uninhabited combat aerial vehicles (International law) |
    Drone aircraft—Law and legislation. | Drone aircraft—Moral and ethical
    aspects. | Robotics—Law and legislation. | Terrorism—Prevention—Law and
    legislation. | Drone aircraft--Law and legislation—United States. | Drone
    aircraft—Government policy—United States. | BISAC: HISTORY / Military /
    General. | TECHNOLOGY & ENGINEERING / Military Science.
Classification: LCC KZ6687 (ebook) | LCC KZ6687 .O54 2018 (print) | DDC
    341.6/3—dc23
LC record available at https://lccn.loc.gov/2018046312

∞ Print editions meet the requirements of ANSI/NISO
z39.48-1992 (Permanence of Paper).
Printed in the United States of America.

26 25 24 23 22 21 20 19 18   9 8 7 6 5 4 3 2 1
First printing

Contents

Foreword

It is a pleasure to have the opportunity to set the stage for the fascinating discussions that will follow in this timely and provocative book. The title, *One Nation, Under Drones*, succinctly describes the world we will encounter in the years to come. Unmanned and robotic technologies are transforming the nature of conflict and competition, forever altering the conduct of military operations. Unmanned systems will make an already challenging security environment exponentially more complicated. In the private sector, robots offer a competitive advantage in the manufacturing of goods, transportation of material and people, and other services. The rate of technological change in the military environment will present both challenges and opportunities for allies and adversaries alike. In the long term, I truly believe that the use of unmanned and robotic systems will change the way our United States Navy and Marine Corps fight. In the maritime arena, the Navy and Marine Corps have a strategic imperative to exploit emergent and rapidly developing unmanned and robotic technologies while building a solid infrastructure upon which our future forces will be based. Unmanned platforms, when employed individually, have significantly enhanced the effectiveness of our naval, air, and ground forces. In the future, when employed in combination with manned platforms in cross-domain applications, unmanned systems will begin to realize their full potential. This combination will provide capabilities that far exceed the effectiveness of systems or platforms employed in isolation. Increased operational use of unmanned and autonomous systems promises to unleash a revolutionary capability for our military forces. But this future is only possible when we think about it today. Robots and artificial intelligence are an inevitable feature of modern warfare regardless of domain. Indeed, they are prevalent today . . . the future employment and integration deserves serious consideration, and our Navy is fortunate that Captain Jackson has done so.

In the chapters that follow, some of the world's foremost experts in the fields of unmanned operations, law, ethics, and innovation will review the conditions we now encounter daily, and they will reflect on the impact that current trends will likely have over the next several decades. These are exciting times, and the way in which men and machines interact will bring about fundamental changes that will improve the lives of our Sailors and Marines and enhance the safety and effectiveness of our warfighters.

Francis L. Kelley Jr.
DEPUTY ASSISTANT SECRETARY OF THE NAVY
(UNMANNED SYSTEMS), 2015–18

Acknowledgments

I would like to acknowledge the remarkable work done by each of the talented chapter authors who worked so diligently to bring this book to fruition. Some of them have served with me on the faculty of the Naval War College, others have been among my brightest students here at the War College, and others have become friends and colleagues in the ever-expanding world of unmanned systems advocates, operators, and futurists.

I am particularly indebted to P. W. Singer, who has done more than anyone to educate me (and my students) about the remarkable path we have before us as we integrate people and machines into society and into our warfighting and security forces. He has been extremely generous with his time and talents and has always been ready to trek to Newport either in person or via his digital avatar.

My thanks go out to the leadership (past and present) of the Association for Unmanned Vehicle Systems International (AUVSI) who have opened many doors for me as they have led the unmanned and robotic community to new levels of professionalism.

I am very grateful to RADM Jeff Harley, USN, the fifty-sixth president of the U.S. Naval War College, for his untiring support of the nation's future warfighters and for appointing me as the college's first Elmer A. Sperry Chair of Unmanned and Robotic Systems. In this position I will encourage faculty, staff, and students (and the Navy at large) to keep a sharp focus on the future challenges that science and technology will bring to the way we fight our wars and the way we live in the robotics age. But as long as I own my little red Corvette, I will *not* be an advocate for driverless cars!

I also express my appreciation to fellow Naval War College faculty members Tim Schultz, Tim Demy, and Mike Sherlock (a *Spy-Pilot*, a *Sky Pilot*, and an *Aye-Aye Pilot*) who helped make this a more interesting and accurate book. And thanks go to LtCol "Rider" Auger, USAF, of the 17th Attack Squadron, who opened the doors to the world of Persistent Attack and Reconnaissance operations.

I also thank C-3PO, R2-D2, WALL-E, Data, Robby, HAL 9000, Johnny 5, T-1000, BB-8, and the Cylons for their fictional inspiration. And to Gort I say, "Klaatu barada nikto."

Finally, I thank my loving wife, Valerie; my brilliant daughter, Gina; and my heroic son, Brian, for their encouragement and support of everything I have ever done. *Je vous aime tous.*

John Edward Jackson
NEWPORT, RHODE ISLAND

01

A Robot's Family Tree

An Introduction and Brief History
of Unmanned Systems | *John Edward Jackson*

No subject has raised more interest in the past two decades than the use of robotic and unmanned systems in military, civilian, and recreational applications. On a nearly daily basis, news stories report the most recent drone attacks on military targets or near misses between a commercial airplane and a hobbyist's drone or the latest proposals for drone deliveries of small packages from a massive automated warehouse (possibly even a huge airship-based flying warehouse) to your front doorstep by services such as Amazon Prime Air. In the chapters that follow, we will look at a broad range of applications in which remotely piloted and machine-intelligent systems are being used to serve the needs of everyone from "modern major generals" to the average citizen. Although many observers think these robots emerged fully operational in just the past few years, humanity has been moving inexorably toward the robotics age for decades, if not centuries.

Terminology

Before proceeding, perhaps it is best to define what we mean when we use the term "robot." Nearly a century ago, Czech playwright Karel Čapek adopted the old Slavic word *robota* (forced laborer) to describe the humanlike automatons in his techno-drama *R.U.R.: Rossum's Universal Robots*. Čapek's play portrayed a global robot-human war that both consciously and subconsciously established in the minds of the common man a deep-seated fear of what technology run amok could mean. According to the *Oxford Dictionary*, "robot" is defined as "a machine capable of carrying out a complex series of actions automatically, especially one programmable by a computer." The key notion is that the machine can do something that is worthwhile automatically and repeatedly, and it can affect things in the physical word. Robots must have sensors, control systems, manipulators, and power supplies all working together to perform a task. Robots can—and do—work on land, on and below the seas, in space, and in the air.

Robots that fly are among the most prolific of all robotic systems and are what most people think about when they consider the world of the future. But most people do not call these machines "flying robots"; they call them "drones." We should note that many scientists, engineers, operators, and proponents of robotic aerial systems hate the term "drone." *Merriam-Webster* defines "drone" as "a stingless male bee" or "one that lives on the labors of others" or "to talk in a persistently dull or monotonous tone." These are hardly terms of endearment! Only in the dictionary's more recent editions is the alternate definition—"unmanned aircraft or ships guided by remote control or through an onboard computer system"—used. Wherever the term came from and however much it is despised, it is here to stay, so in this book we will call flying robots "drones."

We must also differentiate between unmanned aerial munitions, such as preprogrammed cruise missiles that fly one-way missions to a target, and drones, which normally return to their launch point and can be dispatched repeatedly on various missions. The reusability of drones is a key factor in their viability as a modern tool of warfare and commerce.

How We Got Where We Are and Where We Are Going
To maintain a tight focus on drones, we will mention only in passing the pioneering work done in unmanned aviation by designers and engineers such as Elmer Sperry and Charles Kettering. The World War I–era pilotless Kettering Bug (or aerial torpedo), controlled by gyroscopes and pneumatic/mechanical sensors, was designed to carry a payload about twenty-five miles from its launch point. U.S. Army Air

Service observer LTC Henry H. "Hap" Arnold (who became the five-star commander of all Army Air Forces during World War II) was so impressed with the Bug that he recommended the procurement of up to 100,000 units. Wiser heads prevailed, and as the war drew down, only seventy-five aerial torpedoes were ordered and forty-five delivered. None saw operational service, but they laid a foundation for what was to come.

Jumping ahead several decades, during World War II, the BQ-7 and BQ-8 aircraft of Project Aphrodite (also known as Project Perilous) used converted B-17, B-24, and Navy PB4Y bombers loaded with up to 25,000 pounds of Torpex high explosives to attack hardened targets in Europe. Under the overall command of MG Jimmy Doolittle, Project Aphrodite had as its primary focus striking German weapon sites along the French beaches of Pas-de-Calais. The operational concept was to have a two-man crew get the aircraft airborne, and after control of the aircraft had been transferred to pilots in chase aircraft, the two-man crew would arm the explosives and then bail out by parachute. The Army Air Corps asked for Navy assistance with these high-priority missions, and on August 12, 1944, a mission was undertaken to attack the V-3 Super-Gun bunker at Mimoyecques. While en route to the target, the PB4Y exploded over the English countryside, killing Navy pilot LT (jg) Joseph Kennedy Jr. (the older brother of the future president) and his fellow crew member. No conclusive cause for the tragedy has ever been determined.

In the Pacific theater, the U.S. Navy operated the TDR-1 drone, which was controlled in flight by a chase aircraft using rudimentary television images to provide midcourse guidance. The aircraft were purpose-built by Interstate Aircraft with the airframe constructed from pressed wood applied over a tubular steel frame. (One measure of the total mobilization of the American industrial base during the war is the fact that the construction of the steel frame was subcontracted to the Schwinn Bicycle Company, and other components were provided by Wurlitzer, a musical instrument company.) During a two-month period in 1944, fifty TDR-1s were flown against Japanese antiaircraft sites, bridges, airfields, and grounded ships. Thirty-one hits were recorded, but the program was canceled because of higher priorities.

The Nazis' deadly use of V-1 Buzz-Bombs and the first long-range ballistic missile, known as the V-2, represented the earliest use of unmanned precision-guided munitions, the forerunners of the ballistic missiles and cruise missiles of modern warfare. Ironically, German scientist and engineer Werner von Braun designed and employed vengeance weapons for Adolf Hitler in 1945 and then sent Americans to the moon just twenty-five years later.

Before we leave the World War II era, we should also consider the use in combat of the first unmanned intercontinental weapon: the Japanese Fu-Go balloon bombs. Over 9,300 bomb-laden paper balloons, designed to ride the prevailing eastward winds over 3,000 miles to attack the U.S. West Coast, were launched from the Japanese home islands in 1945. The thirty-two-foot-diameter balloons were carried aloft by 18,000 cubic feet of hydrogen. It is estimated that nearly 10 percent reached the United States, some landing as far east as the Mississippi River. This rather quixotic attack resulted in the only known fatalities on the U.S. mainland during the war. One adult and five children were killed near Bly, Oregon, on May 5, 1945, when they encountered a crashed balloon in a forest. In direct contrast to precision-guided weapons, the Fu-Go balloons were launched with no knowledge of where they would detonate and whom they might injure or kill. They surely violated the law of war by being blatantly indiscriminate.[1]

Drones Debut in Hollywood

Returning to the pre–World War II period of drone development, early steps were taken in the 1930s by motion-picture actor Reginald Denny, who spent much of his spare time off the soundstage building and flying radio-controlled model aircraft. Seeing the potential for miniature airplanes to be used for aerial target practice, Denny demonstrated his model OQ-2 Dennymite to the U.S. Army and Navy in 1940. Both services saw value in the concept and placed small orders from Denny's Radioplane Company. Once World War II commenced, additional orders followed until a total of more than fifteen thousand units were produced. Late in the war, an Army photographer visited Radioplane's Van Nuys, California, plant and photographed an assembly line worker named Norma Jeane Dougherty. The photographer thought Dougherty had potential as a model, and his photos led to a screen test for this drone builder who later changed her name to Marilyn Monroe. So, we can credit two stars and thousands of drones for contributing to the ultimate victory by the greatest generation.

The next significant branch of the robot/drone family tree is the Ryan family. After World War II, the Ryan Aeronautical Company (which was eventually acquired by Northrop Grumman) built jet-powered recoverable aerial training targets known as the Ryan QC-2 Firebee series. In 1948 Ryan won a tri-service competition to build this high-speed jet-powered target drone, beating out thirty-seven other bidders. The first Firebee flight took place in the spring of 1951, and the aerial targets were produced for the Army, Air Force, and Navy. Building on the success of the Firebee airframe, in 1960 Ryan engineers pitched the possibility of using modified Firebees to conduct intelligence-gathering reconnaissance to the U.S. Air Force. The classified code name Lightning Bugs was chosen for these unmanned aerial vehicles (UAVs).

During the Vietnam War, a total of 3,435 operational reconnaissance sorties were flown. High-altitude flights above 50,000 feet provided high-quality photo images of targets of interest. Many drones were launched from converted DC-130 aircraft and recovered by parachute. Others were launched from the ground using jet-assisted takeoff (JATO) rockets. Others were used for gathering electronic intelligence and for performing electronic countermeasure missions. Later versions of the Firebee II drone series flew at supersonic speeds. Collectively, more than seven thousand airframes were manufactured over five decades, and they continue to be used today by the U.S. military and those of our allies. The DNA of the Ryan drones can be found in the well-known Global Hawk UAV.

No history of UAVs would be complete without mention of Israeli aeronautical engineer Abraham Karem, who is often called "the Drone father." Karem built his first drones for the Israeli air force during the Yom Kippur War. He immigrated to the United States in the 1970s and founded Leading Systems Inc. in his garage. There he built the Albatross drone, followed by the more capable

Amber drone and the Gnat-750 version of the Amber, designed for export. Karem's company was eventually purchased by the enigmatic Blue brothers, who had previously purchased the fledging General Atomics Company from Chevron for a sum reported in the popular press to be $50 million. This proved to be a good investment since the company sold $2.4 billion worth of UAVs from 1999 to 2009. General Atomics' operating division, General Atomics Aeronautical Systems Inc. (GA-ASI), refined Karem's designs to build the Predator drone, which virtually revolutionized the conduct of aerial warfare.

But before the Predator there had been the Boeing Condor and the Lockheed Dark Star. Both aircraft contributed to the maturation of long-range and high-altitude UAVs. Boeing's Condor was built at the request of the Defense Advanced Research Projects Agency (DARPA), which wanted an extremely high-altitude unmanned aircraft with extremely long flight endurance. This category of drones is referred to generically as high-altitude, long-endurance (HALE). The Condor first flew in 1988 and established the altitude record for propeller-driven flight at 67,028 feet. Its design was developed with input from aeronautical genius Burt Rutan, the designer of the Voyager aircraft, which flew around the world, nonstop and un-refueled, in 1986. The Condor's two-hundred-foot wingspan made it the largest UAV ever flown. Long wings provide the lift necessary for long missions; the Air Force's manned U-2 strategic reconnaissance aircraft, for example, has a wingspan of 103 feet. This long-wing characteristic continues to be seen on modern UAVs.

DARPA's RQ-3 Dark Star program sought to examine the flight characteristics of a low-observable, or "stealthy," UAV. The project was of interest to the U.S. Air Force, the Central Intelligence Agency (CIA), and the National Reconnaissance Office (NRO). Led by Lockheed Martin (in partnership with Boeing), the jet-powered aircraft was relatively small, with a fifteen-foot length and a wingspan of sixty-nine feet. Its cruising speed was 288 miles per hour, and it had a range of 575 miles. Dark Star first flew in 1996, but the program was canceled in 1999, when it was determined that the UAV was not aerodynamically stable. Dark Star did, however, demonstrate an ability to operate for extended periods of fully automated flight, from takeoff to landing, using the Global Positioning System (GPS).

The robots/drones family tree extends its strongest branches in time of war, as we have seen in World War II, the Vietnam War, and the Cold War. The period following the terrorist attacks of September 11, 2001, is no exception.

Drones That Observe and Drones That Attack

It is difficult to find any event in American history that has had more effect on the United States than the 9/11 terrorist attacks. Since that day Americans' daily lives and collective sense of safety and security have been irrevocably altered. The 9/11 tragedy, combined with the elimination of the Soviet Union a decade earlier, reshaped many of the roles and missions of U.S. military forces. New tools were needed to discover and track individual terrorists in desert hangouts vice to monitor huge tank formations in Eastern Europe. The master technologists toiling in the twenty-first-century version of "the arsenal of democracy" were fully prepared to add robotic tools to soldiers' tool kits.

What Is Over the Next Hill?

The history of warfare demonstrates that the warrior has always had a great interest in what enemy forces and geographical conditions exist over the next hill from where he or she is standing. Taking the high ground has always been a key military objective because, from the highest vantage point, one can discern the potential nature of the upcoming battle. In the past when the terrain failed to provide adequate elevated views, armies often built towers to serve the purpose. The French Aerostatic Corps used balloons for reconnaissance at the Battle of Fleurs in 1794. Later, during the American Civil War, aerial observation was conducted by the Union Army Balloon Corps, under the direction of Chief Aeronaut Thaddeus S. C. Lowe. Thaddeus Lowe's hydrogen gas–filled balloons were launched either from land or from a converted coal barge that some consider the world's first aircraft carrier.

Once heavier-than-air flight was developed, airplanes were first used by the military as observation tools. A century later the unquenchable thirst for battlefield reconnaissance motivated engineers to create observation satellites (usually called spy satellites). The first of these systems were known as the Corona KH-1 through KH-3 series; they flew into orbit in 1960–62. Since then, billions of dollars have been spent on a series of increasingly large and capable systems, many of which have been, and still are, highly classified. Given the U.S. investment in this technology, it is fair to ask, Why do we need observation drones? The answer usually comes in three parts: drones cost less than other observation technologies, they can photograph smaller objects than space-based systems can, and they can be where the drone operator needs them to be for as long as necessary to meet mission objectives.

Today, no drone is more sophisticated, capable, or expensive than the Northrop Grumman RQ-4 Global Hawk. The Global Hawk was conceived in the 1990s as a high-altitude reconnaissance platform able to accomplish many of the missions then being performed by the U.S. Air Force's U-2 manned spy plane. The belief was that such missions could be completed without risking a pilot's life and at lower costs. With a wingspan of 130 feet, the Global Hawk can reach altitudes of up to 65,000 feet and can remain aloft for up to 42 hours. Powered by high-capacity turbo-fan jet engines, it operates at a maximum speed of 350 miles per hour and can carry a 3,000-pound payload at distances of more than 12,300 nautical miles. Such remarkable performance does not come cheap, with costs per aircraft of $120–200 million, depending on how developmental and maintenance costs are calculated. In the twenty years since its first flight in February 1998, the Global Hawk has provided commanders with unprecedented intelligence, surveillance, and reconnaissance capability. It is still in regular service today, and the U.S. Navy has purchased a navalized variant of the Global Hawk for open-ocean surveillance. Known as the Triton, it will operate with the Navy's other shore-based patrol aircraft, the manned P-8 Poseidon.

With apologies to any apologists among our readers, we now turn to drones with stingers and we look back to January 1994, when GA-ASI received a contract to build a medium-altitude long endurance (MALE) UAV to conduct surveillance missions for commanders of the various military services. GA-ASI, which then owned Karem's designs for the Amber and Gnat, responded with an advanced concept technology demonstrator (ACTD) aircraft called the Predator. At this stage the Predator was still an observation aircraft, not a strike plat-form. The MQ-1 Predator completed its first flight in June 1994, and less than a year later, it greatly impressed military leaders with its capa-bilities during an air defense demonstration called Roving Sands 95. Although it is exceedingly rare for an ACTD system to immediately transition to operational status, the Predator flew over what is often called the Valley of Death (where most technology demonstrators meet their demise) when it deployed to the Balkans in July 1995. There it flew fifty-two combat missions, observing and reporting the activi-ties of Serbian forces against other factions in the Yugoslavian conflict. In the years that followed, leading up to the end of hostilities in 1999, hundreds of additional Predator sorties were conducted. When Pope John Paul II visited war-ravaged Bosnia in April 1997, Predators from the U.S. Air Force's 11th Reconnaissance Squadron flew two dedicated security surveillance missions. The learning curve for these systems was steep, and nineteen of sixty-eight aircraft were lost during this period to enemy fire and, more often, to mechanical failure or operator error. Experience using these large-scale UAVs was accumulating, however, and they were ready to serve when once again called to war, this time in the Middle East.

As military planners began to see the utility of UAVs for recon-naissance, they started to also consider a role for unmanned com-bat air vehicles (UCAVs). The Joint Unmanned Combat Air Systems (J-UCAS) team was developing designs, but many planners recog-nized that a near-term solution could be more quickly found by arming the existing Predator. In June 2000 General Atomics was asked to add reinforced wings and weapon pylons to the airframe and a laser target designator to the ball turret, and on February 16, 2001, the first firing of a Hellfire missile from a Predator was con-ducted successfully. The first operational strike, directed by the CIA, occurred after 9/11.

The MQ-1 Predators and the larger more capable MQ-9 Reap-ers served as invaluable assets for the decade and a half of combat in Iraq and Afghanistan and in other countries. Millions of combat hours have been accumulated, and thousands of strikes have been conducted. In 2014 the Air Force was maintaining sixty-two combat air patrols, meaning that sixty-two Predators or Reapers were airborne twenty-four-hours a day, seven days a week. A U.S. Army version of the Predator, known as the Gray Eagle, supports organic Army missions, and the U.S. Navy has operated Predators for a variety of missions. These aircraft and equipment are unique, but no more so than the revolutionary operating concept that keeps them over their targets for extended periods.

The Long-Distance Cockpit
To more efficiently operate the remotely piloted aircraft (RPA) fleet, the U.S. Air Force developed a concept called remote-split operations that allows pilots and sensor operators to control air vehicles in combat situations thousands of miles away from the location of the ground control system (GCS). By using a network of fiber-optic undersea cables and satellite communications, the Predator/Reaper crews can observe the target area using real-time color video imagery, command the remote aircraft's movements, and when desired, engage targets. In July 1995 the 11th Reconnaissance Squadron was activated at Creech Air Force Base (formerly Indian Springs Auxiliary Airfield) outside Las Vegas, Nevada. This was the first RPA squadron, and although RPA missions are now flown from more than a dozen locations, Creech remains a crucial hub for RPA activities today.

Operational missions are flown by RPA crews from various stateside locations, and accommodations must be made for the unavoidable time delay inherent in any globe-spanning telecommunications infrastructure. The time it takes a signal generated in the RPA GCS stateside location to reach the vehicle in flight in its theater of operations can be as much as 1.5 seconds. Such signal lags have little effect when crews are commanding the aircraft at altitude, but they can prove disastrous during the critical periods of takeoff and landing. For this reason the Air Force deploys launch-and-recovery elements to overseas locations. These airmen use virtually instantaneous line-of-sight communications to fly the drone off the runway. After takeoff, control is assumed by the flight crews in a stateside GCS who fly the assigned missions. Control of the aircraft is surrendered to the launch-and-recovery personnel when the time comes for landing.

This unique operational concept has many benefits. It significantly reduces the number of personnel put at potential risk of attack in the area of conflict, and it reduces the cost and complexity of overseas locations. Additionally, the stateside RPA crews can be assigned to fly missions in whatever area is of most concern at any given time. In fact, the same RPA pilot might fly a mission over Afghanistan in the morning and another over Somalia in the afternoon. Another key benefit is that training and administration issues are more effectively managed because a large population of RPA crews are colocated at Creech Air Force Base or other locations, as opposed to being located in smaller groups on bases around the world. Finally, morale is improved and stress is reduced because the RPA crews can return to their families at the end of a lengthy work shift.

There is significant controversy about the role of these warriors who, in effect, move from peacetime to wartime on a twenty-four-hour cycle. The drone revolution has altered the very concept of going to war. Throughout recorded history, warfighters have always packed their weapons, left their homes and families, and traveled to the war front, where they were subjected to the rigors of the battlefield and the potential for injury or death. At the end of the conflict, they returned, carrying their shields or lying on them. This is not the case in the RPA community. RPA pilots leave home each morning, fly missions (and potentially slay opponents), and return home that night. Owing to the incredible optics of their systems and the ability to linger over the target both before and after an attack, they witness firsthand the death and destruction they have caused on behalf of their fellow citizens. The pilots of manned bombers rarely see the impact of their weapons, and battle damage assessment (BDA) is conducted by other personnel in the air or on the ground. By contrast, RPA crews perform their own BDA and must deal with the psychological impact of their actions. Some people find it hard to believe aircrews that never leave the United States can have post-traumatic stress disorder (PTSD), but an honest appraisal of the facts indicates these RPA crews do have to deal with significant warfighting issues. They are warriors by any definition.

Small Wings, Big Missions

Most news stories and discussion in the mainstream press have been about long-range, long-endurance drones such as the Predator, Reaper, and Global Hawk. However, in sheer numbers flown and in the level

of direct support provided to soldiers, sailors, and marines, the proliferation of small, inexpensive, and versatile drones is noteworthy.

The history of UAVs is replete with stories of creatively adapting
existing systems for new uses. The highly successful ScanEagle, produced by Insitu (now a subsidiary of Boeing), is such a story of adaptation. Originally, the drone, at the time called the SeaScan, was designed
to provide weather data and help locate schools of tuna for commercial fishermen in the U.S. Pacific Northwest. It was simple, rugged, and
inexpensive to operate. After 9/11 it was transformed into a portable
unmanned aerial system (UAS) that could provide autonomous surveillance on the battlefield. First deployed as the ScanEagle in August
2004, during the Iraq War, it has a wingspan of 10.2 feet, a length of
4.5 feet, and a weight of 44 pounds. It can operate at speeds up to 92
miles per hour, with a cruise speed of about 55 miles per hour. The
early version flew on converted weed whacker engines and could fly
for 10–12 hours on a gallon of gas. Newer versions using task-built
engines have flown in tests as long as 22 hours. Using sophisticated
instrumentation, it returns real-time video signals to the operators in
the nearby ground control station.

The ScanEagle can be launched from ships, small boats, and shore.
It uses a patented pneumatic launcher known as SuperWedge, which
catapults the aircraft into the air. This launcher is portable, can be
rolled on board ship for operations, and can be removed if necessary
without significant shipboard alterations. It is recovered by the Sky
Hook retrieval system, which uses a hook on the end of the wing-
tip to snag a rope hung over the side of the ship (or from a tall pole
ashore). Ship's captains like this system because the ScanEagle never
needs to point directly at the ship; instead, it flies alongside the ship to
be captured and then swung on board. Landing a manned aircraft with
a tailhook on an aircraft carrier is a sight to behold. So is recovering a
fast-moving drone with a wing hook on a rope.

The ScanEagle is operated by or for over a dozen nations, and by
2017 it had flown over 1 million flight hours and more than 56,000
combat sorties. One of the most memorable ScanEagle operations
was in April 2009, when the drone provided overhead imagery of the
actions between Navy ships and the pirates holding Captain Richard
Phillips, the master of the container ship *Maersk Alabama*, hostage. Navy

SEALS on board USS *Bainbridge* (DDG 96) used the situational awareness provided by the drone and other sources to target and kill the three
Somali pirates in an enclosed lifeboat and safely rescue the hostage.

In the small UAS category, AeroVironment, based in Simi Valley,
California, has dominated the market with a family of small, mini,
and micro drones. The company was founded in 1971 by aeronautical engineering pioneer Paul B. Macready Jr. and produced a series

Rent-a-Drone

The U.S. Navy has had great success with Boeing/Insitu's
ScanEagle but has never owned one. For more than two decades,
the service neither bought a drone nor trained or paid for drone
operators. Instead, the Navy purchased, on an hourly basis, what
the ScanEagle produced: intelligence, surveillance, and reconnaissance (ISR) data. Sometimes informally called "rent-a-drone" or
"buy the pixels, not the plane," this fee-for-services model is a
contractual arrangement known as contractor owned/contractor
operated (CO-CO). Per a standing agreement with the Navy,
Insitu provided the drones, the operating equipment, and the
personnel necessary to deliver to the Navy a specific number of
hours of ISR support on a weekly or monthly basis. The Navy
used the valuable end product without having to be concerned
about how the product was produced. All mechanical problems
were corrected by the contractor, all training and personnel costs
were managed by Insitu, and engineering changes and improvements were funded by the company. Since the program began
in 2005, over thirteen hundred engineering improvements have
been made to the engine, sensors, ground control, and launch-
and-recovery systems. This highly flexible contractual arrangement was an effective work-around to the extremely complex
specification process and long lead times inherent in the government procurement process. Although Boeing/Insitu pioneered
the CO-CO approach for UAS, many other vendors now also
offer fee-for-services ISR to the Department of Defense, the
Coast Guard, and allied customers.

of human-powered manned aircraft, including the Gossamer Condor, which won the Kremer Prize in 1977 for human-powered flight, and the Gossamer Albatross, which crossed the English Channel in 1979, winning what was then the largest prize in aviation history, the £100,000 Kremer Prize. AeroVironment built other innovative research aircraft run on solar power and other alternative fuels but set production records in the area of small hand-launched drones. More than 19,000 RQ-11 Raven drones have been built since the aircraft was introduced in May 2003, and they are used in twenty-five different countries. The RQ-11 Raven has a wingspan of 4.5 feet, is 3 feet long, and weighs 4.2 pounds. Powered by batteries, it has a cruising speed of 18 miles per hour, a range of 6.2 miles, and an endurance of 60–90 minutes. It can provide day or night aerial intelligence, surveillance, target acquisition, and reconnaissance.

AeroVironment also markets the Wasp, Puma, Switchblade, and Blackwing UAS. The Switchblade is more appropriately labeled a loitering munition because it carries an explosive warhead with a charge equivalent to a forty-millimeter grenade. Also referred to as a tactical missile system, the Switchblade launches from a tube and its wings and tail structures fold out in flight, similar to the operation of the folding knife of the same name. Switchblade operators use downloaded video images to attack the target during a ten-minute flight time. The Switchblade is particularly popular with Navy SEALs and other special operating forces.

In some circumstances, such as shipboard operations off small vessels, operators do not have the luxury of using a runway for launch-and-recovery operations. In these cases alternative methods, including vertical lift (to be discussed later), must be used. Ashore Army, Marine, and Air Force units can rely on another class of small UAVs including AAI (Textron) RQ-7 Shadow, first used by the U.S. Army in 2001 for tactical reconnaissance and targeting. With a recognizable twin-boom, inverted V tail and pusher propeller configuration, the Shadow has a maximum takeoff weight of 328 pounds, a speed of 130 miles per hour, and an operating ceiling of 15,000 feet. It uses a catapult system for launch, flies for up to seven hours, and lands on any reasonably flat surface of at least 330 feet in length. Textron announced an advanced design based on the successful Shadow, called the Nightwarden, in June 2017. The company is promoting the Nightwarden as a lower-cost alternative to larger systems such as General Atomics' MQ-1 Predator. Lockheed Martin has produced a family of small UAS, including the Desert Hawk, the Vector Hawk, the Fury, and other cutting-edge systems that are in use around the world.

Spinning Wings

All the drones discussed thus far have one factor in common: they use wings (some long, some short) to achieve flight. Whether pulled through the air by tractor propellers, projected forward by rear-mounted pusher propellers, or moved rapidly forward by jet engines, they all require continual forward movement to remain airborne. An alternative method of achieving flight is with rotary wings, like those on helicopters. By using rotating blades to provide lift and thrust, rotorcraft can take off and land vertically and can also hover over a specific location. The German Focke-Wulf Fw-61 first flew in 1936, and small numbers were used by Nazi Germany during World War II for observation, transport, and medical evacuation. In the United States, Russian-born engineer Igor Sikorsky designed the R-4, considered the first large-scale mass-produced helicopter. Over four hundred were produced before the end of the war. Manned helicopters have been used extensively around the world and were particularly useful during the Vietnam War. Nearly 12,000 were used in Vietnam for observation, transportation, and attack missions. Experimentation was undertaken to operate unmanned helicopters as early as 1959, when the Gyrodyne QH-50 Drone Anti-Submarine Helicopter (DASH) flew from Navy ships.

Despite the limited success of DASH, the Navy continued to seek a method to operate drone aircraft from sea. In the spring of 2000, the U.S. Navy conducted a competition to design and fly an unmanned helicopter that could take off from a shipboard flight deck with a 200-pound payload, fly 125 miles, and return to the launch point after a three-hour mission. The competition was won by a team from Teledyne Ryan (later Northrop Grumman) and Schweizer Aircraft that produced the RQ-8A Fire Scout. Later versions of the Fire Scout

Cold War Killer Robots at Sea

Often when you think you have a new idea, you discover that someone tried it years, if not decades, ago. This is the case with unmanned helicopters flying from ships. The U.S. Navy's MQ-8C Fire Scout rotary-wing UAS, built by Northrop Grumman, is now deployed afloat and ashore in support of a wide range of missions. Few remember, however, that over a half century ago, the first armed UAS in history, the Gyrodyne QH-50 DASH was deployed on U.S. Navy and Japan Maritime Self-Defense Force ships. From 1960 to 1969, a total of 755 DASHs were built. Each half-ton aircraft was able to carry two Mark-44 torpedoes or a single nuclear depth charge that could be flown out more than twenty miles from the launching ship and dropped on potentially hostile Soviet submarines. (The once-classified nuclear option was never certified for operational use.) Later versions of DASH carried television cameras to serve as airborne spotters for naval gunfire. Some flew logistics resupply missions between ships. And reportedly, at least one U.S. Marine in Vietnam was flown to safety hanging onto the skids of the mini-copter!

Looking back, in many ways the DASH program was doomed from the beginning. Its greatest weakness was that to save costs and developmental time, the DASH command-and-control links were adapted from off-the-shelf surplus World War II–era electronics with zero redundancy. Estimates are that over 80 percent of operational aircraft losses could be traced to single-point failures of the electronics. DASH developed a widely held, if perhaps unjustified, reputation for frequently losing contact during flight and rarely returning to the launch platform. Complicating operators' ability to master their trade was the fact that carrier battlegroup commanders were highly concerned about the possibility of a collision between a manned aircraft and the drone and severely limited DASH flights in proximity of carriers.

On closer review, records show that successful operations could be accomplished when the operators had adequate training and flight experience. For example, USS *Steinaker* (DD 863) flew 344 DASH missions over sixteen months without a mishap. As with any new technology, accidents and crashes occurred, and by the time the program was canceled in 1969, over three hundred aircraft had been lost for a variety of reasons (but not a single pilot or crew member was injured). Some observers attribute much of the DASH program's failure to the cultural rivalry between the Navy's aviators, who saw themselves as the rightful owners of air systems, and members of the Navy's surface warfare community, who sought to use these organic assets to extend their combat reach. The conflict was ultimately settled by replacing DASH with manned helicopters; the Light Airborne Multipurpose System (LAMPS) assigned qualified pilots to destroyer-sized ships.

Today's Fire Scout is often humorously referred to as "DASH That Comes Back," and although the MQ-8C is an ISR platform, tests have been conducted with weapons on board, thus potentially returning to the Navy a killer robot at sea. Technological advancements have allowed operators to master the task of controlling the drone from ship to target and back. The Navy's surface-versus-aviator cultural issues have become less significant as the officers from both communities have become comfortable with operating together to support evolving missions.

were designated as the MQ-8B, which had a length of twenty-four feet, a width of six feet, a height of nine feet, and a rotor diameter of twenty-seven feet. The payload capacity increased to 250 pounds. The MQ-8B was flown successfully both from ships and from locations ashore. It was also tested as an attack aircraft using the Advanced Precision Kill Weapons System (APKWS). In 2013 the Navy ordered a more advanced Fire Scout based on the Bell 407 helicopter and designated it the MQ-8C. This version doubles the range and endurance and triples the payload of the MQ-8B. Since the first flight, the various Fire Scout versions have completed over 17,000 flight hours and deployed afloat and ashore.

A much larger drone helicopter has been flown by the U.S. Marine Corps. The Lockheed/Kaman K-MAX is a large experimental unmanned helicopter with intermeshing rotors (known as a synchropter) that was operated in combat operations in Afghanistan. It is fifty-one feet long and has a rotor diameter of over forty-eight feet. Since it flies with intermeshed blades, it has no need for a tail rotor to counteract the torque of the spinning rotors. The Marines tested K-MAX as a flying logistics transportation vehicle, thus reducing the number of ground vehicle convoys necessary to support remote-operating bases and avoiding the potential damage to ground convoys caused by improvised explosive devices (IEDs). Derived from Kaman's aerial logging aircraft, K-MAX weighed six thousand pounds and could lift six thousand pounds of cargo. Two K-MAX "helo-drones" were deployed to Afghanistan in 2011 for a six-month test program, but owing to their successful operations, they were extended in theater until May 2014. A total of 2,250 tons of matériel were delivered in real-world combat support missions. K-MAX flew autonomously both day and night and required only a spotter with a laser designator at the receiving location. Although the test program was considered very successful, it is unclear if the Marines or U.S. Army will procure autonomous aerial logistics drones in the future.

In-flight stability for rotorcraft relies on counterrotating blades in the K-MAX and traditional tail rotors in the Fire Scout system, but a remarkable level of stability can be achieved by using multiple rotors operating in tandem. The most common form of rotorcraft with multiple rotors has four rotors and is widely referred to as a "quad-rotor." The U.S. Marine Corps has begun equipping every deploying squad with an InstantEye hand-launched quad-rotor in a program that has become known as "Quads for Squads." Millions of quad-rotors are flown today, the vast majority by hobbyists. The Federal Aviation Administration (FAA) estimates the hobbyist drone fleet will increase to 3.4 million by 2020. The Chinese company DJI has developed an extensive stable of drones for both the recreational and the commercial markets. Its Phantom and Mavic Pro account for more than 60 percent of the U.S. market and a similar share around the world. Other configurations with eight or more rotors have been flown, increasing the lift as the rotor count expands.

Most quad-rotors are used for aerial photography (by both amateurs and professionals) and skill-based precision flying in drone racing, a growing sport often conducted under the auspices of the fledgling Drone Racing League (DLR), whose lucrative television contracts promise to bring the sport to an increasingly larger audience. The DLR drones accelerate from zero to eighty miles per hour in one second, and three-dimensional indoor race courses have sprung up around the world. Intel Corporation uses quad-rotors for nighttime light displays that it hopes will challenge traditional fireworks. Intel has simultaneously flown more than five hundred Shooting Star drones in choreographed aerial dances over events like the Super Bowl and at Disney theme parks. Even larger drone constellations are planned.

Not all quad-rotors, however, are used for business ventures or for fun and games. Relatively powerful quad-rotor drones can be purchased for only a few thousand dollars, and as a result, they are being converted to attack aircraft in the world's battlefields. Beginning in 2015 Islamic State of Iraq and Syria (ISIS) forces in the Middle East used commercially available drones, both fixed-wing and quad-rotor, to observe and attack coalition forces aligned against them in Syria and other locations. Countering the threat of such "homebuilt systems" is the Israeli armed forces' IAI Rotem-L. This drone can be operated by a single soldier and carry a one-kilogram warhead for thirty to forty-five minutes until it strikes a target or returns safely to be used again. The ability to recover and retarget Rotem-L separates it from the previously discussed Switchblade, which must be detonated once launched.

There is also a category of surveillance drones smaller than quad-rotors, the so-called nano-drones. The most widely deployed nano-drone is the PD-100 Personal Reconnaissance System (PRS) known as the Black Hornet. This tiny drone is four inches long and one inch wide. Including its camera, it weighs only half an ounce. Its rotor diameter is 120 millimeters, and its electric motor gives it a flight time of about twenty-five minutes. The air vehicle fits into a small pouch worn on a soldier's vest, and it can be airborne in less than a minute. The handheld control unit receives full-motion video and still images. Over three thousand units had been produced by the end of 2016. The Black Hornet has been used by the militaries of nineteen NATO-allied nations. The primary competitor for the Black Hornet is the Snipe Nano UAS from AeroVironment. It weighs five ounces, flies for about fifteen minutes, and carries both electro-optical and infrared cameras for day and night operations. It is intended to support ground troops by providing critical situational awareness whenever and wherever it is needed.

No Wings at All

We have discussed the use of fixed wings and rotary wings to achieve flight, but there is a third method to get into the air: the aerostatic lift of lighter-than-air gases. The notion of hanging suspended in the air without the noise, turbulence, and fuel consumption of engines, propellers, or rotor blades has always been attractive. The immutable laws of physics dictate that a mass of gas lighter than the air around it and enclosed in a lightweight bag or envelope will rise through a column of air until it reaches a point of equilibrium. Hot air will lift paper lanterns and recreational balloons; hydrogen gas lifted the German zeppelin *Hindenburg* and carried it across oceans; and nonflammable helium gas provided the aerostatic force used to loft the U.S. Navy's rigid airships USS *Akron* (ZRS 4) and USS *Macon* (ZRS 5), a fleet of more than 160 smaller nonrigid blimps during World War II, and the Goodyear advertising blimps of today.

The post-9/11 military turned to large tethered aerostats to provide long-endurance (twenty-two to thirty days) aerial observation over bases and other critical infrastructure in Iraq and Afghanistan. The Lockheed-built Persistent Threat Detection System (PTDS) has been in use by the U.S. Army since 2004. It consists of a large blimp-shaped balloon with a gas volume of 74,000 cubic feet. The envelope is 115 feet long, and with an operating altitude of 5,000 feet, it can scan more than 100 miles from its fixed operating base. It is tethered with a strong Kevlar-based cable that carries power up to the aerostat and data (visual and radar) down to the operators. Reportedly, the PTDS has also had a deterrent effect because many attackers, aware that they were being observed, have avoided the areas under its coverage. The Department of Homeland Security uses a much larger

420,000-cubic-foot version, known as the Tethered Aerostats Radar Systems (TARS), in the continental United States for counterdrug and counter-narco-terrorism missions.

The robot's family tree has many other branches and twigs, but we will pause here and allow our distinguished panel of authors take us through a detailed look at the world of drones as it exists in the first decades of the twenty-first century.

This book is the product of the editor's decade of study, research, and teaching about the ways in which unmanned and robotic systems have become integral to how the developed world's citizens go about their daily business and how military forces and armed groups are fighting on battlefields near and far. Understanding the hundreds of designs and thousands of pieces of hardware being used is important, but more important is developing an awareness of how these revolutionary systems are reshaping the legal, ethical, and operational nature of both war and peace. This chapter set the stage for the chapters that follow by documenting the history of unmanned aerial systems and ground systems going back to the earliest days of the twentieth century.

In chapter 2, "Drones: The Science Fiction Technology of Tomorrow Is Already Here Today," Konstantin Kakaes and P. W. Singer argue that people are comfortable with thinking about robots and autonomous creatures as characters in a movie or book but do not realize that what was once fiction is now reality. In chapter 3, "Rise of Terror/Rise of Drones: A World View," Bard College's Dan Gettinger, cofounder of the highly regarded Center for the Study of the Drone, details the degree to which nations and groups, both friendly and not, have become caught up in the robot revolution. In chapter 4, "State of the Operational Art: Maritime Systems," Arthur Holland Michel, cofounder of the Center for the Study of the Drone, provides a comprehensive look at the variety of maritime-based systems being developed in the United States and around the globe. Since three-quarters of the Earth's surface is covered by water, he appropriately considers the range of systems being used by the world's navies and by the commercial maritime industry. In chapter 5, "When Robots Rule the Waves?" well-known drone ethicist and author George Lucas and Australian researcher Robert Sparrow consider the degree to which unmanned systems may alter the very nature of war at sea.

In chapter 6, "The U.S. Marine Corps, the Evolving Amphibious Task Force, and the Rise of Unmanned Systems," talented and prolific author Robbin Laird offers a case study of how the Marines are integrating drones into every aspect of their warfighting missions. Many of their applications involve ground robots, for explosive ordnance disposal, scouting, and materials transport. In chapter 7, "Defeating the Threat of Small Unmanned Aerial Systems," U.S. Air Force major (and RPA pilot) Dillon Patterson looks at the unique challenges military forces in the field face from small UAVs.

In chapter 8, "Narrowing the International Law Divide: The Drone Debate Matures," noted legal scholar Michael Schmitt discusses the legality of the use of unmanned systems under international laws of war and international humanitarian law. In chapter 9, "Autonomous Weapons and the Law," U.S. Army lieutenant colonel Christopher Ford discusses some of the more challenging legal issues military leaders are encountering in using lethal autonomous weapons. In chapter 10, "Lethal Autonomous Systems and the Plight of the Noncombatant," world-renowned roboticist Ron Arkin reflects on how robots on the battlefield could prove to be more ethical and less destructive than humans to civilian populations located in areas of conflict. In chapter 11, "The Ethics of Remote Weapons: Reapers, Red Herrings, and a Real Problem," U.S. Air Force major Joseph Chapa, himself a qualified RPA pilot, speaks to the ethical issues inherent in the use of drones.

In chapter 12, "Techno-Partners All Around Us: Civilian Applications," Brian Wynne, president and chief operating officer of the Association of Unmanned Vehicle Systems International, the world's largest robotic trade association, provides a look at how the civilian world is also wrestling with the changes being brought about by the use of robotic systems in the commercial and public service fields.

In chapter 13, "The View Downrange: The Decades Ahead," I draw some conclusions and offer some thoughts about the possible future we have before us in a world in which man and man-like machines exist (hopefully) in peace for the benefit of humanity.

The story of drones is the story of the creative application of emerging technology to meet the challenges of national defense and our rapidly changing society at large. The pages that follow will tell this story from the perspective of some of the men and women who have been most closely aligned with this effort over the past several decades. Enjoy!

Notes

1. Robert C. Mikesh, *Japan's World War II Balloon Bomb Attacks on North America* (Washington, DC: Smithsonian Institution Press, 1973).

02

Drones

The Science Fiction Technology of Tomorrow Is
Already Here Today | *Konstantin Kakaes and P. W. Singer*

The Jordanian desert town of Fifa is just south of the Dead Sea and has been inhabited for over five thousand years, as demonstrated by a cemetery full of early Bronze Age ceramic pots. Hundreds of kilometers north, the Syrian town of Raqqa has been inhabited just as long, as shown by the archaeological sites of Tall Zeidan and Tall al-Bi'a. But above both ancient cities now flies a technology only recently from the world of science fiction, robotic planes known as unmanned aerial systems (UAS), or more popularly, drones. The drones above Fifa are being flown by a team of archaeologists from DePaul University in Chicago and the University of Connecticut to make maps of ancient sites. The skies above Raqqa have seen drones flown by armed groups that range from the Syrian air force and the Islamic State in Iraq and Syria (ISIS) to the U.S. military to map out where foes are in order to strike them. These diverse uses and users illustrate not just the proliferation of drones but also the challenges that this novel and powerful technology poses for policymakers.

World of Drones

One can measure the proliferation of UAS technology in several ways. According to New America's World of Drones database, some 80 countries have utilized unmanned systems in their military, and over 65 countries produce and export them. There are at least 680 active drone development programs run by governments, companies, and research institutes around the world. But to perceive robotic planes as military in nature might miss an even greater shift: the technology has increasingly become a civilian one. A related New America project documented over 120 civilian use projects around the world, which is but a small fraction of the growth under way. Governments are using drones to undertake surveillance for military and law enforcement, but also to fly into hurricanes and gather data to improve weather forecasts or to count wild animals. Utilities are using drones to monitor oil pipelines, roads, and rail lines that extend over hundreds of miles. Community groups are using drones in Peru, Guyana, and Indonesia to map out their lands in efforts to protect them from illegal encroachment. Real estate agents around the world are using them to take fetching snapshots; Hollywood filmmakers to get previously impossible shots. And a vibrant and growing hobbyist community is using drones for everything from filming their children's football games to racing them in contests. The use of drones for package delivery is potentially a major new market. If companies like Amazon can make the technology work economically, it will dwarf other applications, like infrastructure inspection or filmmaking. The large number of delivery drones could fundamentally change what it is like to look up in the sky.

Part of what is driving this proliferation of users and uses is the many new sizes, shapes, and forms of the technology. At one end of the spectrum are micro drones like the DD-1000 Black Hornet, which weighs eighteen grams and can fit into a pocket. At the other end are systems like China's Divine Eagle drone, which carries seven radars and reputedly has a fifty-meter wingspan. These systems, in turn, can operate for anything from just a few minutes to eighty-one hours in the case of the 6.8 kilogram Atlantiksolar, which set a record for lightweight drones in July 2015. Even as there is fervid experimentation in new designs, the more powerful shift may be in the software that powers the systems. The Predator, for example, began as a highly improvised system in the 1990s, when engineers hacked together satellite links and flew the drone without the Global Positioning System (GPS) (meaning that the Predator's early video camera–style sensor could see a target at a distance but not precisely identify where in the world it was). Today, the drone not only operates as part of a global communications architecture, but also carries powerful sensors like

Gorgon Stare, which can monitor a 100 square kilometer area with 368 cameras, each capturing 5 million pixels of imagery.

The biggest shift, however, may be in the systems' ability to operate with less and less human control, better known as autonomy. Some of this is playing out in drones' actual flight operations. To maintain stability in flight, drones have to correct their motion without human input. Multirotor drones—small helicopters—must constantly vary the speed of the various rotors to compensate for small imbalances; small delta-wing drones made from foam have simple airframes that are stable only because their ailerons are constantly in motion, keeping the wing level. If drones did not have to share the air with others—other drones and manned aircraft—this capacity for autonomy would be enough to allow them to fly their routes. However, drones do have to share increasingly crowded airspace. Several distinct technologies currently being developed are all focused on figuring out how to share effectively. One approach is to put more and more intelligence on the drone itself so that it can autonomously sense and avoid obstacles. Another (the two are complementary) is to create a comprehensive traffic management system that communicates with drones and keeps track of their positions. Small drones will far outnumber manned aircraft and cannot carry heavy transponders like those used by passenger jets. (The transponders are heavy for a drone that weighs five pounds, though not for a 747.) A traffic-management system for drones might use many of the same technologies that allow mobile telephones to effectively share the radio spectrum.

The other aspect changing in autonomy is the mission itself. To illustrate, the early Predator drone was almost completely operated from afar. Systems like the X-47 unmanned combat aerial system (UCAS) have been able not only to take off and land on their own from an aircraft carrier at sea, perhaps the toughest human pilot task, but also to fly mission waypoints and refuel in midair. Ultimately, the plan for the plane is that it will be able to penetrate enemy airspace on its own and even react to air defenses. A British parallel, the Taranis, is even designed to identify and prosecute targets on its own. This autonomy growth is important. A feedback loop in which more people use drones because the drones are more capable has taken hold. The increasing number of users then drives innovation. Military programs pursuing autonomy are now complemented by Silicon Valley startups after the same goal. This is important, as a new development in the twenty-first century is the power of the consumer market in driving progress in a way that the military market has proved unable to do in recent years. For example, the iPhone has capabilities, and ease of use, that far more expensive defense contractor communications programs were not able to provide for years. That same effect is now being seen in drones, from small systems all the way up to Facebook's new Aquila drone. The size of a passenger jet and solar powered, it is designed to fly for three months at a time and beam down Internet access to remote areas.

Key Questions for Policymakers

These are exciting times but with them come a number of pressing, unresolved questions facing policymakers. With respect to armed conflict, drones are a revolutionary technology for warfare, like the steam engine, machine gun, or computer. Drones raise questions that range from how units that use the technology should be trained, recruited, organized, and commanded to what the best doctrine for battlefield effectiveness is. But perhaps the most controversial question has been the essential one: When is lethal force deemed morally and legally permissible? So far, only the United States, United Kingdom, Israel, Pakistan, Iraq, Nigeria, Iran, Turkey, and Azerbaijan have used armed drones in combat, but these uses have already raised a series of issues. Just to name a few: Does drone warfare make war more likely? How should the battlefield be defined when drones expand the reach of governments? Must targeting decisions be made by human beings, or can algorithms be trusted to make life-and-death decisions under certain circumstances? As armed drones proliferate, these questions will become relevant to more and more governments and non-state actors. Unarmed drones raise different, but no less pressing, questions. As Professor Ryan Calo of the University of Washington has written, drones are a "privacy catalyst." Many of the questions they raise may be similar to those other technologies, such as mobile phones, bring up; however, drones provoke a more pronounced public reaction because of their ability to provide wide area, close up, and persistent surveillance of any and all, not just agreed users. As U.S. Supreme Court justice Sonia Sotomayor has asked in *United States v. Jones*, does there exist "a reasonable societal expectation of privacy in the sum of one's public movements"?

Drones also raise purely practical questions about air safety. Work by regulatory agencies over the last century has made air travel the safest form of mass transportation. And yet drones are now a potential disruptive force for this domain. Airliners are increasingly reporting drones flying in airspace where they are prohibited, as in a July 2015 incident at the Warsaw airport when the pilots of a Lufthansa regional jet said they nearly collided with a drone as they were coming in to land. Drones reportedly got in the way of firefighting helicopters attempting to put out a wildfire near Los Angeles in July 2015. Of course, in turn, drones have also proved to be a powerful new tool for firefighting. This confluence of more drones and more drone users is raising many policy questions. Who should be allowed to operate the systems and with what training or licensing? Ought airspace be segregated? Will, as companies like Amazon have mooted, regulators create segregated bands of airspace dedicated to unmanned aircraft? Amazon has suggested that two hundred to four hundred feet above ground level be reserved for drones. Is that altitude high enough to protect the property rights to airspace of people whom Amazon is flying over? As drones acquire increasingly sophisticated detect-and-avoid and autonomy capabilities, how good must those capabilities be in comparison with manned aircraft? How can one even meaningfully evaluate the difference—and must drones of different sizes be held to the same standards?

The question of who should be allowed to the use the system is not just an issue of air safety and liability, but also one of security. These new capabilities often have incredibly low barriers to entry, which complicates efforts to regulate them effectively and to limit the access of malevolent actors. For instance, non-state actors ranging from ISIS to criminal gangs in Russia, Mexico, and the United States are already using drones. So far their use has been for surveillance and smuggling, not for airstrikes. Nevertheless, as drones become easier to use and more capable, governments may press for more stringent artificial limits on drones' capabilities. So-called geofencing, in which drones are prevented with built-in mechanisms (of various degrees of efficacy and stringency) from flying into particular regions, will likely

become more prevalent. For example, after one of its drones accidentally crashed into the White House lawn, DJI put out a mandatory
firmware update that prevents its drones from flying within the Washington, DC, area. This again raises difficult questions about the balance
between freedom and security.

Conclusions

The proliferation of drones is opening up a powerful new technology
to the world. But this proliferation is also leading to new questions
across areas ranging from military tactics to privacy laws to airspace
deconfliction. Around the world, the sky is set to fill with robotic aircraft, and policymakers will have to sort out what those aircraft will be
allowed to do and how they will be permitted to do it.

Rise of Terror/ Rise of Drones

A World View | *Dan Gettinger*

Alvin Ellis and Abraham Karem were both expatriates at the time of their inventions. Working in their garages—Ellis, an American, in Haifa and Karem, an Israeli, in Los Angeles—the two men built the prototypes for what became the first proliferated drones: the Mastiff and Predator. The Mastiff, a midsize surveillance drone with a twin-boom tail and spindly wheels, was among the first drones used in modern combat. The Mastiff's utility in combat convinced Israeli—and subsequently, American—military planners of the importance of unmanned aerial vehicles (UAVs). These developments in turn fueled the eventual success of Karem's invention, the predecessor to the U.S. Predator drone. The legacy of the Predator, of course, is evident in the myriad U.S. drone units currently active and in the number of similar UAVs that have been developed by a host of other nations.

The development and acquisition of unmanned systems has long been an international affair. This chapter is a guide to some of the forces that have shaped and are shaping the spread of unmanned systems today. Each section aims to situate drone proliferation in the context of major developments, such as the wars in Afghanistan, Iraq, and Syria; the rise of non-state actors like the Islamic State in Iraq and Syria (ISIS); and China's burgeoning drone industry.

The first section examines how multiple ongoing conflicts in the Middle East and Southwest Asia are fueling drone proliferation. The NATO-led intervention in Afghanistan and the ongoing wars in Syria and Iraq have led many countries to acquire unmanned systems and learn from the experience of deploying these systems in combat. However, while the proliferation of drones in Afghanistan underlined the early dominance of U.S. and Israeli drone manufacturers, the conflict in Syria and Iraq illustrates how many new countries and companies are fielding drones.

Meanwhile, owing to the availability and affordability of consumer drones and drone components, non-state actors are recognizing that drones can significantly add to their capabilities. The section titled "Drones for Terror and Insurgency" looks at the way non-state actors are using consumer drones to gain an advantage on the battlefield and the technical innovations that are fueling this trend.

China is becoming a significant drone power in terms of domestic drone production, design, and deployments. In a 2012 report, the U.S. Defense Science Board noted that the "scope and speed of unmanned-aircraft development in China is a wakeup call that has both industrial and military implications" and that China is "moving rapidly to catch up—and perhaps overtake—the West" in the unmanned systems sector.[1] The section titled "A Rising Drone Power" examines China's role as a drone producer and exporter.

Early Drone Proliferation

Until the late 1970s and 1980s, most reconnaissance UAVs were based on designs for target drones and cruise missiles. Beginning in 1964, the United States deployed the Teledyne-Ryan Model 147 Lightning Bug, a turbojet-powered target drone outfitted with camera equipment to conduct reconnaissance missions in Vietnam. Although the drone was difficult to control and produced images of varying quality, the Lightning Bug could fly fast and low, making it difficult for North Vietnamese radar to identify. Beginning in the 1970s, variants of the Model 147 were among the first drones to proliferate to other militaries. In the 1973 Yom Kippur War, Israel deployed the BQM-34 Firebee drones—relatives of the Lightning Bug—to locate Syrian antiaircraft systems and to act as decoys for Israeli fighters. Another variant of the Lightning Bug, the Teledyne-Ryan Model 324 Scarab, was exported in the 1980s to Egypt, where they remained in service up to the mid-2000s.

Like the United States, the Soviet Union also began producing jet-powered reconnaissance UAVs that were based on target drones.

The Tupolev Tu-143 Reys (also known as the DR-3) proliferated widely to Soviet partners and remained in use as recently as 2014, when one of the drones crashed in eastern Ukraine. This proliferation, however, did not escape the attention of the U.S. intelligence community, which tracked the Tu-143 and other Soviet drones like the Lavochkin La-17M, an early Soviet ramjet-powered target drone, within the Soviet Union and across the Middle East and Asia. One 1983 report identified the DR-3 deployed to thirteen locations in the USSR, as well as to locations in East Germany, Czechoslovakia, and Mongolia. Meanwhile, a 1983 cable notes the likely deployment of DR-3 reconnaissance drones to Tartus, Syria, and a second cable from 1983 identifies possible Soviet drones in Libya. A Russian DR-3 even made it to North Korea, the result of a Syrian export of the Russian drones to the DPRK in 1993.

China's acquisition of a Lavochkin La-17 from the Soviet Union in the 1950s provided the origins for their drone development program.[2] The ChangKong-1 (CK-1), China's first indigenously produced drone, was based on the Soviet La-17. China's drone program accelerated when it acquired a U.S. Teledyne-Ryan Model 147 reconnaissance drone that was shot down in North Vietnam in the 1960s, as well as other U.S. drones that were shot down over mainland China. These acquisitions contributed to the development of the Wu Zhen 5 (WZ-5) air-launched reconnaissance drone, a copy of the Ryan 147 that served with Chinese units beginning in the 1980s.

In the late 1970s and 1980s, UAVs started to become something more than U.S. and Soviet modified target drones. Alvin Ellis, a Californian who served in World War II, developed what would become the Mastiff 1 UAV in Israel and sold the design to Israel's Tadiran Electronic Industries. The Mastiff 1, which first flew in 1973, and the Israel Aerospace Industries (IAI) Scout, a competitor to the Mastiff, played a pivotal role in the 1982 Lebanon War by identifying Syrian surface-to-air missile sites in the Bekaa Valley, an engagement that is widely viewed as the origins of the modern combat drone. The success of the Mastiff in Lebanon convinced then–secretary of the Navy John Lehman to make a deal with Israeli defense minister Yitzhak Rabin to secretly acquire the Mastiff, leading to the creation of a joint U.S.-Israeli drone similar to the Mastiff called the Pioneer.[3]

Abraham Karem, an Israeli engineer living in California, built the Amber, the predecessor to the U.S. Predator drone, in a garage outside Los Angeles.[4] The Predator, of course, went on to make history as the premier U.S. counterterrorism weapon.

Ellis' and Karem's garage creations gave way to an entirely new sector in the aerospace industry. In the late 1980s and 1990s, drone development and proliferation began to accelerate. In 1984 Tadiran joined with Israel Aerospace Industries to create a dedicated UAV division, known at the time as Mazlat and today as Malat.[5] Israel began exporting IAI Scout and its successor, IAI Searcher, to a growing number of countries, including South Africa, Singapore, India, and Sri Lanka.[6] The IAI Searcher is perhaps the most widely exported drone in history and remains active in multiple militaries around the world. Variants of the Tadiran Mastiff and IAI Scout, like the U.S. AAI Pioneer, South African Denel Dynamics Seeker, and Swiss RUAG Ranger, entered into service in the 1990s. Together with a growing ecosystem of light, medium, and heavy UAVs, these drones laid the groundwork for the modern fleet of unmanned aircraft that we know today.

Drones on the Battlefield
Drones in Afghanistan
Today's drones were, in many cases, designed for the Afghan theater. In 2000, in its push to locate and kill Osama bin Laden, the Central Intelligence Agency (CIA) and the U.S. Air Force deployed an RQ-1 Predator drone over Afghanistan. In October 2001 Air Force pilots made history when, sitting in a control station thousands of miles away, they launched a Hellfire missile from a Predator at a compound in Kandahar.[7] In the intervening years since those seminal moments, drones have been cemented as the critical counterterrorism and counterinsurgency weapon. This is due largely to their ability to loiter over a target area for a long period and to deliver real-time intelligence to commanders, two traits that appealed to the CIA in its search for Osama bin Laden. Afghanistan, as Benjamin S. Lambeth notes in *Air Power against Terror*, "offered a laboratory for testing, in a live combat setting, some of the most significant air power advances to have taken place in more than two decades."[8]

The uncontested airspace and permissive weather conditions of the Afghan theater contributed to the proliferation of unmanned aircraft.

The United States is not the only nation to deploy drones in Afghanistan. Unmanned aircraft are now a critical piece of equipment for any North Atlantic Treaty Organization (NATO) country forces deployed in this theater. Since the start of the NATO-led intervention in Afghanistan in 2001, at least eleven countries—Australia, Canada, the Czech Republic, Denmark, Germany, the Netherlands, Norway, Poland, Romania, Spain, and the UK—have acquired drones specifically for use in Afghanistan.[9] Some of these acquisitions were direct purchases, while others were leased from the manufacturer or included in U.S. foreign military assistance. For example, the United States has provided the Boeing Insitu ScanEagle drone to Romania and the Czech Republic to support operations in Afghanistan. In preparation for the Afghan deployment, NATO countries have acquired a variety of light, medium, and heavy unmanned aircraft that range from the hand-launched AeroVironment Raven to the IAI Heron medium-altitude, long-endurance (MALE) surveillance drone. With the exception of Canadian-made Sperwer drones, all of these acquisitions were drones of either U.S. or Israeli origin.

For many of these countries, the war in Afghanistan highlighted a crucial deficiency in their capabilities and tested their ability to rapidly acquire, field, integrate, and sustain new technologies and operating concepts into their forces. In 2003 General Patrice Klein, the French air force deputy head of operations, told *FlightGlobal* that France's involvement in Afghanistan had demonstrated that its lack of MALE drones was a significant detriment to its ability to acquire and process intelligence.[10] However, it was not until 2008 that French forces in Afghanistan received medium and heavy unmanned surveillance aircraft. An ambush in Afghanistan's Uzbin Valley in August 2008 that resulted in the deaths of ten French soldiers prompted the French military to rapidly deploy the Sagem Sperwer, a rail-launched tactical surveillance drone, to Afghanistan.[11] In the wake of the ambush, the Ministry of Defense also pushed forward the acquisition of the EADS Harfang, a MALE UAV based on Israel's Heron drone; the first Harfang was deployed to Afghanistan in 2009.

Still, France's introduction of UAVs in Afghanistan was not always smooth. The French lost at least twelve Sperwers in Afghanistan, and owing to the expensive Ka-band commercial satellite communications, Paris found that Harfang operations were unexpectedly costly.[12] In the absence of an indigenous or non-U.S. MALE drone, the Ministry of Defense in 2010 began to consider acquiring the General Atomics Reaper as a supplement or potential replacement for the Harfang. The United States approved the sale of unarmed Reapers to France in 2013, and as of 2017 the Reaper had replaced the Harfang as France's forward-deployed heavy unmanned system. France has selected the domestically produced SAGEM Patroller UAV as a replacement for the Sperwer.

The deployment to the Afghan theater is rapidly turning some countries with little prior experience with drones into regional drone powers. In the late 1990s and early 2000s, Australia was known for its role in the development of several important unmanned aircraft. In 1998 an Australian-made Aerosonde drone made a transatlantic flight, the first for a drone. Then, in 2001, a U.S. Northrop Grumman RQ-4 Global Hawk made another historic flight crossing the Pacific to land in Australia. Aside from some target drones and a few Aerosonde UAVs, however, the Australian Defence Force (ADF) had not invested heavily in unmanned systems. That all began to change with its deployment to Iraq and Afghanistan. The ADF began acquiring a variety of small and medium tactical UAVs to support ground operations in Iraq and Afghanistan. In 2005 it fielded the Israeli Elbit Systems Skylark IV mini UAVs with troops deployed to Iraq. It also acquired the AeroVironment Wasp, Insitu ScanEagle, and AAI Shadow. In 2009 Australia deployed a squadron of three IAI Heron long-range surveillance drones to Afghanistan.

The ADF obtained valuable operating experience from these deployments. Between 2007 and 2012, ADF-operated ScanEagles racked up an average of twenty-two flying hours per day, and between 2009 and 2014, the ADF's IAI Herons flew more than 27,000 flying hours. Following Australia's drawdown from Afghanistan in 2014, success of the IAI Herons in Afghanistan led the Department of Defence to retain two Herons for continued training and evaluation.

Propelled by the experience gained in Afghanistan, Australia is now seeking to apply unmanned aircraft to new missions and to augment its current fleet of drones with new aircraft. While Australia's drone acquisitions have so far been aimed at supporting its ground forces in Iraq and Afghanistan, future drone acquisitions will also include a suite of maritime reconnaissance and surveillance drones. In the "2016 Integrated Investment Program," the Australian Department of Defence outlined plans to invest a total of AUD 5.2–7.7 billion in new unmanned aircraft including a shipboard tactical UAV, long-range maritime surveillance drones, hand-launch reconnaissance drones, and a strike-capable MALE drone.[13] Australia has already selected the Northrop Grumman MQ-4C Triton to fulfill its long-range maritime surveillance requirement and the AeroVironment Wasp as the infantry's new reconnaissance drone.

Drones in Syria and Iraq

If Afghanistan illustrated the dominance of U.S. and Israeli drone manufacturers, the conflict in Syria and Iraq shows that the market for military drones is no longer the domain of these two countries. Drones have been a fixture of the Syrian Civil War and counter-ISIS campaign in Syria and Iraq. Virtually every state and non-state actor operating in Syria and Iraq has adopted some form of unmanned systems technology. In a 2016 guide to drones operating in the region, the Center for the Study of the Drone identified thirty-two systems made in six countries, as well as a handful of homemade drones.[14] In addition to the familiar U.S. and Israeli systems, such as the AeroVironment Puma and Elbit Systems Skylark, there are drones in Syria and Iraq that have been produced in China, Russia, Iran, and Turkey.

The conflict in Iraq and Syria is the first time that many of these systems have been deployed in a significant way to an active battlefield. This is particularly true for systems made in Iran. Although Iran has previously exported drones, like the Ababil and Mohajer tactical UAVs, to partners and allies around the world, Iranian-made systems have appeared in growing numbers in both Syria and Iraq. The Ababil-3, a tactical UAV made by the Iran Aircraft Manufacturing Industrial Company, has appeared repeatedly in Iraq and Syria. The hand-launched Iranian Oghab-1 and Yasir drones, the latter believed to be a copy of the U.S. ScanEagle, made their conflict debut in videos produced by Shiite militias in Iraq.

The conflict in Syria and Iraq has witnessed many notable firsts in the history of drones. New strike-capable drones made in Iran and China are believed to have launched their first strikes in Syria and Iraq. In December 2015 an Iraqi-owned Caihong-4 Rainbow, a surveillance and strike drone made by the China Aerospace Science and Technology Corporation (CASC), reportedly launched a strike in Ramadi. In February 2016 Iranian state media released a video that appeared to show the Shahed-129 drone strike targets in Aleppo Province in Syria. Meanwhile, in August 2015 in Syria, the United Kingdom, which operates the MQ-9 Reaper drone, launched its first targeted killing using a drone, killing UK national and ISIS propagandist Reyaad Khan.

Drones for Terror and Insurgency

In September 2016 a quad-rotor drone flown by militants belonging to Jund al-Aqsa, an al-Qaeda affiliate in Syria, released a small bomb on Syrian regime forces in Hama Province. Although the bomb did not appear do more than surprise the individuals below, this was not the last time terrorist groups used drones to deliver ordnance. In fact, the al-Aqsa drone incident illustrated a trend that had been building for some time: non-state actors are turning to remote-controlled drones to conduct reconnaissance, film propaganda videos, and launch attacks. This trend has accelerated over the course of the war in Syria and Iraq. Both remote-controlled ground vehicles and unmanned aircraft are appearing with greater frequency on the battlefield. In a lecture at the Special Operations Forces Industry Conference in May 2017, GEN Raymond Thomas, the head of U.S. Special Operations Command (SOCOM), said that the threat posed by ISIS drones in Iraq was the most "daunting problem" of 2016.[15]

The use of drones by non-state actors is not, however, a threat without precedent. An October 2016 report by the Combating Terrorism Center at West Point traces the history of the trend and its implications for modern warfare.[16] The first known attempt by a non-state actor to use drones was in the mid-1990s, when the Japanese religious cult Aum Shinrikyo tested using remote-controlled helicopters to deliver sarin gas. The experiment ended when the drones crashed, and the group used Tokyo's subway system to launch the attack. Drone experimentation among terrorist groups moved to the Middle East. Hezbollah, the Lebanon-based Shiite militancy bankrolled by Iran, began its drone program by hacking into the feeds of Israeli drones in the late 1990s. The group went on to become one of the prime innovators in the non–state-actor drone field. In 2004 Hezbollah flew a drone from Lebanon into northern Israel. Meanwhile, the Gaza-based Palestinian militant group Hamas has also experimented with drones and has repeatedly flown drones into southern Israel. Israeli fighter jets are reported to have shot down a Hamas drone in February 2017. The Hamas and Hezbollah drone programs have benefited from Iranian technology. Both groups are believed to have assembled variants of either the Iranian Mohajer or Ababil tactical surveillance drones.

The rise of consumer unmanned aircraft platforms and the availability and affordability of drone technology have reshaped the threat posed by non–state-actor drones. Before the rise of the consumer drone, non-state actors typically had to rely on the availability of drone technology from a third-party patron like Iran or on the technical expertise of an individual to build and use remote-controlled aircraft. Quad-rotors from popular manufacturers like China's DJI have significantly lowered the bar to access to unmanned aircraft systems (UAS). In addition to name-brand consumer drones, fixed-wing remote-controlled aircraft like the Skywalker X8 and Skyhunter, two drones that can be found in most hobby shops in the United States, offer terrorist and insurgent groups larger platforms that can carry larger payloads than quad-rotors. These fixed-wing drones have also been deployed extensively in Iraq and Syria and regularly appear in ISIS propaganda videos.

Remote-controlled ground weapons are also taking a toll on the battlefield in Syria and Iraq. These systems include tele-operated rifles and machine guns, rudimentary unmanned ground vehicles, and remote-controlled vehicle-borne improvised explosive devices (VBIEDs). A 2016 report by the U.S. Army Foreign Military Studies Office found that non–state actors in Libya, Syria, and Iraq were increasingly using improvised tele-operated weapons and had advanced technical knowledge of these devices.[17] One ISIS propaganda video from May

2017 showed a small, tracked unmanned ground vehicle not unlike the World War II–era German Goliath unmanned ground vehicle. ISIS has also outfitted VBIEDs with driverless steering and power so that the vehicle can be remotely driven toward its destination. The types of vehicles outfitted with this technology can vary widely. One remote-controlled improvised explosive device (IED) that was discovered outside Mosul in December 2016 appeared to be little more than a modified trolley.

In the hands of terrorist and insurgent groups, unmanned vehicles on the ground and in the air can be utilized for a variety of missions. Tele-operated machine guns can give attacking or defending forces the impression of greater numbers or distract the enemy from the true objective. Unmanned aircraft can be used to conduct reconnaissance and surveillance, battle damage assessment, strategic messaging and propaganda, package delivery, IED delivery, and weapons of mass destruction delivery and can be made a weapons platform for bombs, rockets, or missiles.[18] Drones are being used by state and non-state actors in Iraq and Syria as spotters to improve the precision of artillery and mortar attacks, as well as guides for VBIEDs.[19] Drones offer non-state actors additional tactical capabilities and enable a greater range of operations, even if they do not necessarily change the strategic situation on the ground.

ISIS has pioneered the development and implementation of cheap, multirole UAVs on the battlefield. Its work in this field was highlighted by an incident in October 2016 in which an ISIS drone carrying explosives rammed into Kurdish and French troops in Iraq, killing two Peshmerga and wounding a French soldier. Over the next few months, ISIS began deploying drones with increasing frequency. Instead of just kamikaze attacks, however, the drones were used to drop tiny bombs on unsuspecting targets below. At one point in the battle for Mosul, explained SOCOM's General Thomas, ISIS fielded seventy drones within a twenty-four-hour period, nearly bringing the Iraqi offensive to a standstill.[20] Documents obtained by the Combating Terrorism Center at West Point show that ISIS implemented a system to manage the development, training, and deployment of drones.[21] This bureaucratic system transformed these unsophisticated remote-control aircraft into strike-capable hobby drones. ISIS created a dedicated unit, the Baraa bin Malek Brigade, to operate the drones.

To turn remote-control aircraft into lethal drones, ISIS and other groups like Jund al-Aqsa have modified quad-rotor and fixed-wing aircraft with a variety of release mechanisms and have developed specialized munitions. Researchers at UK-based Conflict Armament Research found that ISIS had developed a multirole IED that could function either as a grenade or as ordnance dropped from a UAV. The 172-millimeter-long munition would be suspended below the consumer quad-rotor and connected to a servomotor by a metal wire loop and rod. "When the UAV is directly above the intended target, the operator lowers the altitude of the UAV and transmits a radio signal to a custom switching circuit on the UAV," write researchers at Conflict Armament Research. "The custom switching circuit actuates the servomotor, which retracts the rod and releases the IED."[22]

Technological advances in commercial drone systems and technology could enable non-state actors to deploy them in increasingly sophisticated ways on the battlefield. Consumer drones have experienced a rapid technological advancement, particularly in the realm of autonomous flight. DJI has prioritized the implementation of autonomous capabilities as a way of lowering the bar to entry for new pilots. DJI's latest drone, the Spark, has four built-in automated flight modes, including a gesture control feature that allows users to control the drone with their hands. Smaller companies specializing in drone software are also developing increasingly sophisticated autopilots. The ArduPilot, a popular open-source autopilot software, and the Pixhawk hardware are able to turn any remote-controlled aircraft into a semiautonomous drone. Other platforms, such as the Triangle UAS Andruav, allow the operator to control multiple vehicles at once from a remote location. These technologies both add capability to non-state-actor UAS operations and remove the vulnerability of the operator.

State militaries and militias are increasingly adopting consumer drones. Iraqi federal police are using DJI drones for artillery spotting and reconnaissance and have established specialized drone units. The Israel Defense Forces have begun equipping their infantry, border defense, and combat intelligence corps with DJI drones. Some countries are choosing to invest in smaller, low-cost unmanned systems rather than in long-range platforms like the Reaper. At the GLOBSEC 2017 Security Forum, Tomasz Szatkowski, the undersecretary of state for Poland's Ministry of National Defence, said that Poland is planning a "massive investment in ISR [intelligence, surveillance, and reconnaissance] drones and kamikaze drones . . . similar to those ISIS is using."[23] This decision reflects the uncertain future facing MALE UAVs like the Reaper, which are not suited for operating in contested environments. Szatkowski envisions that consumer reconnaissance drones and lethal loitering munitions, like the Polish WB Electronics Warmate, are a deadly combination.

The growing prevalence of small unmanned systems on the battlefield has alarmed U.S. military planners. The Navy is concerned that swarms of low-cost unmanned air or maritime platforms could penetrate the defenses currently on board today's ships. The Air Force is similarly considering a future in which armed, low-cost drones could be used to attack vulnerable aircraft parked on the tarmac of an airfield. In the popular 2016 novel *Ghost Fleet: A Novel of the Next World War,* Peter W. Singer and August Cole explored some of these possibilities, describing swarms of autonomous quad-rotor drones overwhelming air base defenses.[24] Although that was science fiction, there are already hints that these scenarios are not too far in the future. In early 2017 researchers in Yemen discovered that Houthi rebels were outfitting drones smuggled in from Iran with explosives and launching them at Saudi air defenses.[25] The rebels were also using remote-controlled boats laden with explosives to attack Saudi frigates off the Yemeni coast, killing one Saudi sailor.

Beyond the battlefield, the possibility that drones may be used in a terror attack against a domestic target has never been far outside the realm of possibility. In the months preceding the 2003 U.S. invasion of Iraq, then–secretary of state Colin Powell expressed concern that Iraqi drones could be used to attack U.S. cities.[26] While this fear turned out to be misplaced, Iraq was indeed developing UAVs under a program known as Al Quds. Following Saddam Hussein's capture in December 2003, the CIA discovered that some of the drones were intended to be delivered to Hamas agents who would use them to attack Ariel Sharon. More recently, terrorism investigations in the

United States and Europe have uncovered plans for potential terrorist attacks using drones.[27]

A 2008 report by the RAND Corporation explored the different ways that drones could be used in a domestic terror attack.[28] The
report focused on the ways that drones could serve as platforms for a
direct attack, an indirect attack, or the dispersal of a chemical or biological agent and compared the utility of UAVs to cruise missiles. It
found that although drones offered terrorists some advantages, there
are usually other cheaper and more effective means of attacking targets for most scenarios.

It wasn't until a stunt at a political rally in Germany in 2013
that the possibility of a domestic terror attack with drones started
to gain public attention. During the September 2013 rally in Dresden, a member of Germany's Pirate Party flew a Parrot AR quad-
rotor drone within feet of Chancellor Angela Merkel. Even though
the incident was never intended to be more than political theater, it
highlighted the potential threat posed by a consumer drone technology that was, at the time, still in its infancy. In 2015 a federal
employee accidentally crashed his DJI quad-rotor drone into the
White House lawn. And one month later, a Japanese man protest-
ing Tokyo's plans to restart nuclear energy plants landed a quad-rotor
drone carrying radioactive sand on the prime minister's residence.
Most concerning, however, was when investigators found two drones
among the belongings of Abdulkadir Masharipov, the suspect in the
2017 New Year's Day terrorist attack in Istanbul that left thirty-nine
people dead. Although the drones do not appear to have been used
in the attack, the discovery suggested drones could be used in future
ISIS-inspired terror attacks.

A Rising Drone Power

On September 9, 2013, the Japanese Air Self-Defense Force
scrambled an F-15 fighter jet in response to an aircraft that had
intruded into Japanese airspace. The offending vehicle: a Chinese military drone. The surveillance drone was spotted flying over the Senkaku Islands—known in China as the Diaoyu

Islands—in the southern region of the East China Sea. The Japanese government was furious; China was unapologetic. . . .

Japan was shaken by the Chinese drone. . . . After the overflight, . . . Japan released new rules of engagement for drones that included the proviso that it would shoot down any unauthorized unmanned aircraft that entered Japanese airspace and ignored warnings to leave.[29]

The Senkaku/Diaoyu Islands incident suggested that drones like the BZK-005 could play a larger role in China's territorial disputes in the East and South China Seas. Since that incident China has revealed new UAS and has deployed the BZK-005 and other drones to surveil domestic targets and conduct border patrols. Today, the Chinese domestic drone industry is competitive with the U.S. and Israel industries, both for military and civilian unmanned systems. Like the U.S. military, the People's Liberation Army (PLA) believes that unmanned systems can augment and, in some situations, replace manned platforms. And as in the United States, unmanned platforms are viewed in China as stepping-stones toward systems that are able to operate with greater autonomy and artificial intelligence, technologies that China views as truly transformational.[30]

Early Chinese drones were based on copies of Soviet and U.S. drones like the Firebee reconnaissance UAV. China's modern military drone industry, however, is the result of a modernization program that began in the mid-1990s and included an emphasis on the development of unmanned aircraft. China's first class of dedicated UAV operators graduated in 1994 from what was at the time the Army Artillery Academy. One of China's most prominent tactical UAVs, the ASN-20X series drones, were first fielded by the PLA in the mid-1990s. The ASN-series drones, truck-launched fixed-wing tactical drones made by Xian ASN Technology Group, continue to remain active in both the PLA and the PLA Navy, providing tactical ISR and serving as communications relays. China also imported the Israeli IAI Harpy loitering munition in the 1990s.

The U.S. Department of Defense 2003's *Annual Report on the Military Power of the People's Republic to China* noted China's investment in unmanned aircraft and in the burgeoning line of ASN-20X series drones.[31] The report argued that China was developing drones that would eventually "enable continual surveillance well beyond China's coastal waters." Indeed, in the early 2000s, China was developing another of the PLA's most noteworthy drones, the Harbin BZK-005. The BZK-005 is a MALE UAV designed for long-range maritime surveillance. It was designed and manufactured by Beihang University, one of China's first centers for unmanned systems research, and Harbin Aircraft Industry. A model of the BZK-005 appeared at the 2006 Zhuhai Air Show.

Along with the ASN-209 Silver Eagle, the BZK-005 has since been deployed extensively by the PLA Navy to coastal bases for maritime border surveillance in the East and South China Seas.[32] Beginning around 2013, a previously abandoned airfield on Daishan Island in Zhejiang Province has served as the East Sea Fleet's primary drone base in the East China Sea. In 2016 the BZK-005 was deployed briefly to Woody Island in the South China Sea and, later that year, to Lingshui Air Base on Hainan Island. These deployments underscore the fact that unmanned aircraft are likely to play heavily into China's maritime border surveillance and, potentially, into the disputes over islands in the East and South China Seas.[33]

In addition to surveillance drones, China has developed several unmanned combat aerial vehicles (UCAVs), namely, the China Aerospace Science and Technology Corporation (CASC) Caihong series and the Aviation Industry Corporation of China (AVIC) Wing Loong series. The CH-4 and Wing Loong resemble the U.S. Predator and Reaper drones, although the Chinese systems are constrained by China's limited satellite communications capabilities. And unlike most U.S. systems, some of these drones appear to have been designed primarily for export.

The development of the CASC Caihong (also known as "Rainbow") drones began in 2000. The first two prototype aircraft, the Caihong-1 and Caihong-2, were mainly for development and testing purposes. The Caihong-3 (CH-3) was larger, and unlike its predecessors, it could be armed. It was first displayed at the 2008 Zhuhai Air Show. The CH-3 does not appear to have been adopted by the PLA. Rather, it is believed to have been exported to a number of international partners, including Nigeria, Pakistan, Turkmenistan, and potentially, Myanmar. The CH-3's successor, the CH-4, is significantly larger than the CH-3 and bears a physical resemblance to the U.S. Reaper drone. A model of the CH-4 was displayed at the 2012 Zhuhai Air Show. The CH-4 has been exported to Iraq, Jordan, and Saudi Arabia. The latest Caihong drone, the CH-5, was unveiled at the 2016 Zhuhai Air Show. The CH-5 is the most heavily armed Chinese UCAV, capable of carrying sixteen air-to-surface munitions.

The AVIC Wing Loong drones are the main competitors to the Caihong series. The Wing Loong (also known as Yi Long, or "Pterodactyl") was unveiled at the 2010 Zhuhai Air Show. The Wing Loong was developed by AVIC's Chengdu Aircraft Design and Research Institute, and although it was intended primarily for the PLA Air Force (PLAAF), it has also been exported to international customers. It was first deployed domestically in Xinjiang Province following unrest among the Uighur population in 2014. The PLAAF has at least one dedicated Wing Loong unit, which is based at Uxxaktal Air Base in the Bayingolin Mongol Autonomous Prefecture in northwestern China. The Wing Loong has been exported to the United Arab Emirates (UAE), which has deployed the drone to Libya and to Eritrea for operations over Yemen. It is also believed to have been sold to Egypt, Saudi Arabia, and Kazakhstan. The Wing Loong II, which is considerably larger than the Wing Loong I, was unveiled in November 2016.

China's UCAV industry accelerated in 2016 in several important areas. In May 2016 a Chinese CH-4 that was controlled via satellite from over a thousand kilometers away conducted a live-fire missile test. Unlike U.S. drones, China's UCAVs are limited by satellite communications infrastructure to an operational range of less than two hundred kilometers. The test in May 2016 signified a major step forward for China's UAV capabilities. Meanwhile, several countries in the Middle East, including the UAE, Saudi Arabia, and Jordan, began deploying Chinese-made drones in 2016, some in active combat zones. These deployments suggest that the Chinese UCAVs are becoming increasingly capable and offer Chinese engineers opportunity to examine how their systems perform in combat. At the 2016 Zhuhai Air Show, CASC and AVIC both unveiled upgraded versions of the Wing Loong and Caihong series combat aircraft that appear to be significantly more capable than their predecessors. Also displayed at Zhuhai 2016 was the AVIC Cloud Shadow, a new strike drone that, unlike the Wing Loong and Caihong, is powered by a turbojet engine. According to *IHS Jane's*, the Cloud Shadow appears designed primarily for export.[34]

Over the past few years, China has unveiled concepts for new drones. Whereas some of the systems do not appear to have progressed much past the prototype stage, others are reported to have recently entered into production, and each of these systems suggests possible directions and roles for the next generation of Chinese UAVs. The Xianlong (Soar Dragon), a large UAV made by Guizhou Aircraft Corporation, could be used to locate targets for the DH-21D antiship ballistic missile.[35] The Xianlong reportedly entered into production in mid-2016. Two stealth UAV prototypes, the Lijian (Sharp Sword) and Anjian (Dark Sword), are reportedly still under development. Although there is little reliable information about either drone, the Lijian was awarded second place in China's National Science and Technology Advancement Prizes competition in 2017. China's largest drone, the Shendiao (Divine Eagle), has a massive forty-five-meter-long wingspan—just longer than the U.S. RQ-4 Global Hawk. The Shendiao reportedly made its first flight in 2015 and appears to remain in development.

New airframes are not the only progress China has made in developing next-generation unmanned systems. China has developed its own family of unmanned ground vehicles, similar to those used by the United States for explosive ordnance disposal. In a demonstration in 2016, the China Electronics Technology Group Corporation (CETC) launched a swarm of sixty-seven drones, potentially breaking the record for the largest drone swarm. "Our swarming drone technology is the top in the world," Zhang Dengzhou, chief accountant at CETC, said in a statement to reporters following the demonstration.[36] China has also progressed in developing ground and maritime unmanned systems. In the monthlong Overcoming Obstacles 2016, a Chinese army contest similar to the U.S. Defense Advanced Research Projects Agency (DARPA) Grand Challenge, competitors tested legged robots, robotic trucks, self-driving cars, and other unmanned and autonomous ground vehicles. Meanwhile, in 2015 an unmanned underwater vehicle developed by Tianjin University completed a field test in which it operated autonomously at sea for twenty-one days. In 2016 the China State Shipbuilding Corporation proposed developing an underwater Great Wall composed of underwater listening posts, unmanned undersea vehicles, and unmanned surface vehicles designed to locate enemy submarines.

Chinese military planners believe that unmanned systems, robotics, and artificial intelligence are part of a revolution in military affairs, the theory that some changes in doctrine and technology can fundamentally change the character of warfare. In the Ministry of Defense's 2015 white paper "National Security Situation," the authors argue, "The world revolution in military affairs (RMA) is proceeding to a new stage. Long-range, precise, smart, stealthy and unmanned weapons and equipment are becoming increasingly sophisticated."[37] Chinese policy documents published in 2016, including the thirteenth Five-Year Plan (2016–20) and the fourteenth Five-Year National Science and Technology Innovation Plan, highlight the importance of achieving a breakthrough in the development of artificial intelligence.[38] The PLA has reportedly established a dedicated unit, the Intelligent Unmanned Systems and Systems of Systems Science and Technology Domain Expert Group, to integrate these new technologies into the future force. In 2017 the *New York Times* reported that China was investing heavily in U.S. artificial intelligence and robotics startups, prompting concerns in Washington that American advances in these technologies could be accessed by the Chinese.[39]

Looking Forward

Internal and peripheral operations such as disaster response and border security are likely to be a significant focus of global drone operations. This is evinced by the acquisition strategies of countries like Australia, which seeks to purchase the Northrop Grumman Triton for maritime border surveillance, as well as by news of drone deployments. France's EADS Harfang drones, for example, which were withdrawn from active overseas operations in 2017, are now expected to be used to provide surveillance for high-profile public events. In 2015 China deployed a Wing Loong to assist in the response to the Xinjiang earthquake—the first acknowledged Wing Loong deployment by the PLAAF—and in 2017, China sent a CH-4 UAV to monitor forest fires in northeastern China. In the United States, there is also growing interest in tasking Predator and Reaper drones operated by the Air National Guard to domestic missions, particularly emergency response. These types of operations are only likely to increase as more and more countries implement domestic drone regulations and as technologies such as sense-and-avoid enhance the safety of drone operations in crowded civilian airspaces.

Drones are well suited to assist with border security and disaster response because of their long dwell time and payload capabilities. Michael Horowitz writes in *International Security* that surveillance drones and other unarmed surveillance platforms have traditionally limited the potential for international disputes over borders and contributed to greater stability.[40] By delivering persistent surveillance and real-time information, drones could remove some of the ambiguity from a crisis situation, reducing the risk that misunderstanding or fear could escalate a conflict. And as more and more countries become accustomed to drones, the loss of an unmanned system is less likely to spark an international incident than the loss of a manned platform. In 2015, for example, Turkey shot down a Russian Orlan-10 reconnaissance drone on its border with Syria without incurring a significant response.

Chinese drone exports will continue to enable a growing number of countries to acquire strike-capable drones. Chinese arms exports are generally aimed at improving ties with partners and as a way to support broader foreign policy objectives. In addition to direct sales, China has licensed some countries to produce their own variants of Chinese drones. In March 2017 China agreed to open a drone factory in Saudi Arabia to produce the CASC CH-4, part of a $65 billion arms deal between the two countries. Saudi Arabia already purchased several Chinese strike drones and has also unveiled its own strike-capable drone, the Saqr-1, which appears similar to the Chinese systems. Owing to U.S., Israeli, and international limitations on drone exports and the affordability of Chinese systems, China is unlikely to face much competition in this space in the coming years. Unlike U.S. drone exports, Chinese exports do not come with the same restrictions on how these systems may be used.

Although the proliferation of surveillance drones may have a stabilizing effect, the spread of strike-capable drones could have the opposite effect. In 2016 alone five countries—Kazakhstan, Jordan, United Arab Emirates, Saudi Arabia, and Egypt—acquired strike-capable drones from China. Some of these drones have already been deployed in active operations over Libya, Yemen, and the Sinai Peninsula and may have engaged in counterterrorism strikes. There is a not insignificant risk that as more countries acquire armed drones and engage in drone strikes, the potential for miscalculation and error could increase. In spite of a successful drone strike just months earlier, in January 2016 an Iraqi CH-4 drone accidentally killed nine Shiite Muslim militia fighters allied with the government. As the Iraqi example and the U.S. targeted killing campaign demonstrate, drone operations frequently rely on a confluence of intelligence sources.

The number of indigenous multirole, strike-capable drones currently under development or deployed is also on the rise and carries similar risks. Turkey has developed two strike-capable drones, the Kale-Baykar Bayraktar and the TAI Anka-S. The Bayraktar is already reported to have engaged in operations against Kurdish rebels, and the Anka-S is expected to do so, potentially with strikes, when it becomes operational in 2017. These systems could potentially enable Ankara to engage in counterterrorism operations that might otherwise be too risky for regime forces.

Even as more and more countries acquire multirole, strike-capable drones, a family of small, lethal drones known as loitering munitions are also gaining in popularity, particularly among countries with less well-funded militaries than Turkey or the UAE. A report by the Center for the Study of the Drone found there are nearly thirty different types of loitering munitions made in eight countries, including the United States, Israel, South Korea, China, Iran, Turkey, and Poland.[41] Because they are armed and offer a low-cost precision-strike capability, the spread of these systems could have an escalatory effect on conflicts. In 2016 Azerbaijan reportedly directed an Israel-made Harpy loitering munition at a bus filled with Armenian volunteers in the Nagorno-Karabakh region, killing seven. Incidents such as these have the potential to exacerbate tensions. Today, Azerbaijan is producing its own armed loitering munitions, a variant—known as Zarba—of the

Israel Aeronautics Defense Systems Orbiter 1K. Meanwhile, Ukraine has acquired the Polish Warmate loitering munition and has developed its own small strike drone called the Yatagan-2.

The proliferation of small, cheap, and lethal drones among both state and non-state actors has accelerated in recent years and shows no signs of slowing down. In Syria and Iraq, ISIS has developed innovative and deadly applications for the same consumer drones that are available to hobbyists in the United States. In the near future, as Paul Scharre notes in a report by the Center for a New American Security, "IEDs will come looking for U.S. forces."[42] Non-state-actor drone tactics and systems on the ground and in the air are likely to become more sophisticated and could transfer from active battlefields to domestic targets. Moreover, developing an effective solution will require both technologies and tactics that are adaptable to evolutions—such as increased autonomy—in drone capabilities.

In the years since the Ellis' and Karem's garage-built creations, unmanned systems have proliferated widely and become standard equipment for militaries around the world. The surge in drone production, acquisition, and deployments has been shaped by the counterterrorism and insurgency conflicts in Afghanistan, Iraq, and Syria, as well as by the rise in non-state-actor drones and China's drone industry. These trends are likely to accelerate the proliferation of unmanned systems, leading to a world that is increasingly crowded with drones.

Notes

1. Defense Science Board, *Task Force Report: The Role of Autonomy in DoD Systems* (Washington, DC: Department of Defense, July 2012), http://www.acq.osd.mil/dsb/reports/2010s/AutonomyReport.pdf.
2. Richard D. Fisher Jr., "Maritime Employment of PLA Unmanned Aerial Vehicles," in *Chinese Aerospace Power: Evolving Maritime Roles*, ed. Andrew Erickson and Lyle Goldstein (Annapolis, MD: Naval Institute Press, 2012).
3. Norman Polmar, "The Pioneering Pioneer," *Naval History Magazine*, October 2013, https://www.usni.org/magazines/navalhistory/2013-09/historic-aircraft-pioneering-pioneer.
4. Richard Whittle, *Predator: The Secret Origins of the Drone Revolution* (New York: Henry Holt, 2014).

5. Laurence R. Newcome, *Unmanned Aviation: A Brief History of Unmanned Aerial Vehicles* (Reston, VA: American Institute of Aeronautics and Astronautics, 2004).

6. Stockholm International Peace Research Institute, SIPRI Arms Transfers Database, https://www.sipri.org/databases/armstransfers.

7. Arthur Holland Michel, "How Rogue Techies Armed the Predator, Almost Stopped 9/11, and Accidentally Invented Remote War," *Wired*, December 17, 2015, https://www.wired.com/2015/12/how-rogue-techies-armed-the-predator-almost-stopped-911-and-accidentally-invented-remote-war/.

8. Benjamin S. Lambeth, *Air Power against Terror: America's Conduct of Operation Enduring Freedom* (Santa Monica, CA: Rand, 2005), https://www.rand.org/content/dam/rand/pubs/monographs/2006/RAND_MG166-1.pdf.

9. Original data collected by the Center for the Study of the Drone, Bard College, Annandale-on-Hudson, NY.

10. Christina Mackenzie, "Intelligence a Key Lesson of Afghanistan for French," *Flight International*, March 3, 2003, https://www.flightglobal.com/Flight PDFArchive/2003/2003%20-%200490.PDF.

11. Jean-Baptiste Jeangène Vilmer, "Proliferated Drones: A Perspective on France" (Washington, DC: Center for a New American Security, n.d.), http://drones.cnas.org/reports/a-perspective-on-france/.

12. Gary Schaub Jr., *Long Time Coming: Developing and Integrating UAVs into the American British, French, and Danish Armed Forces* (Copenhagen: Centre for Military Studies, 2014), http://cms.polsci.ku.dk/publikationer/longtimecoming/Long_Time_Coming.pdf.

13. Department of Defence, *2016 Integrated Investment Program* (Canberra: Commonwealth of Australia, 2016), http://www.defence.gov.au/WhitePaper/Docs/2016-Defence-Integrated-Investment-Program.pdf.

14. Dan Gettinger, "Drones Operating in Syria and Iraq," Center for the Study of the Drone Field Guide, December 13, 2016, http://dronecenter.bard.edu/drones-operating-in-syria-and-iraq/.

15. David B. Larter, "SOCOM Commander: Armed ISIS Drones Were 2016's 'Most Daunting Problem,' " *Defense News*, May 16, 2017, http://www.defensenews.com/articles/socom-commander-says-isis-drones-were-2016s-most-daunting-problem.

16. Don Rassler, *Remotely Piloted Innovation: Terrorism, Drones and Supportive Technology* (West Point, NY: Combating Terrorism Center, October 2016), https://www.ctc.usma.edu/v2/wp-content/uploads/2016/10/Drones-Report.pdf.

17. Robert J. Bunker and Alma Keshavarz, *Terrorist and Insurgent Teleoperated Sniper and Machine Guns* (Fort Leavenworth, KS: Foreign Military Studies Office, August 22, 2016), https://community.apan.org/wg/tradoc-g2/fmso/m/fmso-monographs/194883.

18. Robert J. Bunker, *Terrorist and Insurgent Unmanned Aerial Vehicles: Use, Potentials, and Military Implications* (Carlisle, PA: Strategic Studies Institute, U.S. Army War College, August 2015), https://ssi.armywarcollege.edu/pdffiles/PUB1287.pdf.

19. Austin Bodetti, "Iraqi Militias Are Using Consumer Drones to Fight ISIS," *Wired*, June 28, 2016, https://www.wired.co.uk/article/iraq-isis-war-consumer-drones.

20. Patrick Tucker, "In Urgent Request US Special Ops Adds 350 Kamikaze Drones to Fight ISIS," *Defense One*, May 18, 2017, http://www.defenseone.com/technology/2017/05/Special-Ops-Gets-350-More-Kamikaze-Suicide-Drones-to-Fight-ISIS/137987.

21. Don Rassler, Muhammad al-Ubaydi, and Vera Mironova, "The Islamic State's Drone Documents: Management, Acquisitions and DIY Tradecraft," Combating Terrorism Center, January 31, 2017, https://ctc.usma.edu/posts/ctc-perspectives-the-islamic-states-drone-documents-management-acquisitions-and-diy-tradecraft.

22. Conflict Armament Research, "Frontline Perspective: Islamic State's Weaponised Drones," October 2016, http://www.conflictarm.com/perspectives/islamic-states-weaponised-drones/.

23. Patrick Tucker, "Poland Is Preparing for 15 Years of Rising Tension with Russia," *Defense One*, June 1, 2017, http://www.defenseone.com/technology/2017/06/poland-preparing-15-years-rising-tension-russia/138337.

24. P. W. Singer and August Cole, *Ghost Fleet: A Novel of the Next World War* (Boston: Mariner Books, 2016).

25. Thomas Gibbons-Neff, "Houthi Forces Appear to Be Using Iranian-Made Drones to Ram Saudi Air Defenses in Yemen, Report Says," *Washington Post*, March 22, 2017, https://www.washingtonpost.com/news/checkpoint/wp/2017/03/22/houthi-forces-appear-to-be-using-iranian-made-drones-to-ram-saudi-air-defenses-in-yemen-report-says/.

26. Bret Baier and Liza Porteus, "Iraqi Drones May Target U.S. Cities," Fox News, February 24, 2003, http://www.foxnews.com/story/2003/02/24/iraqi-drones-may-target-us-cities.html.

27. Rassler, *Remotely Piloted Innovation*.

28. Brian A. Jackson, David R. Frelinger, Michael J. Lostumbo, and Robert W. Button, *Evaluating Novel Threats to the Homeland: Unmanned Aerial Vehicles and Cruise Missiles* (Santa Monica, CA: Rand, 2008), https://www.rand.org/content/dam/rand/pubs/monographs/2008/RAND_MG626.pdf.

29. Dan Gettinger, "'An Act of War': Drones Are Testing China-Japan Relations," Center for the Study of the Drone Field Guide, November 8, 2013, http://dronecenter.bard.edu/act-war-drones-testing-china-japan-relations/.

30. Elsa B. Kania, *Battlefield Singularity: Artificial Intelligence, Military Revolution, and China's Future Military Power* (Washington, DC: Center for a New American Security, November 28, 2017), https://www.cnas.org/publications/reports/battlefield-singularity-artificial-intelligence-military-revolution-and-chinas-future-military-power.

31. Department of Defense, *Annual Report on the Military Power of the People's Republic of China* (Washington, DC: Department of Defense, July 28, 2003), http://www.globalsecurity.org/military/library/report/2003/20030730chinaex.pdf.

32. Dan Gettinger, "Drone Bases Updates," Center for the Study of the Drone, October 2, 2016, http://dronecenter.bard.edu/drone-bases-updates/.

33. Elsa Kania, "China's Employment of Unmanned Systems: Across the Spectrum from Peacetime to Wartime," *Lawfare* (blog), May 22, 2017, https://www.lawfareblog.com/chinas-employment-unmanned-systems-across-spectrum-peacetime-wartime.

34. Ibid.
35. Jonathan Ray, Katie Atha, Edward Francis, Caleb Dependahl, James Mulvenon, Daniel Alderman, and Leigh Ann Ragland-Luce, *China's Industrial and Military Robotics Development* (Vienna, VA: Center for Intelligence Research and Analysis, Defense Group Inc., October 2016), https://www.uscc.gov/sites/default/files/Research/DGI_China%27s%20Industrial%20and%20Military%20Robotics%20Development.pdf.
36. David Hambling, "If Drone Swarms Are the Future, China May Be Winning," *Popular Mechanics*, December 23, 2016, http://www.popularmechanics.com/military/research/a24494/chinese-drones-swarms/.
37. Ministry of National Defense, People's Republic of China, "National Security Situation," May 26, 2015, http://eng.mod.gov.cn/Database/White Papers/2015-05/26/content_4586688.htm.
38. Elsa Kania, "China May Soon Surpass America on the Artificial Intelligence Battlefield," *National Interest*, February 21, 2017, http://nationalinterest.org/feature/china-may-soon-surpass-america-the-artificial-intelligence-19524.
39. Paul Mozur and Jane Perlez, "China Bets on Sensitive U.S. Start-Ups, Worrying the Pentagon," *New York Times*, March 22, 2017, https://www.nytimes.com/2017/03/22/technology/china-defense-start-ups.html?_r=0.
40. Michael C. Horowitz, Sarah E. Kreps, and Matthew Fuhrmann, "Separating Fact from Fiction in the Debate over Drone Proliferation," *International Security* 41, no. 2 (Fall 2016): 7–42, https://www.mitpressjournals.org/doi/abs/10.1162/ISEC_a_00257.
41. Arthur Holland Michel and Dan Gettinger, "Loitering Munitions in Focus," Center for the Study of the Drone, February 10, 2017, http://dronecenter.bard.edu/loitering-munitions-in-focus/.
42. Paul Scharre, *Uncertain Ground: Emerging Challenges in Land Warfare* (Washington, DC: Center for a New American Security, December 10, 2015), https://www.cnas.org/publications/reports/uncertain-ground-emerging-challenges-in-land-warfare.

04

State of the Operational Art

Maritime Systems | *Arthur Holland Michel*

Introduction

If the first chapter of the modern drone revolution was written in the skies over Central Asia and the Middle East, the next chapter will be a seafaring tale. The maritime domain is set to witness an explosion in the development and use of a whole range of unmanned systems that will likely have just as much of an impact on future conflicts as the aerial Predators, Reapers, and Shadows had on the overland wars of the past two decades.

All the markers of a looming drone revolution at sea are already evident, particularly when it comes to the U.S. Navy. Billions of research and acquisition dollars are being funneled into maritime drone projects, and military leaders are emphasizing the need for an unmanned pillar in every conceivable type of operation, from antisubmarine warfare in open waters to amphibious assaults. It seems that no naval vision document can pass muster with the top brass anymore without making some mention of the need for autonomous unmanned systems. "There is no question," wrote Chief of Naval Operations Adm. John Richardson in one such vision document, from 2017, charting the course for the future of the service, "that unmanned systems must . . . be an integral part of the future fleet."[1]

Unlike the first wave of the drone revolution, the maritime drone revolution will take place across all domains: not just under the oceans but also on the surface of the sea and in the air. The Navy is actively developing a dizzying array of unmanned systems—ranging from small, motorless sea-glider submarines to 130-foot ghost ships to high-altitude, long-endurance reconnaissance drones—along with elaborate concepts of operations that seek to take advantage of the "unmanned-ness" of these new vehicles as a means of maintaining superiority over the seas for many years to come.

Of course, like the aerial drone revolution, the maritime drone revolution has a long history. Navies first took an interest in drones—aerial drones for target practice, in particular—as early as the 1910s. Shortly after World War I, the UK's Royal Navy tested a number of drones, including the Royal Aircraft Establishment Larynx, an ambitious and complex explosives-laden aerial torpedo that is considered to be one of the earliest "strike" drones (it was in fact more like a modern-day cruise missile than a Reaper), from the deck of ships like HMS *Stronghold*. The Larynx never made it past the developmental stage, but the maritime services' interest in unmanned aircraft was firmly cemented.[2]

In the late 1930s, the U.S. Navy developed the TDR-1, an unmanned aerial strike fighter built by Interstate Aircraft equipped with a 1,000-pound weapon payload and an advanced guidance system created, in secret, by the Radio Corporation of America. A fleet of TDR-1s was deployed in 1944 to the Pacific, where they completed fifty sorties (thirty-one of which resulted in target hits), but the Navy was focused on other efforts, and the airplanes were soon retired and largely forgotten.[3]

Investment in unmanned aerial technology continued among the U.S. military services throughout the second half of the twentieth century. In 1946 the Navy used drones—essentially old manned warplanes that had been equipped with remote-control systems—to take measurements from inside atomic mushroom clouds at Bikini Atoll during Operation Crossroads. The most notable aerial maritime drone of the twentieth century was undoubtedly the Gyrodyne QH-50 Drone Anti-Submarine Helicopter (DASH), an outlandish and startlingly modern weaponized helicopter drone first deployed in 1962. A number of QH-50 variants were produced, including several intelligence, surveillance, and reconnaissance (ISR) models and even a nuclear strike–capable system, making it the first and only drone (so far) to carry a nuclear bomb. Though the system never saw active combat, it remained in service, primarily as a target practice drone, until May 2006.[4]

While aerial drones like the DASH tend to dominate histories of military unmanned systems technology, undersea drone development was also active during this period, and the history of drones under the waves is almost equally as varied as that of their unmanned counterparts in the air.

The sea itself is an ideal environment for drones. It is dull, it is dear, it is dirty, and it is dangerous—the four *D* jobs for which unmanned systems are particularly useful. The first military submersible drone was the U.S. Navy's Cable-Controlled Underwater Recovery Vehicle, which was designed and deployed in the 1960s to recover unexploded ordnance from the sea floor at depths of up to two thousand feet. In one particularly heroic mission that served as early proof of the benefits of going unmanned under the sea, the submersible drone was used to retrieve an unexploded hydrogen bomb from the bottom of the Mediterranean following an air accident involving a nuclear bomber off the southern coast of Spain in 1966.[5] In the following decade, the Defense Advanced Research Projects Agency (DARPA) engaged in a lengthy research effort to develop technologies for long-endurance unmanned submarines for a variety of missions.

The commercial sector—specifically the oil and gas industry—as well as the scientific research community, also energetically pushed the development of the technology forward. Some of the earliest widely used systems—such as the University of Washington Applied Physics Laboratory's Special Purpose Underwater Research Vehicle, the U.S. Navy's Deep Drone, and the Argo, a deep-sea drone that made headlines when it discovered the wreckage of the *Titanic* in 1985— were conceived for research purposes (though their development was funded, in all three cases, by the Navy).

In the final years of the twentieth century, and the early years of the twenty-first, the commercial sector, specifically the oil and gas industry, also contributed to the field. By 2006 the sector was routinely using no fewer than ten distinct types of remotely operated vehicles for a range of missions.[6] Indeed, in 2000 a U.S. Navy committee advised the service that it had fallen far behind the commercial and scientific sectors in the development of unmanned undersea vehicles and needed to catch up fast.[7] In the years since, the Navy has done exactly that.

Undersea Systems

Indeed, one of the most storied unmanned submarines in the current U.S. Navy arsenal was conceived not in a defense lab, but in the scientific research community. Remote Environmental Monitoring Units, better known as REMUS, are a family of small, long-endurance torpedo-shaped unmanned submarines designed by the Woods Hole Oceanographic Institution for a wide range of data collection roles. The systems were initially developed for remote-sensing operations, but they were light, reliable, and highly capable—one early REMUS variant, REMUS 100, weighed just eighty pounds and could remain submerged for nearly a full day—and in the 1990s the Navy quickly took an interest in the technology.

The service had a number of potential roles in mind for the system, including reconnaissance operations for amphibious special operations assaults. One of the principal applications of this class of drones is underwater mapping, a difficult and tedious exercise that is nevertheless crucial if you want to know what's going on around you during maritime operations. Another concept for a proposed mission that is gaining popularity is choke point control, in which a group of unmanned submarines patrols a narrow channel of water in order to surveil all vessels that pass through it.

Operational deception, another mission for which the technology is thought to be well suited, involves using undersea drones equipped with transducers that transmit phony signals to confuse or mislead the adversary. For example, a vessel might transmit signals that make it look to adversary forces like a large manned attack submarine or an advanced torpedo in order to fool them into believing they are under attack so that they will flee.[8]

But one mission in particular quickly rose to the top: mine countermeasures. The mine countermeasure mission is a fairly easy one to comprehend, though in reality it is extremely difficult and danger-ous to execute. Before a naval force can move through any contested or denied environment—say, as part of a landing operation—advance teams must quickly and methodically ensure that it is clear of defen-sive ordnance.

Traditionally, the Navy employed a combination of expert human divers and trained marine mammals to sniff out underwater mines, which can be notoriously difficult to spot in the murky littoral waters where they are most often used. These operations are almost always covert, as the presence of a mine-clearing team is an obvious indication of a looming offensive.[9] In the 1990s the service increas-ingly began to recognize that an unmanned vehicle might make more sense for the role. A 2000 Navy planning document described mine countermeasures as a core focus for its future force of under-water drones.[10]

The small, portable, and eminently replaceable REMUS proved to be adept at the task. The system's first mine-hunting mission took place during Operation Iraqi Freedom, when it was deployed by Spe-cial Clearance Team 1. The task was to clear the Khor Abd Allah water-way, a crucial artery connecting to the port of Umm Qasr, which had been heavily wired with mines by Iraq's retreating Navy in the first weeks following the U.S. invasion. Working alongside human divers, the drones not only located numerous mines within the 2.5 million square meters of real estate that they scanned, but they also discovered several unreported wreckages.[11] Officers who used the systems had high praise for REMUS, which they described as being "undeterred by cold temperatures, murky water, sharks, or hunger."[12]

As they have become more popular, the family of REMUS-based vehicles has grown in every sense. One model, the REMUS 600, has an endurance of nearly three days and a range of up to 286 nautical miles.[13] In 2013 the U.S. Navy deployed a variant of the REMUS 600, the MK 18 Mod 2 Kingfish, which weighs six hundred pounds.

The unmannedness of vehicles like the REMUS makes all the difference in these missions, which are dangerous for human div-ers and trained marine mammals; drones do not return in caskets to grieving families. There are other benefits to going unmanned. And if, as one declassified report explained, a mission has to be clandestine, a small remote submarine that can be operated from a standoff distance "is the only solution."[14] In short, the mine–countermeasures mission is to unmanned submarines what the find, fix, finish mission is to the Predator.

This fleet of fearless mine hunters will soon be joined by a new generation of much heftier craft. Though the REMUS's compact size can be useful for certain roles, there are plenty of reasons one might also want a larger submersible. It can travel to greater depths and carry more fuel for longer missions and a greater variety of payloads, meaning that it could be useful for much more than just mine hunting.

Among other efforts, the Navy has been exploring the viability and potential of large unmanned undersea vehicles with a prototype system called the Large Displacement Unmanned Underwater Vehicle (LDUUV). The goal of the initiative, broadly speaking, is to build a large system that can nevertheless be launched from a wide range of manned host platforms, including littoral combat ships and nuclear submarines. In 2017 LDUUV development was split into two parallel programs. One system will be used to further the development of autonomous features, while the other, designated the Snakehead Large Displacement Unmanned Underwater Vehicle, is being developed specifically for littoral combat ships.

Initially, the Snakehead program, which is scheduled to field a Phase 1 prototype by 2019, will focus on intelligence surveillance and reconnaissance missions. It is envisioned that a littoral combat ship, seeking to build a more complete picture of the battlespace, particularly in a contested area, might send out a Snakehead to more closely track an adversary escadrille. The final system will have a modular configuration, allowing it to carry out a range of missions, including mine countermeasures, mine warfare, and electronic warfare.[15]

No system reflects the thinking behind this new class of giant unmanned submarines more spectacularly than Boeing's Echo Voyager, a bright yellow 80-foot behemoth that offers a glimpse of the type of drone sub that may well serve as the backbone for a future unmanned undersea fleet. Funded entirely in-house by Boeing, which has been building unmanned undersea vehicles since the 1960s, the

Echo Voyager is designed to be highly autonomous and capable of conducting missions extending over many months without needing to return to port.

In particular, the Echo Voyager stands apart from other unmanned undersea systems—including its Boeing predecessors, the Echo Seeker, which was 32 feet long, and the Echo Ranger, which measured 18 feet—in that it can be deployed from ports and does not rely on the manned host platforms, such as littoral combat ships or submarines, that are required to launch smaller unmanned submarines closer to the mission area. With a modular design, the Echo Voyager could be configured for a range of different missions, and thanks to its 1,000-gallon fuel tank, it has a range of 6,500 miles.[16]

To function as intended, the Echo Voyager will need to be highly autonomous. But as many observers have noted, the challenges of developing autonomous systems that can execute high stakes missions reliably and consistently without the need for significant human supervision are manifold. What's more, the ethics and legality of leaving potentially high stakes life-and-death decisions—such as where to deposit a set of mines or whether to classify a foreign vessel as a military target or simply a civilian craft—up to a drone's algorithmic judgment remains hotly contested.

Undersea drones do not necessarily need to be 80 feet long to attain the level of endurance that can really set an unmanned system apart from a manned one, nor will all unmanned undersea systems spend their days engaged in high stakes mine-hunting sweeps or covert reconnaissance missions. The U.S. Navy's Littoral Battlespace Sensing-Glider (LBS-G), manufactured by Teledyne Brown, moves through the water by automatically adjusting its buoyancy, and its principal role is a peaceful one. First deployed operationally in 2012 by the Naval Oceanographic Office (NAVOCEANO), the LBS-G collects a range of unclassified oceanographic data, including water temperature, ocean depth, and water salinity, which is then incorporated into NAV-OCEANO's operational models of the seas. Dozens of LBS-Gs now patrol oceans across the globe, helping to feed the Navy's increasingly sophisticated models of this complex environment.

In 2016 an LBS-G became the focal point of a minor diplomatic crisis when a Chinese navy vessel seized the glider as it was conducting a routine oceanographic mission in international waters. After the U.S. Navy submitted a formal protest to the Chinese government, the glider was returned, though not, some have speculated, before the drone's temporary custodians gleaned valuable design information to be used in the development of a similar system of their own.[17]

Other unmanned subs generate propulsion using the sea itself. Known as wave gliders, these peculiar systems consist of a floating surface platform connected by a tether to a multiwinged propulsion mechanism that moves the device forward at a slow but steady pace on the relative motion of waves. The most widely recognized system, simply called Wave Glider, is produced by Liquid Robotics, which was acquired by Boeing as part of the aerospace giant's bid to solidify its position in the maritime unmanned vehicle market.

Boeing is pitching the Wave Glider, which has already been used extensively by the National Oceanic and Atmospheric Administration for remote-sensing missions, as a communications hub linking a range of other manned and unmanned platforms operating in the maritime environment. In one test Boeing demonstrated that it could link a Wave Glider with an Echo Ranger unmanned undersea vehicle, a submarine, and a manned surveillance aircraft.

Surface Systems
The Boeing Wave Glider is somewhat a hybrid of an undersea drone and a drone boat, and while a majority of the U.S. Navy's current and planned unmanned systems do indeed live underneath the waves, the service has shown a growing interest in unmanned surface vehicles. Like their undersea kin, these ghost ships will perform a variety of roles, from fleet protection to patrol, surveillance and reconnaissance, and antisubmarine warfare.

The Navy's Sea Hunter, a 130-foot-long warship that originated within DARPA as the Anti-Submarine-Warfare Continuous Trail Unmanned Vessel (ACTUV), will be the largest, most capable unmanned surface vehicle ever developed. Like the Echo Voyager, the Sea Hunter's size affords it enormous endurance and range compared to smaller systems. Capable of carrying up to forty tons of fuel, the system has a range of roughly 10,000 nautical miles, which, according to Scott Littlefield, DARPA's ACTUV program manager, means that it can reach anywhere in the maritime world from U.S. territory.[18]

And like large unmanned undersea systems, the Sea Hunter will be highly autonomous. As envisioned by its creators, the craft will operate as a man-on-the-loop system rather than a man-in-the-loop system. That is to say, the human pilots will not really be piloting the craft; they will merely be supervising it. The ship will autonomously execute a range of directions—"go to these coordinates" or "look for this kind of vessel"—and then await further instructions upon completing each task. And because the Sea Hunter has been programmed to comply with the full set of collision regulations established by the International Maritime Organization, there's little danger that it will crash into anything while it is out doing its thing.

As the Sea Hunter's previous name suggests, DARPA originally envisioned that the craft would serve a single purpose: hunting submarines, particularly diesel submarines, which are quiet and thus hard to track.[19] Using a submerged sensor, the Sea Hunter would autonomously patrol a designated segment of maritime territory until it discovered a submarine. Once it did so, it would autonomously commence moving in a "continuous trail" pattern, following the submarine at a set standoff distance wherever it went.

Because the system is unmanned, and therefore "attritable" (though not expendable—each platform will reportedly cost about $20 million, much less than a manned alternative, but not an insignificant amount of money), it can be held much closer to adversary vehicles than manned ships and submarines, giving commanders persistent eyes on a target without endangering human lives (or large expensive vessels) in the process.

A similar concept of operations is also likely to be applied for unmanned undersea systems, which can likewise be kept much closer to enemy vessels without endangering one's own soldiers. In the Pentagon's 2011 *Unmanned Systems Integrated Roadmap*, strategists presented a future vignette in which an unmanned glider covertly attached itself to an adversary's nuclear submarine, periodically extending its tether in order to reach the surface of the water to transmit its position.[20]

When the Sea Hunter is eventually deployed, it will serve a far wider range of purposes than just antisubmarine warfare. Since the program was first conceived, DARPA and the Navy have broadened the system's planned mission sets. "The Navy doesn't want it to be a 'one-trick pony,'" explained Littlefield at the time of the vessel's christening.[21] Shortly after receiving the Sea Hunter program from DARPA, the Office of Naval Research (ONR) said that it would soon equip the vessel with powerful daylight and infrared sensors for long-range target detection and also put it through its paces in a range of simulated mine countermeasure operations.[22]

The vessel has already proved to be quite versatile. In one set of tests, in October 2016, the Sea Hunter successfully launched a prototype of DARPA's Towed Airborne Lift of Naval Systems, a tethered parachute designed to hold surveillance systems aloft for extended periods.[23] Engineers and program managers began referring to the system as a "truck," something that will be happy to take whatever load you put on it.[24]

The Navy is actively developing smaller unmanned boats too. Indeed, most of the future fleet's unmanned boats will be relatively small. In the early 2000s, the Naval Sea Systems Command experimented with the Spartan Scout, a 23-foot-long unmanned surface vehicle technology demonstrator equipped with a .50-caliber gun. The command envisions using such a system to steam ahead of a group of manned ships to conduct reconnaissance and force protection missions.

The Navy also imagined that the Scout might be useful for anti-submarine warfare and precision strike operations.[25] The newer Common Unmanned Surface Vehicle, billed as a versatile workhorse for a range of missions, will soon be integrated at scale into the U.S. fleet. The Navy's first planned operational variant of the system, the Barracuda, will be initially used for mine countermeasures.

Though these systems are not as far ranging and versatile as larger vessels such as the Sea Hunter or Echo Voyager, some will be capable of a very unique and potentially transformative trick. ONR runs a program that uses software originally developed for the Mars Rover to convert traditional small manned surface vessels such as rigid-hulled inflatable boats into autonomous unmanned surface vehicles that can operate together in swarm formations without human operator control. According to ONR, these boat swarms could be useful for everything from protection missions to reconnaissance, escort, and lethal strike missions.[26]

In a typical reconnaissance mission, for example, a swarm might receive a simple high-level order from a human operator ("search this area for adversary vessels," for instance) and execute said order autonomously, with each craft playing a unique role. In an escort operation, the boats might autonomously identify adversary light attack vessels speeding toward the force and rapidly execute a swarmed interdiction that "overwhelms" the incoming craft.

In tests on the James River in 2014, ONR ran a swarm of thirteen boats that autonomously executed a range of complex maneuvers, including protection of a friendly manned vessel and coordinated interdiction of an enemy craft. In further tests in the Chesapeake Bay in 2016, an updated boat swarm tasked with a simulated harbor defense mission demonstrated the ability to identify a range of adversary vessels and even allocate tasks to individual vessels in the swarm autonomously. The project remains active and seems to be growing. To further develop the technology, ONR has partnered with the Strategic Capabilities Office, a once-secret Pentagon unit working on a range of technologies for use in a potential future conflict against a large technologically advanced adversary force.

Undersea drones may someday work in coordinated swarms too. A 2012 Naval Research Advisory Committee report on autonomy in naval operations describes how a small swarm of unmanned submarines could effectively execute the various steps of a broad mine countermeasures operation with only high-level human input. Given the instruction "Eliminate mines," a Knifefish scanning an area for mines could autonomously direct a second unmanned neutralizer system to each mine without having to inform human operators. With a scalable system, the report states, one could cover much more ground than one currently can with more traditional techniques.[27]

Airborne Systems
The Navy is also pursuing unmanned technology in the air with just as much energy and optimism as it has invested in unmanned systems for use on and under the surface of the sea. Some the Navy's most

important aerial unmanned systems have been in service for years and already play a key, routine role in maritime operations.

One such system that is already firmly established in the service's arsenal is the Boeing Insitu ScanEagle. Originally designed for hunting schools of tuna for the commercial fishing industry, the forty-pound ScanEagle and its newer, larger variants, the Blackjack and Integrator, have become popular tools in the Navy and the Marine Corps (as well as a number of foreign militaries) since they were first deployed with the Marine Expeditionary Force in Iraq in 2004.

With an endurance in excess of twenty hours, these systems are primarily used for ISR missions, though they have also seen action in search-and-rescue and antipiracy missions. (A ScanEagle even played a key role in the rescue of Captain Richard Phillips, who was taken hostage by Somali pirates in 2009.) Launched by a catapult and retrieved with a hook system, they are well suited for ship-based deployments and have flown several hundred thousand flight hours in recent years.[28]

The MQ-4 Triton is another beast altogether. It weighs 30,000 pounds and has a wingspan of 131 feet. All that size and weight is necessary for the Triton's unique mission: reconnaissance and surveillance of very large ocean areas. Flying at altitudes at 50,000 feet, the multi-sensor Triton can remain airborne for up to 24 hours across an effective range of 2,000 nautical miles, with its radar and electro-optical/infrared sensors tracking everything from nuclear submarines to destroyers to small expeditionary vessels. (If it looks familiar, that's because it is; it is based on the Air Force's storied RQ-4 Global Hawk.)

Because they are expensive, the Navy will only operate about sixty-eight Tritons when fully operational. The Navy would someday like to be able to give individual combat ships their very own persistent eye in the sky. That means a drone small enough to launch from deck but large enough to remain airborne for twenty-four hours with a heavy suite of sensors. Currently, the Navy does not have such a drone. Its MQ-8 Fire Scout series of helicopter drones, introduced in 2009, can be launched from littoral combat ships and other vessels of that size, but because they are rotary aircraft, they do not have the endurance, range, or persistence necessary for true persistent surveillance.

The most capable Fire Scout variant, the MQ-8C, is likely to have an endurance of twelve hours at most. Meanwhile, existing fixed-wing persistent surveillance drones, like the Triton or the Air Force's Reaper, need a full-length runway.

DARPA's Tactically Exploited Reconnaissance Node, now known simply as the Tern, may be just what the Navy is looking for. Slated to begin flight-testing in 2018, the Tern is a large fixed-wing unmanned aircraft that can take off and land vertically from the deck of a small ship and yet fly faster and longer than any rotary aircraft.[29] This is thanks to the Tern's unique "tail-sitter" design. When it is on the deck of a ship, the aircraft sits on its rear, with its nose pointing vertically into the air. When it takes off, a pair of large contra-rotating propellers on the nose provide lift, a bit like a helicopter or the Marine Corps' V-22 Osprey. Once the Tern reaches altitude, it flips ninety degrees and transitions to horizontal flight, with the same pair of propellers providing forward thrust.

For decades, the tail-sitter design had been written off as a technological dead end. In the 1950s the Navy enlisted Lockheed Martin and Convair to build two experimental manned tail-sitter aircraft for similar missions to those currently envisioned for the Tern. With the exception of the cockpit, these systems bear a striking resemblance to the DARPA drone, which the agency claims has "been on the U.S. Navy's wishlist since World War II."[30] But the two projects stalled because, as military aviation expert Richard Whittle explains, "it would be devilishly hard for a pilot to land on a pitching ship deck—already one of the most stressful tasks in aviation—while looking *backwards* as if parallel parking." The Tern, however, does not need to rely on fallible human pilots. Autonomous control systems will allow the aircraft to take off and land far more reliably and safely than a human ever could.[31]

The Tern is intended to be operated from three types of forward-deployed ships, littoral combat ships, *Arleigh Burke*–class destroyers, and expeditionary fast transports, with minimal modifications to the host ship's deck. It will have a persistent coverage range of up to 600 nautical miles from the host ship while carrying at least 500 pounds of payload.[32]

These specifications put the Tern on a par with the Air Force's land-based Predator, which can carry up to 450 pounds at a range of 675 nautical miles, giving the Navy a significant capability, not just for maritime operations, but also overland missions.[33] As the program's manager has pointed out, 87 percent of the world's land area is less than 500 nautical miles from a coast, meaning that a Tern based on a forward-deployed vessel could potentially access a far wider range of theaters across the globe than its cousins the Predator and Reaper.[34]

In addition to persistent surveillance and reconnaissance, the agency has stated that it intends to develop an airframe that can also "strike mobile targets anywhere, around the clock," meaning that armed versions of the Tern could be in the works.[35] The sea may become the new front in the global drone war.

When the Tern prototype completes its first successful tail-sitter landing on a pitching ship deck, it will be a historic moment, though it will not be the first occasion on which an unmanned aircraft autonomously accomplished a piloting feat that was previously only possible in the hands of human pilots with superhuman skills. That honor goes to a Navy drone that has arguably captured the public imagination more than any other developmental unmanned vehicle to date, the X-47B.

On July 10, 2013, this futuristic jet-powered carrier-based strike drone demonstrator, which emerged from a 2005 Department of Defense Quadrennial Defense Review directing the Navy to develop a long-range carrier-based drone "to increase naval reach and persistence," achieved the unthinkable and made a perfect autonomous arrested landing on USS *George H. W. Bush* (CVN 77).[36] It was the first time that a fixed-wing unmanned aircraft autonomously landed on an aircraft carrier. (Two months earlier, the X-47B had also made a perfect catapult takeoff from the carrier, another historic first.)

Mary "Missy" Cummings, a robotics researcher and former F-18 Navy pilot who has made countless carrier landings over the course of her career, says that when she heard about the X-47B's autonomous landing, she knew that the future of military aviation was unmanned and that the days of the human pilot were numbered.[37] But shortly after the X-47B prototype successfully executed, in 2015, an air-to-air refueling exercise with an aerial tanker—yet another tricky maneuver—the Navy retired the two X-47B airframes and canceled the program. It was an unexpected move that some fans of the futuristic drone described as "strategic malpractice."[38] According to CAPT Beau Duarte, the initiative's program manager, however, this was a logical move: "The program met all of its demonstration objectives within its allocated level of funding and transferred lessons learned to reduce the technical risk of future operational unmanned platforms."[39] In the X-47B's place, the Navy unveiled a less showy program, the Carrier-Based Aerial Refueling System (CBARS).

Instead of serving as a stealthy reconnaissance and strike platform capable of penetrating deep into enemy territory, this new drone, which was designated the MQ-25A Stingray, will primarily serve as a tanker to refuel carrier-based strike aircraft in blue water operations.[40] This will free up the manned F/A-18E/F, which reportedly spends a significant portion of its time in that role.[41] As a tanker the Stingray would undoubtedly play an important part in these missions, but it will not be the star of the show. It likely will not have stealth, and though the Navy is still leaving the door open to giving the Stingray some surveillance capabilities, the priority is to make a tanker.[42]

The tumult experienced by the program in recent years is emblematic of how the road to an unmanned future is not always an easy one. In 2016, the same year that it reconfigured its carrier strike drone, the Navy canceled its ambitious and long-running Remote Mine-Hunting System (RMS) program, which sought to acquire fifty-four large, potentially transformative unmanned mine-countermeasure submarines built by Lockheed Martin.[43] After seventeen years of development, and a total program cost of over $700 million, the Navy acquired just ten systems, prompting Senator John McCain (R-AZ) to lambast the RMS as "indefensible" in one of his famous "America's Most Wasted" reports.[44] In 2016 the Navy also eliminated the Unmanned Warfare Systems Directorate, a large office intended to manage the Navy's wide range of drone programs that had been announced, to much fanfare, just one year earlier.[45]

And even though it is tempting to assume that unmanned systems will increasingly replace manned systems—former secretary of the Navy Ray Mabus once famously said that the F-35 Lightning "almost certainly will be, the last manned strike fighter aircraft the Department of the Navy will ever buy or fly"—the reality is that the emerging ecosystem of unmanned systems across domains will cohabitate with, rather than entirely displace, traditional systems.[46]

Manned-unmanned teaming (MUM-T), the idea of developing concepts of operations in which unmanned systems collaborate with manned systems, has become a firm paradigm that is likely to define the next chapter of the unmanned revolution. While unmanned systems have operated in conjunction with manned vessels in operations such as specialized mapping and object detection and localization for decades, MUM-T emphasizes a much more fluid collaboration between manned and autonomous—that is, not merely remotely piloted—unmanned systems, in which, as an Air Force chief scientist report put it, "functions and situation awareness flow smoothly, simply, and seamlessly between" the manned and unmanned systems.[47]

Much work has already been done in the Navy to push the needle in that direction. The Helicopter Sea Combat Squadron has demonstrated how an MQ-8B Fire Scout can effectively serve as a laser designator for Hellfire missiles fired from manned rotary aircraft such as the MH-60S Knighthawk. ONR's boat swarms are capable of serving as an autonomous protection entourage for manned vessels. In a test in the Mediterranean in 2015, the Navy even demonstrated how it can launch a REMUS 600 from an attack submarine.

Under a program called Advanced Weapons Enhanced by Submarine UAS against Mobile Targets (AWESUM), the Navy is looking to equip a number of its attack and guided missile submarines with canister-launched Blackwing unmanned aerial vehicles that would orbit overhead providing crews in the water with a real-time aerial view of the surrounding environment.

In some cases the collaboration will be not only between unmanned and manned systems, but between unmanned systems and other unmanned systems. Some of the most potentially transformative planned collaborative operations will pair different unmanned platforms across domains. In the 2011 *Unmanned Systems Integrated Roadmap* vignette, the small drone sub following the enemy nuclear submarine beamed its location data directly to "an extreme-endurance

UAS, capable of operating for two months on station without refuelling." Later in the vignette, an unmanned surface vessel deployed an unmanned undersea vehicle to explore the ocean floor.[48]

These types of complex drone-to-drone collaborations have already moved beyond the page and into reality. In the summer of 2016, the Naval Undersea Warfare Center demonstrated how a Blackwing aerial drone could serve as a communications relay between a manned submarine and a swarm of unmanned undersea vehicles.[49] That same year, at the Annual Navy Technology Exercise, an unmanned surface vehicle relayed instructions from human operators in a ground control station to a Marlin MK2 unmanned submarine, which then successfully launched a Vector Hawk unmanned aerial vehicle, which in turn proceeded to engage in line-of-sight communications with other vehicles in the exercise.

Future naval operations, then, will see a diverse range of unmanned systems collaborating in complex teams both with each other and existing and future manned platforms. The operations that these systems execute will be as diverse as the platforms themselves. While a Sea Hunter ghost ship tracks diesel-powered adversary submarines in a continuous trail pattern, relaying intelligence to operators via an MQ-4C Triton flying at 60,000 feet somewhere over the East China Sea, a swarm of rigid-hull inflatable boats might escort an amphibious landing group to a combat theater while a team of Knifefish unmanned undersea vehicles map the landing zone and search for underwater mines. It sounds like science fiction, but it is all already in the works.

Maritime drones will also begin to proliferate globally. The United Kingdom, Israel, France, the Netherlands, and a host of other countries have all invested heavily in recent years in unmanned aircraft, boats, and submarines of their own. China and Russia have both begun a number of unmanned systems programs for the maritime domain. Maritime unmanned technology will therefore likely proliferate rapidly in coming years, and the effect on future engagements will be profound. The U.S. Sea Hunter may one day have to contend with swarms of adversary boats that autonomously escort the submarines it is meant to hunt, and DARPA's Tern might have to share its airspace with uncooperative high-altitude reconnaissance or strike drones.

There is also a sense that we are only now just scratching the surface of what's possible. The field is moving so quickly that it can be hard to keep track. Each week seems to bring developments that continue to push the Navy toward a future in which unmanned systems play an integrated, routine, and indispensable role in maritime operations. New technologies emerge, new tests confirm proofs of concept, demonstrations prove that these systems actually work the way that they are intended, new deals are inked, and the Navy shows no sign of slowing down.

And these are just the projects that are known publicly. In its 2018 budget, the Navy announced the creation of an entirely new $206 million program managed by the Strategic Capabilities Office that seeks to develop a "fleet-integrated" operational prototype drone to fill a range of existing roles. The program is called "Ghost Fleet" and is highly classified. There is always more happening beneath the surface than meets the eye.[50]

Notes

1. Adm. John Richardson, "The Future Navy," Department of the Navy, May 17, 2017, 6, http://www.navy.mil/navydata/people/cno/Richardson/Resource/The FutureNavy.pdf.
2. Kenneth P. Werrell, *The Evolution of the Cruise Missile* (Maxwell Air Force Base, AL: Air University Press, 1985), 21, 23.
3. Naval Aviation Museum, "TDR-1 Edna III," n.d., http://www.navalaviation museum.org/attractions/aircraft-exhibits/item/?item=tdr.
4. Samuel S. Evans, "The Incredible Story of the QH-50 DASH," *Vertiflite*, Spring 2011, www.aero.psu.edu/Facilities/images/36_DASH_QH-50.pdf.
5. Ocean Engineering Division, *Naval Ocean Systems Center Underwater Vehicle History* (San Diego: Naval Ocean Systems Center, April 1989), 1.
6. Robert W. Button, John Kamp, Thomas B. Curtin, and James Dryden, *A Survey of Missions for Unmanned Undersea Vehicles* (Santa Monica, CA: Rand, 2009), 42.
7. Carl Posey, "Robot Submarines Go to War," *Popular Science*, April 2003, 72.
8. John Jackson, ed., *The U.S. Naval Institute on Naval Innovation* (Annapolis: Naval Institute Press, 2015), 84.
9. Department of the Navy, *The Navy Unmanned Undersea Vehicle (UUV) Master Plan* (Washington, DC: Department of the Navy, 2004), 10–11, http://www.navy.mil/navydata/technology/uuvmp.pdf.

10. Robert L. Wernli, "Low Cost UUV's for Military Applications: Is the Technology Ready?" (San Diego, CA: Space and Naval Warfare Systems Center, July 2000), 3.
11. Douglas H. Stutz, "UUV Use in Support of Operation Iraqi Freedom Recounted," Department of the Navy, August 29, 2003, http://www.navy.mil/submit/display.asp?story_id=9079.
12. Woods Hole Oceanographic Institution, "REMUS," http://www.whoi.edu/main/remus.
13. Woods Hole Oceanographic Institution, "REMUS 600," http://www.whoi.edu/main/remus600.
14. Naval Research Advisory Committee, Unmanned Vehicles (UV) in Mine Countermeasures (U) (Washington, DC: Department of the Navy, November 2000), 5, https://www.nrac.navy.mil/docs/2000_rpt_unmanned_vehicles_mine_countermeasures.pdf.
15. Anika Torruella, "Surface Navy 2017: USN LDUUV to Receive Multiple Mission Packages," IHS Jane's International Defence Review, January 12, 2017, http://www.janes.com/article/66901/surface-navy-2017-usn-lduuv-to-receive-multiple-mission-packages.
16. Olga Kharif, "Echo Voyager: 50-Ton Drone Sub Can Go Six Months without Refueling," Bloomberg Businessweek, May 5, 2016, https://www.bloomberg.com/news/articles/2016-05-05/innovation-echo-voyager.
17. Jane Perlez and Matthew Rosenberg, "China Agrees to Return Seized Drone, Ending Standoff, Pentagon Says," New York Times, December 17, 2016, https://www.nytimes.com/2016/12/17/world/asia/china-us-drone.html.
18. Scott Littlefield, "Anti-Submarine Warfare (ASW) Continuous Trail Unmanned Vessel (ACTUV)," Defense Advanced Research Projects Agency, http://www.darpa.mil/program/anti-submarine-warfare-continuous-trail-unmanned-vessel.
19. Ibid.
20. Office of the Under Secretary of Defense (Acquisition, Technology, and Logistics), Unmanned Systems Integrated Roadmap FY2011–2036 (Washington, DC: Department of Defense, 2011), 6.
21. Scott Littlefield, DARPA program manager, speaking at ACTUV Christening Media Roundtable, April 6, 2016.
22. Katherine Owens, "Navy Anti-submarine Drone-Ship Conducts Minehunting Testing," Defense Systems, May 4, 2017, https://defensesystems.com/articles/2017/05/04/seahunter.aspx.
23. Defense Advanced Research Projects Agency (DARPA), "ACTUV Unmanned Vessel Helps TALONS Take Flight in Successful Joint Test," press release, October 24, 2016, http://www.darpa.mil/news-events/2016-10-24.
24. Rachel Courtland, "DARPA's Self-Driving Submarine Hunter Steers Like a Human," IEEE Spectrum, April 7, 2016, http://spectrum.ieee.org/automaton/robotics/military-robots/darpa-actuv-self-driving-submarine-hunter-steers-like-a-human.
25. Ernest Marvin III and Mark Wasilewski, "Unmanned Surface Vehicles: Reducing Risks for Joint Surface Force Protection Operations" (Newport, RI: Naval Undersea Warfare Center, November 28, 2006), http://www.dtic.mil/dtic/tr/fulltext/u2/a630564.pdf.

26. Jeremy Hsu, "U.S. Navy's Drone Boat Swarm Practices Harbor Defense," IEEE Spectrum, December 19, 2016, http://spectrum.ieee.org/automaton/robotics/military-robots/navy-drone-boat-swarm-practices-harbor-defense.

27. Naval Research Advisory Committee, *How Autonomy Can Transform Naval Operations* (Washington, DC: Department of the Navy, October 2012), 31, https://www.nrac.navy.mil/docs/NRAC_Final_Report-Autonomy_NOV2012.pdf.

28. Colin Clark, "Scan Eagle Stars in Piracy Fight," DOD Buzz, March 8, 2011, https://www.dodbuzz.com/2011/03/08/scan-eagle-stars-in-piracy-fight/.

29. DARPA, "Tern Moves Closer to Full-Scale Demonstration of Unmanned VTOL Aircraft Designed for Small Ships," press release, October 28, 2015, http://www.darpa.mil/news-events/2015-12-28.

30. Ibid.

31. Richard Whittle, "Tern Tailsitter Drone: Pilot Not Included," Breaking Defense, December 6, 2016, http://breakingdefense.com/2016/12/tailsitter-drone-tern-pilot-not-included/.

32. Daniel Patt, "TTO Proposers Day 2016" (PowerPoint presentation, April 21, 2016), http://www.darpa.mil/attachments/TTOProposersDay2016PresentationFINAL.PDF.

33. U.S. Air Force, "MQ-1B Predator," fact sheet, http://www.af.mil/About-Us/Fact-Sheets/Display/Article/104469/mq-1b-predator/.

34. Patt, "TTO Proposers Day 2016."

35. Graham Drozeski, "Tern," Defense Advanced Research Projects Agency, http://www.darpa.mil/program/tern.

36. Department of Defense, "Exhibit R-2, RDT&E Budget Item Justification: PB 2017 Navy," February 2016, http://www.fi-aeroweb.com/Defense/Budget-Data/FY2017/UCAV-NAVY-RDT&E-FY2017.pdf.

37. Mary Cummings, remarks at the Intrepid Sea, Air and Space Museum, May 9, 2017.

38. Shawn Brimley and Robert Martinage, "The Navy's New Museum Drone and Strategic Malpractice," *War on the Rocks* (blog), April 28, 2015, https://warontherocks.com/2015/04/the-navys-new-museum-drone-and-strategic-malpractice/.

39. Beau Duarte, email to the author, October 12, 2017.

40. Department of the Navy, *U.S. Navy Program Guide 2017* (Washington, DC: Department of the Navy, 2017), 16, http://www.navy.mil/strategic/npg17.pdf.

41. Sydney J. Freedberg, "Navy Hits Gas on Flying Gas Truck, CBARS: Will It Be Armed?" Breaking Defense, March 11, 2016, http://breakingdefense.com/2016/03/navy-hits-gas-on-flying-gas-truck-cbars-will-it-be-armed/.

42. Chief of Naval Operations, "MQ-25 Concept Refinement," memorandum, August 24, 2015.

43. Megan Eckstein, "Navy's Remote Minehunting System Officially Canceled, Sonar May Live On," U.S. Naval Institute News, March 24, 2016, https://news.usni.org/2016/03/24/navys-remote-minehunting-system-officially-canceld-sonar-may-live-on.

44. Lance M. Bacon, "McCain Slams Remote Minehunting System as a Failure," *Navy Times*, September 14, 2015, https://www.navytimes.com/story/military/capitol-hill/2015/09/14/mccain-slams-remote-minehunting-system-failure/72018764/.

45. Megan Eckstein, "Navy Eliminates Unmanned Systems Office, Moves Programs to Other Directorates," U.S. Naval Institute News, February 8, 2017,

https://news.usni.org/2017/02/08/navy-staff-reorganization-eliminates-opnav-n99-unmanned-warfare-systems-office.

46. Todd Harrison, "Will the F-35 Be the Last Manned Fighter Jet? Physics, Physiology, and Fiscal Facts Suggest Yes," *Forbes*, April 29, 2015, https://www.forbes.com/sites/toddharrison/2015/04/29/will-the-f-35-be-the-last-manned-fighter-jet-physics-physiology-and-fiscal-facts-suggest-yes/#cbcfbcb95fa1.

47. Office the Chief Scientist, *Autonomous Horizons: System Autonomy in the Air Force—A Path to the Future*, vol. 1, *Human-Autonomy Teaming* (Washington, DC: U.S. Air Force, June 2015), iv, http://www.af.mil/Portals/1/documents/SECAF/AutonomousHorizons.pdf?timestamp=1 435068339702.

48. Office of the Under Secretary of Defense, *Unmanned Systems Integrated Roadmap*, 6.

49. Naval Undersea Warfare Center, "United States Navy Demonstrates Cross-Domain Communications, Command and Control via AeroVironment Blackwing Submarine-Launched UAV," press release, September 7, 2016, http://www.businesswire.com/news/home/20160907005733/en/United-States-Navy-Demonstrates-Cross-Domain-Communications-Command.

50. FY 2018 President's Budget, PE 0604250D8Z: Advanced Innovative Technologies, https://www.gpo.gov/fdsys/browse/collectionGPO.action?collectionCode=BUDGET.

05

When Robots Rule the Waves?

Robert Sparrow and George R. Lucas Jr.

R obotic weapons are widely believed to be the future of war. Dramatic progress in the science and engineering of robotics, alongside the perceived success of the United States' Predator and Reaper drones in Iraq and Afghanistan, has led many commentators to conclude that the wars of the twenty-first century will increasingly be fought, by industrialized nations at least, using remotely piloted and autonomous weapon systems (AWS). This belief is also playing an important role in shaping the thinking and practice of militaries around the world, which are scrambling to purchase drones and to develop and deploy robots for both combat and combat-support roles. Thus, for instance, all the U.S. armed services have published "road-map" documents detailing ambitious plans to integrate unmanned maritime systems (UMS) into their forces.

The new enthusiasm for robots in military and policy circles has been accompanied by increased philosophical and ethical attention being paid to issues surrounding the military uses of robots. In particular, there is now a flourishing literature on the ethics of drone warfare and an emerging literature on the ethics of the development and deployment of AWS. However, the high profile of aerial drones in

---

This chapter is a substantially abridged version of the authors' original article published in the U.S. government publication *Naval War College Review* 69, no. 4 (Autumn 2016): 49–78.

the public eye—along with the fact that these are the systems that have seen most active service—has led to the latter literature focusing almost entirely on the ethical issues raised by autonomous unmanned aerial vehicles (UAVs) and unmanned combat aerial vehicles (UCAVs).

To date there has been comparatively little discussion of the ethical issues raised by the prospect of autonomous submersibles or autonomous surface vessels. We seek here to address this lacuna, especially given the rapid development and military potential of autonomous unmanned underwater vehicles (UUVs) and unmanned surface vehicles (USVs). There are a number of ethical dilemmas specific to these technologies, owing to the unique and distinctive character of war at sea. A number of unique and complex ethical questions are likely to arise regarding the applications of autonomous UUVs and USVs, including

- whether (as the comparatively modest body of legal literature to date has posed the problem) armed autonomous UUVs and USVs should be understood as "vessels" or as "weapons";
- what sorts of operations autonomous UUVs and USVs might legitimately be tasked with in international, as opposed to territorial, waters;
- whether the operation of armed autonomous systems is compatible with freedom of navigation in international waters; and
- whether future maritime and underwater autonomous systems will have the capacity, when weaponized, to abide by the requirements of distinction and proportionality in naval warfare.

Distinctive Ethical Character of War at Sea

While aerial drones may have been hogging the limelight thus far when it comes to the military uses of robotics, there is currently an enormous amount of interest in the development and application of remotely piloted, semiautonomous, and autonomous weapons to fight wars on and under the sea.

The existence of waves, currents, tides, and submerged obstacles, and the difficulties of maintaining reliable communications through water, in some ways makes the oceans a more difficult environment for robots than the air. However, remaining afloat or submerged at a given depth is less technically demanding than remaining airborne, while surface vessels only need to move in two dimensions rather than the three required of aerial vehicles. The relatively small number of terrain types in war at sea, the virtual nonexistence of legitimate commercial traffic beneath the sea, and the fact that blue-water operations may often proceed without regard to concerns about running aground also mean that the oceans are a more tractable environment for robots than land. Moreover, the results that might be achieved through the further development and deployment of UUVs and USVs are substantial. Operations at sea—and especially underwater—are always dangerous and often dull, and they are arguably also often dirty, at least in the sense of being wearing and uncomfortable for those involved in them. Thus, many missions at sea are well suited to being assigned to robots. The military advantages to be secured by the development of autonomous systems for war on and under the seas, in particular, are enormous.

Unmanned surface vehicles have enormous potential in naval operations, although this potential is just beginning to be explored. The fact that these UMS operate on the surface means that maintaining a human being in (or on) the loop is more feasible than it is for submersibles. Nevertheless, as in the case of UMS more generally, there are still powerful military and economic dynamics pushing toward the development of systems that are capable of fully autonomous operations. The U.S. USV inventory already includes a number of systems of different sizes—and intended for different roles—with more under development. Most of these systems are described and discussed elsewhere in this volume.

Likewise submarine operations are notoriously dangerous, so removing human crews from submersibles wherever possible is arguably a moral imperative; it also has a number of other benefits. Because UMS do not carry a crew, they can be significantly smaller than the manned systems required to carry out similar operations. In turn, this permits UUVs to operate more quietly, for longer periods, and with a longer range. Autonomous UUVs in particular show enormous potential for operating for very long periods without needing to surface to replenish oxygen or fuel supplies or to return to base to rotate crews. This renders them ideal for roles in which the capacity to loiter undetected is an advantage. Indeed, because any emissions risk giving away two of the most vital secrets of a submersible—its presence and its location—the capacity to operate autonomously is a requirement for an effective unmanned submersible. It is therefore no surprise that the U.S. Navy has an ambitious program for research and development of UUVs and especially autonomous UUVs, as well as a number of existing systems already deployed.

There has been a small—but productive—discussion in the literature of the legal status of UUVs and USVs. However, to date there has been little discussion of the ethical issues raised by these systems. Our concern here is primarily with the latter topic. The law does not exhaust ethics. Provisions of the law not only fail to address ethical concerns; those very legal constraints may pose moral dilemmas that will need to be addressed in operational policy and naval warfare strategy. In addition, there may be obvious ethical demands on warfighters that are yet to be adequately codified in existing law. Indeed, there may be activities that are legally permitted but that are not morally permissible. Ethical principles may therefore provide useful guidance to warfighters where current law is silent or lacking. They may also motivate and inform attempts to revise, extend, or supplement existing law.

One reason to believe that the development of robotic weapons for naval warfare might raise new ethical issues is that war at sea differs in important respects from war in (most) other environments. As a result, the moral norms and customs that have evolved to regulate naval warfare are arguably more demanding than those regulating warfare elsewhere, are more deeply entrenched in the consciousness of warfighters, and have distinctive elements. Four features of war at sea, in particular, are found to play a key role in shaping the ethical (and legal) codes that regulate the activity of naval combatants.

1. In wartime as in peacetime, the sea itself is a deadly adversary of those who travel on (or under) it. Even in peacetime, hazards, in the form of strong winds, rough seas, and hidden

reefs abound while shipwreck and drowning are an ever present danger. In wartime, seafarers who are forced to abandon ship after an enemy attack may find themselves facing nearly certain doom alone in freezing waters or floating in a small life raft thousands of miles from land.

2. Because of the hostile nature of the marine environment, life at sea is primarily a collective life in which men (and increasingly, now, women) are thrown together in a mutual endeavor framed by the possibility of misadventure. Few people go to sea by themselves. Rather, people go to sea together in vessels, which then form miniature—or even, on modern capital ships, quite large—societies in the midst of a hostile environment.

3. The sea is more sparsely populated than the land, and in wartime the vessels that sail on or under it divide more-or-less naturally into those that are actively participating in the conflict and those that are not. That is to say, especially with the benefits of modern sensor packages, military vessels are more easily distinguished from civilian vessels than are groups of armed men from civilians in land warfare, and it is more difficult for combatants to hide among the noncombatant population. Thus, with the exception of merchant vessels (of which, more later), which might have been pressed into service to carry cargo or personnel for military purposes, it is generally much easier to distinguish legitimate from illegitimate targets at sea than it is in other forms of warfare.

4. The comparatively featureless nature of the oceans and the lack of local geographical reference for national and other relevant political boundaries means that it is harder to separate combatants and noncombatants geographically. This problem is exacerbated by the fact that oceangoing commerce is essential to the flourishing—and even to the survival—of modern nations, with the consequence that, even during wartime, merchants will continue to ply the seas with their goods and passenger ships and ferries will continue to transport civilians. At least partially in recognition of this fact, the high seas remain a "commons," owned by no one and available for use by everyone.

The first two of these four facts already have two important consequences for ethical understandings regarding war at sea. First, the
collective nature of life at sea and the shared vulnerability of all seafarers to misadventure and drowning means that a strong expectation
of mutual aid has grown up among those who go to sea. In particular, all those who go to sea are understood to have a duty to come to
the aid of those who are lost at sea wherever possible without serious danger to themselves—a duty that transcends ordinary national
loyalties and has no direct analogue in land warfare.[1] The development of this expectation may be accounted for as a function of the
need for a form of social insurance for this risky endeavor; each and
every person at sea is safer if there is an expectation that everyone will
come to the rescue of anyone as required, and consequently, it is in
each and every individual's interests if this expectation is widely pro-
mulgated and if failures to live up to it are subject to sanctions, both
formal and informal. Obviously, war—and the dehumanization of
the enemy that often accompanies it—places this expectation under
stress. Nevertheless, because enemy sailors in the water are no longer combatants by virtue of being hors de combat—and because
the risk of being in need of rescue is higher for all seamen during wartime—the expectation remains that vessels will render aid to,
and will attempt to rescue, individuals lost at sea regardless of their
nationality *when they have the capacity to do so and as long as doing so
would not jeopardize the safety of the vessel and those on board*. Moreover,
the extent to which all those who go to sea share a distinct way of
life compared to those who remain on land—and the solidarity that
this encourages—along with the constant danger posed by the sea to
all combatants ensures that this duty of rescue remains central to maritime culture even in wartime.[2]

Second, the ethical and legal codes that govern war at sea are primarily concerned with the activities and fate of "vessels." As a ship's
operations are the result of a cooperative activity, it is often not possible to distinguish between the intentions of the commanding officer
and those of his or her crew. Nor is it usually possible to attack some
persons on board a vessel without targeting the vessel as a whole and
thus risking the lives of everyone on board. For these reasons, seamen
literally sink or swim together. Thus, it is both natural and appropriate

that the vessel be the primary locus of attention in ethical (as well as legal) deliberation about naval warfare.

The last two of these four features of war at sea have led to the development of a sophisticated set of practices and agreements around the activities of belligerent and neutral parties intended to allow peaceful navigation of the seas by neutral parties to continue even when wars are being fought. Customary international law relating to naval warfare attempts to balance the competing demands of national sovereignty and freedom of navigation; distinguishes between belligerent and neutral nations' internal waters, territorial waters, and exclusive economic zones (EEZs) and the high seas; and places limits on the sorts of activities that may be legitimately pursued in each. Understanding the competing considerations informing these treaties will also, as we shall see later, prove useful to resolving ethical issues relating to the areas and roles in which UUVs and USVs may legitimately be deployed.

We do not wish to exaggerate the extent to which the ethics of war at sea differs from the ethics of fighting wars in other environments. The fundamental moral framework for naval warfare, as for land or air warfare, is outlined in just war theory. The special features we have highlighted here may be accounted for as consequences of the application of just war theory to the peculiar character of war at sea. Moreover, each of the various features of war at sea highlighted previously may have some counterparts in other domains of warfare. Nevertheless, drawing attention to the way in which the ethics of war at sea is structured by its special contextual circumstances may productively inform deliberation about the ethics of the development and deployment of robotic weapons in this context.

Status of Armed USVs and UUVs: Vessels or Weapons?

As we noted previously, the legal and ethical codes that govern war at sea are mostly concerned with the activities of ships and submarines and place demands on individuals primarily—although not exclusively—through their role on these vessels.

A number of legal authorities have already begun to consider whether—or when—UUVs and USVs should be considered "vessels" under the law of the sea. The emerging consensus seems to be that autonomous UUVs and USVs, at least above a certain size, should be classed as vessels.[3] While remotely piloted vehicles (RPVs) might plausibly be held to be extensions of the vessel from which they are operated, systems capable of extended autonomous operations should be understood as vessels in their own right.[4]

As we shall see later, the question of how we understand USVs and UUVs is also central to the ethics of their design and application. The more we think of these systems as autonomous and controlled by an onboard computer—and the more roles they become capable of fulfilling—the more natural it is to think of them as vessels. However, as the following discussion highlights, understanding them as vessels appears to impose demanding ethical requirements on their capacities and operations, especially relating to distinction, proportionality, and the duty of rescue.

An alternative way of addressing these requirements, in the light of such conundrums, is to think of armed autonomous USVs and UUVs themselves instead as weapons, which may be deployed by warfighters, who then become responsible for ensuring that the use of the weapon meets the requirements of distinction, proportionality, and so forth. Yet as we shall see, this way of proceeding generates its own challenges. An important early finding of our research then is that much work remains to be done to clarify the best way of understanding the status of armed UUVs and USVs in the context of the larger ethical framework governing war at sea (as opposed merely to their current legal status).

Deployment: Where, When, and Why?

The Law of the Sea Convention attempts to balance the competing claims of national sovereignty and freedom of navigation in peacetime by distinguishing between the status of different sorts of waters and the permissibility of different sorts of activities therein. Customary international law relating to naval warfare extends this to regulate the relations between belligerent and neutral parties insofar as this is possible. The research and analysis required to assess the operations of USVs and UUVs within these frameworks is now beginning to be undertaken, and some initial results are starting to emerge. Thus, for instance, Henderson suggests that "UUVs may operate freely in both the high seas and the EEZ while exercising the requisite due regard for the interests of other vessels and posing no threat to the territorial integrity of the coastal state" and remain submerged while exercising transit passage in international straits and archipelagic sea lanes. In territorial seas, he suggests, UUVs must operate on the surface in order to exercise the right of innocent passage and display appropriate lights and make sound signals in order to facilitate safety of navigation.[5] Gogarty and Hagger also suggest that USVs and UUVs are restricted in the activities that they can undertake while exercising the right of innocent passage.[6] McLaughlin emphasizes that USVs and UUVs are clearly subject to the Convention on the International Regulations for Preventing Collisions at Sea (COLREGs) and must be capable of avoiding collisions to such a degree that they could be said to maintain a "proper and sufficient lookout." He also allows that the presence of a foreign submerged UUV within a nation's territorial waters might constitute a sovereign affront justifying the use of armed force.[7]

We leave the task of settling the legal questions raised by the deployment of UUVs and USVs in various sorts of waters to others qualified to complete it. However, some discussion of the deeper ethical questions underpinning and surrounding the relevant legal frameworks is appropriate here and might, we hope, usefully inform the ongoing legal debate.

It does seem reasonable, for instance, that the moral right nations have over their territorial waters and (to a lesser extent) continental shelves and EEZs should exclude USVs and UUVs conducting—or perhaps even just capable of conducting—certain sorts of operations. If nations have a right against other nations that they not conduct mining or survey operations in their EEZs or carry out operations injurious to their security in their territorial waters then this right would surely carry over consistently to exclude unmanned vessels just as much as manned vessels. Indeed, arguably the fact that UUVs and USVs are unmanned makes their use in these sorts of waters more suspicious and threatening to the interests of sovereign governments on the assumption that other nations will be more likely to deploy vessels in hazardous environments that might generate a military response given that doing so will not place a human crew at risk of death or capture. Requiring such systems to confine themselves to innocent passage through territorial waters is at least a partial solution to this problem.

The ethics of the use of autonomous UUVs and USVs on the high seas remains an open—and controversial—matter. At first sight at least, the right to freedom of navigation in international waters appears to extend to include these systems, presuming that they do not pose too much of a navigational hazard to other vessels. However, interestingly, this presumption rests on an understanding of them as vessels and may be unsettled when we start to consider the prospect of armed autonomous UUVs and USVs and whether such systems should be thought of, instead, as weapons.

Roughly speaking, the operations of vessels in international waters are permissible as long as they are compatible with the right of free navigation of other vessels through the same waters. Thus, if they are to operate on the high seas, UUVs and USVs must have the capacity to reliably avoid posing a hazard to other vessels. At a bare minimum, this requires taking the appropriate measures to minimize the risk of collision. While the COLREGs spell this out as requiring all vessels to "at all times maintain a proper lookout by sight and hearing," which phrasing encourages the reader to presume a human being on board (or at least supervision by a remote operator), we can see no reason why a fully autonomous system that proved equally capable of avoiding collision with other vessels without human supervision should not be judged to meet the appropriate standard.

Of course, armed UUVs and USVs operating on the high seas would appear to pose risks to commercial shipping and to the warships of neutral nations beyond simply the risk of collision: they might (accidentally) fire on them, for example. Their significance for the right of freedom of navigation is therefore likely to depend on their capacity to distinguish between legitimate and illegitimate targets of attack as discussed in the following sections.

A key question in the larger debate about the ethics of autonomous weapons concerns whether—by analogy to what we suggested was the case with regard to the capacity to avoid collision—it would be sufficient to render the use of such weapons permissible if they were capable of achieving results similar to the standard required of human beings with respect to compliance with the moral principles of distinction and proportionality. That is, would we regard maritime autonomous systems as likewise subject to what has come to be called the "Arkin Test" for ethical use of lethal force by autonomous systems.

Those adhering strictly to the original moral intentions of the Law of Armed Conflict (*jus in bello*) to provide protections for war's most vulnerable victims are prone to believe that satisfaction of the Arkin Test would be sufficient to render the use of AWS permissible. Indeed, owing to the (thus far unrealized) promise of AWS to comply more perfectly with legal demands of proportionality and distinction than combat systems controlled by human operators, they may be tempted to the conclusion that their use will become mandatory. On the other hand, a number of authors have suggested that a strict focus on the requirement of human autonomy and accountability central to the moral (as opposed to the legal) structure of *jus in bello* itself may conclude that the absence of a human will at the moment the attack is carried out means that the Arkin Test is irrelevant, since autonomous weapons cannot be said to comply with that stipulation at all. Insofar as our concern is with the compatibility of the operations of AWS with the right to freedom of navigation rather than with the wider conceptual debate concerning the ethics of autonomous targeting, though, it appears that the relevant standard of discrimination is just that required of human beings in similar circumstances (as the Arkin Test seems to stipulate).

However, there is another reason to worry that achieving a high standard when it comes to the capacity to distinguish between legitimate and illegitimate targets may not be sufficient to render the use of AWS ethical on the high seas. The presence of AWS operating in particular waters might exercise a "chilling" effect on commercial shipping over a wide area—and thus impinge on the right of freedom of navigation—even if the chance of an accidental attack by AWS was extremely remote given the capacities of these systems. This possibility seems especially likely if we think of autonomous UUVs and USVs as weapons rather than vessels. Indeed, one might well argue that armed autonomous UUVs at least should be understood as sophisticated versions of free-floating mines and consequently should be prohibited.[8] The use of drifting mines that do not disarm themselves within an hour is prohibited under international law because of the threat they pose to freedom of navigation.[9] The fact that the chance of any particular ship being struck by any particular drifting mine is small does not seem to affect the force of this concern.

An important point of reference for our intuitions here is the United States' Mk 60 Captor deep-water mine, which is a moored torpedo launch system capable of detecting the acoustic signature of approaching enemy submarines and firing a torpedo to destroy them. This system is arguably already autonomous insofar as the "decision" to launch a torpedo is made without direct human input at the time. Versions of the system have been in use since 1979 without causing significant international outcry, which suggests that concerns about freedom of navigation in the open waters need not rule out the deployment of AWS.

However, there are at least three reasons to be cautious about this conclusion. First, because as the Captor is itself fixed—even if its range of operations is extended—the system would appear to pose less of a danger to navigation than hypothetical free-ranging AWS.[10] Second, insofar as this weapon is advertised as an antisubmarine system, those plying the surface of the waters may feel that they have little to fear from it. International opinion might be very different should it become common knowledge that similar systems are being tasked with destroying surface vessels. Finally, the absence of any outcry against Captor and similar systems needs to be understood in the context of a history in which—to date—they have not been responsible for any noncombatant casualties. The first time an AWS deployed at sea attacks a commercial or—worse—passenger vessel, we might expect public and international opinion about their legitimacy to change dramatically.

Even very reliable AWS may therefore jeopardize freedom of navigation if vessels are unwilling to put to sea in waters in which AWS are

A General Atomics MQ-1 Predator operated by the 163rd Reconnaissance Wing flies near the Southern California Logistics Airport in
Victorville, California. *TSgt Sgt. Effrain Lopez/U.S. Air Force*

A General Atomics MQ-9 Reaper flies near Creech Air Force Base,
Nevada, on June 25, 2015. *SrA Cory Payne/U.S. Air Force*

A pilot and sensor operator for the MQ-9 Reaper during a training mission at Hancock Field Air National Guard Base, New York. *TSgt Ricky Best/U.S. Air Force*

A Northrop Grumman RQ-4 Global Hawk lands taxiing at an undisclosed location in Southwest Asia on March 8, 2015. *TSgt Marie Brown/U.S. Air Force*

A Northrop Grumman MQ-4C Triton lands at Naval Air Station Patuxent River, Maryland, on September 18, 2014. *U.S. Navy*

The Northrop Grumman MQ-8C Fire Scout on board the USS *Montgomery* (LCS 8) on March 27, 2017. *PO3 Zachary S. Eshleman / U.S. Navy*

A Kaman K1200 lands at Marine Corps Air Station Yuma, Arizona, on May 7, 2016. *PFC George Melendez / U.S. Marine Corps*

The X-47B unmanned combat aerial system demonstrator launches from the flight deck of the aircraft carrier USS *George H.W. Bush* (CVN 77) on May 14, 2013. *PO2 Anthony Curtis / U.S. Navy*

The X-47B receives fuel from an Omega K-707 tanker on April 22, 2015. *Elizabeth A. Wolter/U.S. Navy*

ET2 Darius Jackman launches a Puma unmanned aerial vehicle on board the USS *Monsoon* (PC 4) on July 22, 2016. *PO2 Ryan McLearnon/U.S. Navy*

A U.S. Marine holds a PD-100 Black Hornet nano-drone during an exercise at Camp Pendleton on July 9, 2016. *PFC Rhita Daniel/U.S. Marine Corps*

The Persistent Threat Detection System at Multi-National Base Tarin Kot, Afghanistan, on December 7, 2010. *SPC Jennifer Spradlin / U.S. Army*

A REMUS 600 autonomous unmanned undersea vehicle at the Naval Air Station Patuxent River, Maryland, on September 20, 2015. *John Williams / U.S. Navy*

Professor John Jackson uses the SkyWall-100 drone capture system during a demonstration at the U.S. Naval War College in October 2017. *Editor's collection*

SrA David Tillery prepares to launch the Desert Hawk unmanned aerial vehicle at Shaw Air Force Base in February 2004. *SSgt. A.C. Eggman/U.S. Air Force*

The U.S. Marine Corps tests the Modular Advanced Armed Robotic System (MAARS) at Camp Pendleton, California, on July 8, 2016. *LCpl Julien Rodarte/U.S. Marine Corps*

The U.S. Marine Corps tests a General Dynamics Multipurpose Unmanned Tactical Transport at Camp Pendleton, California, on July 13, 2016. *PFC Rhita Daniel/U.S. Marine Corps*

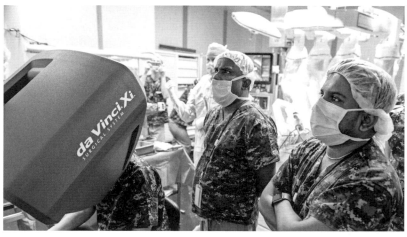

USNS *Mercy* surgical team and a Sri Lankan surgical team perform the first robot-assisted surgery in a ship using the Da Vinci Robot Surgical System. *PO2 Kelsey Adams*

U.S. Marines with the 15th Marine Expeditionary Unit retrieve an Insitu RQ-21A Blackjack UAV on board the USS *San Diego* on October 2, 2017. *LCpl Jeremy Laboy/U.S. Marine Corps*

The Defense Advanced Research Project Agency's Fast Lightweight Autonomy project is designed to enable small drones to autonomously navigate complex and crowded environments. *Timothy Sandland/U.S. Air National Guard*

Professor John Jackson (*fourth from left*) and other Navy representatives attend the "roll-out" of the Echo Voyager XLUUV in Huntington Beach, California. *Editor's collection*

Cadets and midshipmen from the Air Force Academy, Military Academy, and Naval Academy participate in the DARPA swarm challenge in April 2017. *DARPA*

Fixed wing drone launched in Army training exercise. *U.S. Army photo from DVIDS*

Sun sets on MQ-1 Predator remotely piloted vehicle at Creech Air Force Base, Nevada. *U.S. Air Force photo from DVIDS*

RQ-4 Global Hawk undergoes maintenance at Warner Robbins, Georgia. *U.S. Air Force photo from DVIDS*

known to be operating. While fear of (accidental) attack by an AWS might appear to be irrational when compared to the risks posed by manned systems, beliefs about risk are notoriously complex and difficult to assess because they often contain hidden value judgments. In this case, a reluctance to risk attack by an AWS may express the value judgment that human beings alone should be responsible for decisions to take human lives. Insofar as what matters for the sustaining of the international commerce that the right of freedom of navigation exists to protect is the willingness of ships to ply the oceans, subjective judgments of risk may be just as—indeed more—significant for the existence of freedom of navigation as the objective risks that ships actually take when they leave port.

It may, therefore, turn out that the international community will be required to adjudicate on the balance of the interests of states in deploying AWS and the civilian vessel operators' desire not to be at risk of attack by an autonomous weapon. Any attempts to embed this judgment in legislation will also need to consider what is realistically achievable in this regard, especially given the military advantages associated with UMS and the force of the logics driving their uptake. In many ways, such a debate would hark back to that which took place with the advent of submarine warfare, which was effectively resolved in favor of permitting the operations of military submersibles. We suspect that this is the most likely outcome with regard to armed autonomous UUVs and USVs as well. However, it is important to acknowledge the competing considerations in this debate, summarized previously.

There are several further questions that may arise concerning the operations of armed autonomous UUVs and USVs in various waters that reasons of space prevent us from doing more than mentioning here. The difficulty in imagining autonomous weapons having the capacity to capture enemy or neutral vessels suggests that they could at most play a limited role in naval blockades or the taking of neutral merchant vessels as prizes. The requirement to record the locations of mines so that they may be removed or rendered harmless after the cessation of conflict would appear to be moot when "mines" are themselves mobile and autonomous, although the considerations motivating this requirement (to reduce the subsequent hazards to shipping postconflict) imply that autonomous weapons must reliably be able to render themselves harmless on instruction or after some defined period. There are undoubtedly also other issues that, along with these, require further investigation.

Distinction

Perhaps the most fundamental ethical requirement in wartime is to confine one's attacks to enemy combatants and as much as possible to try to avoid civilian casualties. Thus, the *jus in bello* principle of distinction requires that warfighters refrain from targeting noncombatants and take appropriate care to try to minimize the noncombatant casualties caused by attacks targeted at combatants.

Much of the current criticism of AWS proceeds from the claim that robotic weapons are unlikely to be capable of meeting the requirements of distinction for the foreseeable future. In counterinsurgency warfare in particular, identifying whether someone is a combatant or not requires a complex set of contextual judgments that look to be beyond the capacity of machines for the foreseeable future. Whether this problem is insurmountable or exists in all of the roles in which we might imagine AWS being used is controversial and a larger question than we can hope to resolve here. In this context we will settle for observing that the problem of distinction is arguably less demanding in naval warfare because there are fewer potential targets and because sonar and radar are more capable of distinguishing between military and civilian vessels than image recognition, radar, and lidar are at distinguishing between targets in land warfare. Indeed, one reason advanced for favoring the use of autonomous systems on or under the sea, especially in blue-water missions, is that (when compared with land or air), the "civilian footprint" on the high seas is comparatively small, even allowing for commercial shipping and recreational boating. Moreover, the problem of distinction looks especially tractable in the context of antisubmarine warfare given the relative paucity of civilian submarines with comparable tonnage or acoustic signatures to military submarines and the fact that those few civilian systems that do exist tend to operate in a limited range of roles and locations (primarily around oil rigs and submarine cables). We might therefore expect that if robots are to become capable of distinction in any context, they will become capable of it in war on and under the sea.

Nevertheless, there are at least five sorts of cases in which the requirements of distinction pose a formidable challenge for the (ethical) operations of autonomous weapons in naval warfare. First, to avoid attacks on military ships of neutral nations, AWS will need to be able to identify the nature and the nationality of potential targets and not just the fact that they are warships. In some cases, where the ships in the enemy's fleet are easily distinguishable from those of other nations owing to distinctive radar or acoustic profiles, this problem may not arise. However, in some circumstances identifying that a ship carries guns or torpedoes or is of a certain tonnage or class will not be sufficient to establish that it is an enemy warship. Instead, making this identification will require the ability to form reasonable conclusions about its identity on the basis of its historical pattern of activity and threat posture within the battlespace. One obvious way to solve this problem would be to program autonomous UUVs and USVs to confine their attacks to targets that are themselves firing weapons. However, this would significantly reduce the military utility of AWS especially in strike and area-denial roles. Whether computers will ever be able to make the necessary judgments to avoid the need for this restriction remains an open question.

Second, AWS must be able to recognize when warships are repurposed as hospital ships and declared as such, in which case they cease to be legitimate targets. This may sometimes happen in the course of a particular engagement, when, for instance, the enemy is forced to draft a ship into service as a hospital ship to treat a large number of their warfighters who have been wounded in the course of the battle. The new role of the ship will be communicated by prominently displaying the Red Cross (or its various equivalents) and radioing the other forces involved in the battle. AWS will need to have the capacity to recognize these signals and the change of status in the vessel concerned.

Third, as enemy vessels that have clearly indicated their surrender are not legitimate targets, AWS must be able to recognize surrender.[11] It is possible that in the future warships may be expected to carry a "surrender beacon" capable of communicating to any AWS operating in the area that they have in fact surrendered. Until that day, however, AWS will need to have the capacity to recognize and respond to the existing conventions about communication of surrender through changes in threat posture and via the display of signal lights or flags. Again, at this stage it is unclear whether or not robots will ever be able to do this reliably.

Fourth, AWS must be able to identify when an enemy ship is hors de combat by virtue of being so badly damaged as to be incapable of posing any military threat. In rare circumstances it may not be possible for a badly damaged and listing ship to signal surrender. Thus, morally—if not legally—speaking, even an enemy warship that has not indicated surrender is not necessarily a legitimate target, if it is no longer capable of engaging in hostilities. Human beings are (sometimes) able to discern when this circumstance applies using their rich knowledge of the world and of the motivations and likely actions of people in various situations. AWS would need to be at least as capable as human beings at making such discriminations before their use would be ethical.

Importantly, these last three issues appear in a different light depending on whether we think of AWS as vessels or as weapons. If an enemy warship surrenders after a torpedo is launched from a manned submarine, for instance, the ship's destruction would be a tragedy but not a crime. However, if a ship fires on an enemy vessel that has clearly indicated surrender, this *is* a war crime. If we think of an AWS as a weapon, therefore, then as long as the officer who deploys it does not do so knowing the intended targets have surrendered or otherwise become hors de combat or have been repurposed as hospital ships, its use will be legitimate even if there is some chance that the status of the targets may change after the AWS is deployed. On the other hand, if we think of the USV or UUV as a vessel, then it seems it must have the capacity to detect whether potential targets have surrendered or otherwise become hors de combat (or have been repurposed as hospital ships) in order to avoid attacks in such circumstances. Of course, if the delay between deploying an AWS understood as a weapon and its carrying out an attack is too long—a matter of days rather than hours, for instance—then this might shake our conviction that it is sufficiently discriminating to be ethical.

Fifth, when it comes to operations to interdict or attack merchant shipping, the problem of distinction is especially challenging just because it is so context sensitive. AWS would seem to be poorly placed, for instance, to make judgments about whether merchant vessels were carrying enemy troops or "otherwise making an effective contribution to military action." The fact that AWS are unlikely to be capable of searching or capturing merchant ships also limits their utility in making this discrimination.

Proportionality

The ethical requirements of proportionality in *jus in bello* ask whether the military advantage to be gained by an attack on a military target is sufficient to justify the death and destruction that might reasonably be expected to be caused by the attack. Importantly, while the *legal* requirement of proportionality is usually understood to require only that the noncombatant casualties ("collateral damage") it is reasonable to expect an attack on a military target to cause are not excessive in relation to the military advantage the attack seeks to secure, the *ethical* principle grants weight to the lives of combatants in this calculation as well. Thus, for instance, a deliberate attack on an enemy military installation housing a large number of enemy warfighters who posed no immediate threat, when it was already known that the enemy had signed an agreement to surrender effective the next day, would be unethical by virtue of being disproportionate.

This important consideration exposes a deep divide between the two authors of this article themselves. Sparrow has previously argued elsewhere that the requirements of proportionality stand as a profound barrier to the ethical use of AWS. The calculations of military advantage required to assess whether a given number of civilian (or military) casualties is proportionate are extremely complex and context sensitive and require a detailed understanding of the way the world works that is, Sparrow has argued, likely to remain beyond the capacities of autonomous systems for the foreseeable future. Lucas is less pessimistic, believing that their potential to exceed the limited abilities of human beings when it comes to making judgments of proportionality is an important part of the promise of AWS.

Regardless, there are reasons to believe that these sorts of calculations of proportionality are likely to be easier in the context of war at sea. To begin with, as noted previously, the relative lack of civilian "clutter" on the oceans means that the risk of civilian casualties in attacks on legitimate military targets in naval engagements is much lower than in land warfare, reducing the number of circumstances in which a judgment of the proportionality of anticipated civilian casualties is required. There are also typically fewer units involved in naval engagements than in land warfare, and the scope of operations available to individual units is less, which makes it more plausible to think that a computer could calculate the military advantage associated with a particular attack and thus whether a given number of military deaths would be justified.

On the other hand, there is another proportionality calculation that is especially difficult in the context of war at sea. Military operations may have significant and long-term implications for civilian life via their impact on the environment. Consequently, combatants are now also held to an obligation to consider and, where possible, minimize the damage to the environment caused by their activities. These obligations must be balanced against considerations of military necessity. In practice, then, combatants are required to make a calculation of proportionality when contemplating an attack in order to determine whether or not the environmental damage it is likely to cause is justified by the military advantage it will achieve. However, the role played by wind, waves, and tides in distributing the debris resulting from war at sea and the complex nature of marine ecosystems make calculations of the environmental impacts of naval operations especially difficult. Moreover, both the intrinsic value of significant features of the environment (such as, for instance, clean rivers, coral reefs, the spawning grounds of fish, etc.) and the instrumental value they have in terms of their contribution to human well-being are controversial. Judgments about such matters inevitably involve balancing a range of complex considerations as well as arguments about matters of (moral) value. For both these reasons, calculations of proportionality in attack in relation to damage to the environment seem likely to remain beyond the capacity of computers for many years yet.

Thus, once we admit that the marine environment and enemy combatant casualties are relevant to the proportionality calculation (in ethics, if not in law) and we take the broader strategic context into account, as well as the possible interactions of naval, ground, and air forces, it once more appears that judgments of proportionality are fiendishly difficult and require knowledge of the world and reasoning capacities that computer systems currently lack and seem likely to lack for the foreseeable future. Thus, at the very least, proportionality appears to remain a more difficult issue for AWS in naval warfare than distinction.

AWS, "Supervised Autonomy," and Precautions in Attack?

Of course, human beings also have significant limitations when it comes to their capacity to achieve distinction and make judgments of proportionality, and it might be argued that machines will eventually be able to perform at least as well as humans at these tasks. This is an empirical matter. However, there is also a deeper philosophical question here regarding the nature and force of the ethical imperatives underpinning the requirements of *jus in bello*. While human beings often fail to behave ethically, when it comes to the duty to avoid taking human life unnecessarily, morality demands perfection. Consequently, it might be argued that there is something troubling about justifying the use of an autonomous weapon solely on the basis that it makes "as few or fewer mistakes" than the alternative.

We cannot hope to settle these questions here. Indeed, the authors themselves disagree sharply on them. A partial solution to both the problem of distinction and proportionality might be achieved by requiring AWS to seek input from a human supervisor whenever the risks of attacking an illegitimate target exceeded some predetermined threshold. A number of authorities already advocate "supervised autonomy" as a way of attempting to combine the benefits of autonomous operations and human decision making in complex environments. Yet there are obvious limitations of this proposal. To begin with, it presumes that the task of accurately assessing the risk of inadvertently attacking an illegitimate target is easier than identifying a potential target as legitimate or not in the first place, which may not be the case. Perhaps more important, relying on human supervision to carry out combat operations ethically would sacrifice two of the key benefits of autonomous operations. It would require maintaining a robust communications infrastructure sufficient to allow the AWS to transmit the relevant data to a base station and receive instructions from a human operator, which is especially challenging in the context of operations underwater. It would also jeopardize the capacity of autonomous systems to conduct stealthy operations. In particular, submersibles would need to transmit and receive signals in real time—and thus risk giving away their location—in order to allow a human supervisor to provide input into their decisions. While supervised autonomy may be a solution in the context of operations against technologically unsophisticated adversaries without the capacity to contest the electronic battlespace or launch kinetic attacks against communications infrastructure, then, it seems unlikely to be an attractive solution in the longer term.

There is, however, a further complexity here. The *jus in bello* principles of distinction and proportionality not only distinguish between legitimate and illegitimate targets but also demand that warfighters make all feasible efforts to avoid attacking illegitimate targets in circumstances where, for various reasons, it is difficult for them to distinguish between the two. Thus, as the *San Remo Manual* notes, warfighters "must take all feasible measures to gather information which will assist in determining whether or not objects which are not military objectives are present in an area of attack" and "take all feasible precautions in the choice of methods and means in order to avoid or minimize collateral casualties or damage."[12] While the question of what sorts of measures or precautions are "feasible" in a given context is obviously complex and often controversial, the level of risk to warfighters involved in the various options available to them is clearly relevant: there must be some limit to the amount of risk that we can reasonably expect warfighters to take on in order to achieve any given degree of confidence about the nature of the targets they intend to attack.

The fact that no human lives would be—directly (discussed later)—placed at risk by requiring autonomous UUVs and USVs to take any given sort of actions to minimize the chance of inadvertently attacking civilian targets or causing disproportionate casualties suggests that the requirements to take "all feasible measures" and "all feasible precautions" might be significantly more demanding for these systems.

Thus, for instance, unmanned submersibles might be required to launch sensor buoys, to use active sonar, or even to surface to facilitate identification of targets. Indeed, AWS might even be required to await authorization from a human supervisor before carrying out an attack. That is, according to the strongest version of this line of argument, fully autonomous operations of a UUV or USV (or, one suspects, any AWS) would be unethical.

There are two obvious ways in which this conclusion might be resisted. First, given the military utility of UMS—and an argument from military necessity—it might be argued that the risk to the "vessel," regardless of the absence of any crew on board, is properly relevant to judgments about feasibility: it would be unreasonable to include in the range of "feasible" precautions those that would be likely to result in the destruction of the system if carried out during an engagement. Second—in addition—while exposing a UMS to risk may not directly threaten any lives, the destruction of the vessel would jeopardize the safety of friendly forces who might have been relying on its carrying out its mission. Thus, human lives may well be at stake when we risk the safety of a UMS. These two considerations speak in favor of allowing autonomous systems to prioritize their own "safety" over the safety of those whose lives they potentially threaten through their targeting decisions.

The capacity of UMS to take more precautions before launching an attack is often cited as an argument in favor of developing and deploying them. The fact that they are unmanned means that they might plausibly be used in more risky operations in order to try to achieve any worthwhile goal. Perversely, when the goal is the preservation of the lives of noncombatants, this might even mean placing (what would otherwise be) autonomous systems at risk by requiring them to seek authorization for each attack from a human operator. Yet this would vitiate many of the military advantages of autonomous opera-tions—including the extent to which the use of UMS reduces the risk to the lives of friendly forces. The advent of armed autonomous systems will therefore require a potentially difficult conversation among the international community about the balance to be struck between military necessity and humanitarian considerations and the role of human supervision of autonomous systems in securing this balance.

Conclusion

Our investigations suggest that the distinctive ethical character of war at sea generates a number of novel ethical dilemmas regarding the design and use of UUVs and USVs, which do not arise for UMS operating in the air or on land. In particular, the importance of freedom of navigation on the high seas and the obligation to come to the aid of those who are shipwrecked or lost at sea pose difficult challenges for the ethical operations of UUVs and USVs—and especially armed and autonomous systems. Moreover, some of the ethical issues that do arise regarding the (hypothetical) operations of armed autonomous systems more generally are differently inflected in the context of war on and under the seas, including the implications of the requirements of proportionality and distinction for the operations of these systems. Finally, what seems clear to both authors, despite specific differences, is that much more work remains to be done to resolve the question of whether—or, perhaps, which—UUVs and USVs should be conceptualized as vessels or weapons and also to settle the role that should be accorded to legal conventions and historical debates about mine warfare in shaping future practice regarding UUVs. The fact that such systems blur the lines between weapons platforms and weapons means that ethical as well as legal frameworks may need to be rethought and refined in the pursuit of an appropriate balance between the demands of military necessity and humanitarian concerns in the naval warfare of the future.

Notes

1. This obligation is reflected in SOLAS, Ch. V, Reg. 10(a); UNCLOS Article 98 (1). For a useful discussion, see M. Davies, "Obligations and Implications for Ships Encountering Persons in Need of Assistance at Sea," *Pacific Rim Law and Policy*

Journal 12, no. 1 (2003): 109–41. Walzer seems to suggest, in his discussion of the Laconia affair, that the duty of rescue only applies to noncombatants and thus to the context of attacks on merchant shipping. Michael Walzer, *Just and Unjust Wars: A Moral Argument with Historical Illustrations*, 4th ed. (New York: Basic Books, 2006), 147. On the other hand, Article 18 of Geneva Convention (II) 1949 refers specifically to shipwrecked members of the armed forces, a matter that for decades complicated the formation of international law governing submarine warfare.

2. The legal formulation of this duty, in Article 18 of Geneva Convention (II) 1949, specifies that it applies "after each engagement," but it is hard to see why this duty should lapse before or between engagements and this restriction is most naturally understood as acknowledging that parties to the conflict are unlikely to have the capacity to safely conduct rescue in the midst of combat rather than as denying the existence of a generalized duty to rescue. For some discussion, see W. Heintschel von Heinegg, "Submarine Operations and International Law," in *Law at War: The Law as It Was and the Law as It Should Be*, ed. O. Engdahl and P. Wrange (Leiden, Netherlands: Koninklijke Brill, 2008), 160–61.

3. There is also a debate about when/if such systems can be considered "warships," especially in relation to the status of merchant shipping (see, for example, R. McLaughlin, "Unmanned Naval Vehicles at Sea: USVs, UUVs, and the Adequacy of the Law," *Journal of Law Information and Science* 21, no. 2 [2011]: 100–115).

4. McLaughlin thinks they should be granted sovereign immunity on the basis that they are "government ship's operating for non-commercial purposes" even though he thinks it is a stretch to argue that they are themselves "warships." He agrees, however, that they are "vessels" under COLREGs. The question, he raises, of whether UMS are "warships" is an issue with implications mostly for the ethics of attacks *on* these systems rather than attacks *by* them and as such is of less interest to us here. McLaughlin, "Unmanned Naval Vehicles."

5. A. H. Henderson, "Murky Waters: The Legal Status of Unmanned Undersea Vehicles," *Naval Law Review* 53 (2006): 68–69.

6. B. Gogarty and M. Hagger, "The Laws of Man over Vehicles Unmanned: The Legal Response to Robotic Revolution on Sea, Land and Air," *Journal of Law, Information and Science* 19, no. 1 (2008): 73–145.

7. McLaughlin, "Unmanned Naval Vehicles," 110–11.

8. *San Remo Manual*, Part 4, Section 1, 79: "It is prohibited to use torpedoes which do not sink or otherwise become harmless when they have completed their run" (L. Doswald-Beck, ed., *San Remo Manual on International Law Applicable to Armed Conflicts at Sea* [Cambridge: Cambridge University Press, 1995], 25). See also Part 4, Section 1, 82, on free-floating mines, which are prohibited unless they are directed against military objectives and become harmless an hour after being deployed. See also Bruce Berkowitz, "Sea Power in the Robotic Age," *Issues in Science and Technology* 30, no. 2 (2014): 33–40.

9. The 1907 Hague Convention VIII prohibited the use of "automatic contact mines." However, as Heintschel von Heinegg notes, these principles "are generally recognized as customary international law and thus also govern the use of modern naval mines." W. Heintschel von Heinegg, "The Protection of Navigation in Case of Armed Conflict," *International Journal of Marine and Coastal Law* 18, no. 3 (2003): 415.

10. Doswald-Beck, *San Remo Manual*, notes that the Captor should arguably be con-
    sidered a system capable of delivering a weapon rather than a weapon itself. Von
    Heinegg, "Submarine Operations" (p. 154), also argues that this system should be
    governed by the rules applicable to torpedoes.
11. Additional Protocol to the Geneva Conventions of 12 August 1949, and Relating
    to the Protection of Victims of International Armed Conflicts (Protocol I), June
    8, 1977, Art. 43, http://www.icrc.org/ihl.nsf/INTRO/470?OpenDocument.
12. Doswald-Beck, *San Remo Manual*, 8.

06

The U.S. Marine Corps, the Evolving Amphibious Task Force, and the Rise of Unmanned Systems

Robbin Laird

For the U.S. Marine Corps (USMC), the use of twenty-first-century unmanned systems involves two strands of development involving larger unmanned systems. The first was the decision during operations in Iraq and Afghanistan to join the U.S. Army in using the Shadow unmanned aerial system (UAS) for land operations. According to a USMC Warfighting Laboratory publication, use of the Shadow UAS was closely tied to the land wars:

> The recent development and fielding of Unmanned Aircraft Systems . . . has delivered even more capabilities to our Marines. One such aircraft, the RQ-7B Shadow, is deployed in squadrons as an asset of the Marine Expeditionary Force or Marine Expeditionary Brigade. Designed to provide reconnaissance, relay communications and assist in target acquisition, the RQ-7B Shadow keeps an eye above the battlefield for extended periods of time, constantly relaying information between Marine air and ground controls. The Shadow enhances the capabilities of Marine commanders across the

spectrum of military operations and was first deployed during
Operation Iraqi Freedom in September 2007.[1]

The RQ-7B Shadow UAS has electro-optical and infrared (EO/IR)
sensors, communications relay payloads, and laser designators to provide commanders on the ground with increased visual reconnaissance
and communications capability. An unmanned aerial vehicle squadron, designated as a VMU, supports the Marine Corps Ground Combat Element (GCE) with route reconnaissance, fire integration, and
force protection before, during, and after a mission.

The second strand of unmanned systems development involved
the introduction of the ScanEagle into the Corps. This system fit the
Corps' evolution from a primary occupation force involved in land
wars to a force planning its "return to the sea." The Amphibious Ready
Group (ARG) and Marine Expeditionary Unit (MEU) have joined to
become a flexible amphibious ready task force. This change was driven
initially by the introduction of the Osprey but is being reshaped as
other manned and unmanned aircraft systems come to the force.

Shaping the Twenty-First-Century Amphibious Task Force
The USMC is evolving as its focus shifts from land wars to full-
spectrum operations. An entire generation of Marines has fought
ashore as a flexible land force; with the drawdown in the land wars
in the Middle East, the Marines have returned to the sea and are now
learning to operate from the sea base. But given the twin impacts of
the Osprey and the F-35B, this new force is unlike any previous Navy–
Marine Corps team that operated from the sea. With new tools Marines
can operate at greater distance and with greater lethality from the sea.
Crucial to the reworking of the sea-based Navy–Marine Corps team
has been the evolution of the amphibious task force itself. The ARG–
MEU is no longer limited to operating within a two-hundred-mile
box dictated by the rotorcraft onboard; the Osprey allows the ships to
operate at much greater distance from one another and even allows for
a disaggregated force to operate alongside the amphibious force.

The amphibious task force is a work in progress as new capabilities—
such as the CH-53K, the heavy lift element, and unmanned systems—
are added. These systems are being incorporated into what is already

the most flexible and lethal insertion force built in history. Although the Marines used the Shadow UAS significantly during their participation in the land wars in the Middle East, this system requires land basing and thus is unusable as the Marines return to the sea. The ScanEagle, whose origin was at sea, was the primary UAS used by the amphibious task force until the advent of the RQ-21A Blackjack in 2014. The Blackjack's commercial variant is known as the Integrator.

Marine UAS are to be understood in the context of the overall evolution of the amphibious task force and the flexibility the force commander will be looking for. The commander may operate the UAS from the ship to assist a Marine inserting force for a short duration mission. Or he or she may take that UAS from the ship and operate it ashore with deployed Marines. The flexibility of the UAS over-watch asset and evolving payload flexibility will be most important to the commander going forward.

A good perspective on the transition from the Shadow land-tethered force to the ScanEagle-Blackjack expeditionary approach was provided by one of the key ground combat marines involved in the transformation of the Osprey. In a 2014 interview, then–major Scott Cuomo, who was head of the Infantry Officer Course (IOC) at Quantico, focused on the overall shift toward empowering the Marines with aviation assets to become a more flexible and lethal ground combat maneuver force. In the interview Major Cuomo described how innovation was being generated and in the process the Shadow was being shed:

> The process started with a bootstrap operation.
> The IOC Team started by simply setting up a training exercise operating from Quantico to Parris Island.

> *We took off from a commercial airport near Quantico.*
> *We flew two Ospreys. We were to fast-rope out of the Ospreys at the "enemy" area on Parris Island; we had to fast-rope in due to suspect enemy mines in the primary LZs [landing zones].*
> *We were doing it at night but one of the Ospreys developed a hydraulic leak, which led to us executing with only 1 Osprey.*
> *We continued on and the 22 guys on the plane fast-roped into the objective area.*

The exercise highlighted two problems which have been addressed in later exercises: given the distance covered by the Osprey, intelligence received at the point of departure is not that accurate on the point of arrival. And given the distance of the Osprey team from the command element, who is giving the fires approval? In other words, the plane can outrun the normal fire controls process.

The IOC Team, led by Captain Deane, published a piece in the *Marine Corps Gazette* in January 2013 which General Schmidle read and then contacted Major Cuomo.

This meant that prior to the second exercise in Camp Blanding, FL that DCA [deputy commandant of aviation] and his team offered IOC their full support. Notably, they were offered a "Shadow," unmanned aerial system (UAS) for the second experiment. The idea was to operate in a very humid and tropical objective area similar to many areas in the Asia-Pacific region.

This exercise was very helpful in highlighting the limitations of the "Shadow" for the type of expeditionary operations being tested in the exercise. And as well, it highlighted what kind of UAS support asset the GCE would find most useful to such operations.[2]

Put bluntly, for the Marines looking to advance their capabilities as an expeditionary force, the Shadow was not on the menu. They instead turned to leverage their ScanEagles, and by working with the company providing the ScanEagle, they generated a new UAS that had even greater flexibility for the evolving USMC expeditionary force.

UAS in the USMC: Perspective
of LtGen (Ret.) George Trautman

LtGen (Ret.) George Trautman, former deputy commandant of aviation and a key figure in generating the USMC's current aviation innovation wave, provided an overview of the evolution of UAS capabilities in the USMC in a 2017 interview by Robbin Laird.

Question: The unmanned aerial vehicles (UAVs) going on ships now really had their origin in the land wars. How did the process get started?

Trautman: It goes back to the time GEN Jim Conway was in Iraq with I Marine Expeditionary Force and he found a little company called Insitu, which was making the ScanEagle UAV.

Believe it or not, the ScanEagle was being used for the albacore fishing fleets up in the Pacific Northwest at the time. In other words, the ScanEagle has a shipboard legacy already built right into it. But the Marines evolved the ScanEagle principally as an asset for land-based operations in Afghanistan and Iraq. And in recent years, with the focus on returning to the sea, it became obvious that a similar capability on board our amphibious task force would be quite useful. That is what led us to make the selection of the Insitu RQ-21 Blackjack, which is now deploying on our Marine Expeditionary Units, and by all accounts it is doing quite well so far.

Question: It is very challenging to operate UAS on board ships. Could you discuss those challenges?

Trautman: Many people who have not spent a lot of time at sea really do not grasp the inherent challenges that you have when you launch and recover from a sea base. The Marines over the years, along with their partners in the U.S. Navy, have built an aviation force that's quite credible from the sea. F-35Bs, MV-22s, H-1s, and the evolving CH-53K all come into the force at a very important time as our nation evolves into a better understanding of the value and proper use of the amphibious task force. In parallel with those developments, we must figure out how to take advantage of UAS. As we do that operationally, we at the same time have to experiment with, learn, and use systems from the sea in ways that cause us to understand what new systems we should procure in the coming decade as well. In other words, the foundation for the future is being built with our experience on board our amphibious ships today as the new aviation assets marry up with the unmanned systems on board our ships.

Question: Having UAS on board allows the Marine Corps commanders to sort out how best to use those assets in operations as well. How might they do that?

Trautman: If I'm a task force commander and I'm deployed somewhere around the globe, I want to be prepared to conduct operations at a moment's notice when the mission dictates. I also want to have the flexibility to conduct all my sorties from the sea or if necessary to transition to an expeditionary land base for short duration operations that make an impact on the enemy before quickly returning to sea.

I want UAS that enable me to do whatever I need to do to accomplish the mission. That means I need range, speed, endurance, the ability to take off and land vertically, a wide range of payloads, nonproprietary payload "hooks," and the best size, weight, and power (SWAP) advantage I can attain. To do that, you have to think long and hard about the types of capabilities that you wish to procure. Whether it is classic UAS capabilities like intelligence surveillance and reconnaissance, the delivery of precision weapons, or electronic warfare, there are a whole host of missions that unmanned systems can do with the right payloads. The key is to have those systems with me, use them, and determine how to get the most effective use from them in the widely varied operations that an amphibious task force will pursue.

Question: When you were DCA, you worked the decision to sunset the Prowler electronic warfare aircraft. That decision clearly has an impact on the payloads that you want to have on a UAS as well.

Trautman: It does. We made the decision in 2009 to sunset Prowler a decade out in 2019. We did that with our eyes wide open, knowing that the F–35B would be coming into the force in a more robust way by that time. There are inherent electronic warfare capabilities resident in the F-35, but our vision also included the need for UAS to proliferate in the battle space to round out the electronic warfare requirements that the force will have. We are in our infancy right now in developing those capabilities, but the first step in achieving something is to get started and to put the capabilities in the hands of young men and women who are in the force and then evolve the capability in a way that makes sense. I'm confident that we are on that trajectory with our UAS and the payloads that we will develop for those systems in the next few years.

Question: And the experience being gained now and in the next decade will clearly shape the way ahead, not only for the amphibious task force but for the unmanned element. In other words, the approach is to experiment by operational use. What happens next?

Trautman: The current DCA has been very prescient in laying out a requirement for a program called MUX (Marine Air-Ground Task Force [MAGTF] Unmanned Expeditionary UAS), which the current aviation plan says will be ready for initial operations in the 2025 time frame. That platform, whatever it becomes, should have the capability to take off and land from the sea base, to take off and land from an expeditionary operating location ashore, and to deliver long-range relatively high-speed service to the fleet so that you can use that range and speed to your advantage. It should also come in with adequate power and nonproprietary "hooks" so that future users can employ whatever payloads make the best sense for the force as it evolves. This is a very exciting time for the development of unmanned systems in support of the amphibious task force and the Marine Corps.

Role of the ScanEagle and Blackjack in USMC Expeditionary Capabilities

Lieutenant General (Ret.) Trautman highlighted both the ScanEagle and the Blackjack as key elements of shaping the transition from land to sea. Art Crowe, a former Marine officer involved in manned and unmanned operations who is now working for Insitu, provided a sense of how this process is evolving in another 2017 interview by Robbin Laird. The second strain of evolution, namely, support to the expeditionary force by a UAS able to operate on board a ship and on shore, has been shaped to date by Insitu's working relationship with the USMC.

Crowe is a former Harrier pilot who became the operations officer of VMU-2 in 2003–4. He participated in the second battle of Fallujah, and his combat experience clearly guides his thinking on how remotely operated aircraft can provide a combat edge for Marines as they build out their amphibious capabilities.

Question: What was the origin of the coming of the ScanEagle to the Marine Corps?

Crowe: General Conway, later commandant of the USMC, was in Iraq in 2004 and was looking for support for his maneuver force. He wanted a way to get support from an effective UAS without having to wait for a long acquisition process. He got that through a services contract with Insitu whereby the company provided ISR [intelligence, surveillance, and reconnaissance] services but operated the assets. The Marines provided security and operational support; the company operated the asset and delivered the product to the Marines.

Question: This was the origin then of a company-operated and company-owned system. What was the advantage to both company and the Corps of such an approach?

Crowe: The company could evolve the capabilities of the ScanEagle in concert with the feedback from their UAS operators and Marines on their operational needs.

Rather than going through a long requirements generation process, the company could evolve the capabilities of the aircraft and the payloads to provide for the services the Marines required. This allowed for rapid innovation and adaptation to customer needs.

The payloads then evolved over time to provide data to meet the evolving needs of the USMC, with the service contract delivering the payoff for the company. The ScanEagle's latest generation of EO/IR sensors is the 900 series of turrets.[3]

And this evolution of capability has been driven by the company in interaction with the USMC, the U.S. Navy, and other DOD [Department of Defense] and foreign customers. The ScanEagle has become a product and capability deployed worldwide. The genesis of the ScanEagle was in fact to support weather reconnaissance and commercial fishing fleets, so it has been a maritime-proven platform from the beginning. The return to the sea for the Marines has provided a venue within which the ScanEagle has returned home—so to speak.

Question: One of the other deployed UAS from Insitu is the RQ-21A Blackjack.

How was this procured, and how is it being used?

Crowe: The Navy and Marines procured the Blackjack through the traditional procurement model. The Navy approved acquisition in 2010 and operated the first early operational capability (EOC) Blackjacks in 2014. The program achieved initial operational capability in 2016. The Blackjack is different from the ScanEagle. While it operates with similar launch and recovery equipment, it is larger and designed to be an air vehicle that can operate a variety of payloads simultaneously. The aircraft is built around a center of gravity payload bay. It is a modular setup in which you can configure a variety of payloads, to include all previously integrated ScanEagle payloads. There is room on the air vehicle for up to thirty-nine pounds of payloads, which operate with up to five hundred watts of power. As long as you can meet those requirements and operate with the interface control, you can integrate various payloads. The Marines have operated it ashore and have now brought it to the amphibious force. Blackjack is configured to operate off *San Antonio*–class L ships. It first deployed last year with the 22nd MEU and is currently operating with deployed forces. Operating a UAS off a ship can be more challenging than operating it ashore. Integrating the air platform in the workflow of the ship is one challenge; operating with the different operational impacts of the air fleet is another. And working the launch and recovery can be more challenging in a dynamic shipboard environment. This continues to be a focus of effort for the Blackjack team.

Question: The sunsetting of the Prowler has set the stage for another key development for the Blackjack, namely, providing support for the MAGTF along with the F-35 for electronic warfare. How do you see this challenge?

Crowe: The sunsetting of the Prowler in 2019 is a key driver of needed capability.

The payload flexibility of the Blackjack means that it could be part of the electronic warfare capability for deployed Marines, and because we are working the shipboard integration, it could be part of that package as well for the at-sea force. It is a work in progress but a key part of the way ahead for the Marines and Blackjack.

VMUs and Innovation in the USMC

As with other services, the introduction of unmanned systems in the USMC requires the development of core training and skill sets both to operate current systems and to shape future innovation in unmanned systems. There are four VMUs in the USMC, and they are geographically located to support their relevant force elements. VMU-1 is part of the 3rd Marine Aircraft Wing and is based at Yuma, Arizona. In 2007 VMU-1 was the first squadron in the USMC to operate RQ-7 Shadows in Iraq. It is now operating Blackjacks as well.[4] VMU-2 is part of the 2nd Marine Air Wing, based at Cherry Point, North Carolina, and is operating Blackjacks.[5] VMU-3 is part of the 1st Marine Aircraft Wing and is based at Marine Corps Air Stations Kaneohe Bay. Its primary mission is to provide support for III Marine Expeditionary Force. VMU-3 operates Shadows but is transitioning to Blackjacks.[6]

VMU-4 is a USMC Reserve unit based in Camp Pendleton, California, and operates Shadows.[7]

The shift from the old to the new was highlighted in an article about VMU-1 written in 2016, when the unit first received Blackjacks:

> "The Blackjack is runway independent, expeditionary, modular and a lot quieter than the Shadow," said Cpl. Preston Martin, a UAS maintainer with VMU-1.
>
> VMU-1 Marines received hands-on mobile training from maintenance instructors from Insitu, the company who developed the Blackjack.
>
> "The Blackjack is faster to set up and tear down," said Cody Cavender, a maintenance instructor with Insitu. "It comes loaded with payload packages, it has a longer endurance, and the training out here is going great."
>
> The Small Tactical Unmanned Aerial System Launching equipment and the STUAS Recovery System require a significantly smaller space to store and set up for operations, explained Capt. Garon Taylor-Tyree, director of safety and standardization for VMU-1 and will be the detachment officer-in-charge for the 15th Marine Expeditionary Unit.
>
> "The fact that our footprint has decreased substantially is the first benefit," said Taylor-Tyree. "The second is that we don't require a runway to operate the RQ-21."
>
> VMU-1 is slated to deploy in summer 2017 in support of the 15th MEU with the new RQ-21A Blackjack UAS which will primarily bring the unit Intelligence Surveillance Reconnaissance.
>
> "The capability of the new aircraft will bring organic ISR to the MEU that is persistent and easy to manage," said Taylor-Tyree.
>
> "We'll be able to distribute that [ISR] feed to other ships, or if satellite capabilities allow, back to the states to various units," continued Taylor-Tyree. "This means that we can provide persistent ISR organic to the MEU instead of having to request it from sister services."[8]

I conducted interviews with members of VMU-2 during 2014 and 2015. These interviews provide a sense of the evolution in the USMC and the operators' perspective on the way ahead for unmanned units.

VMU-2 on the Future (2014)

The commanding officer (CO) of VMU-2 in 2014 was LTC Kris Faught. Faught had most recently served with VMM-266 as the air combat element operations officer for the 26th MEU. The mission statement for the squadron highlighted its contextual support role, both now and in the future: "To support the MAGTF Commander by conducting electromagnetic spectrum warfare, multi-sensor imagery reconnaissance, combined arms coordination and control, and destroying targets, day or night, under all-weather conditions, during expeditionary, joint and combined operations." Faught highlighted some key limitations facing UAVs in the USMC and identified what he saw as a solid path for future growth. He started with a discussion of the value of the Shadow and the USMC's experience with the UAV. Clearly, the Shadow provided important operational experience, yet it is not congruent with where the USMC is headed. According to Faught, "It is clearly not expeditionary and looks like it has been designed by a tanker."

Faught went on to say the squadron was working with the RQ-21A Blackjack to evolve an expeditionary support capacity. Notably, the 2nd Marine Air Wing Forward was working with an EOC run-up to the RQ-21A in Afghanistan to gain operational experience and help shape the UAV role in the USMC. The principle differences between the EOC system and the RQ-21A system are software and ship compatibility issues with launcher and retriever. A key quality of the Blackjack is its nonproprietary payload system. Said Faught, "The payload bay is not patent-protected. This means that L-3 is building payloads. Lockheed Martin is building payloads. Little one-off shops in San Diego are building payloads." And clearly the trend line, which the Marines would like to see, is an ability to shape modular payloads to provide for the support missions envisaged for UAVs.

At the time of the interview, the Blackjack carried the following types of payloads:

- electric-optical,
- midwave infrared,
- infrared marker, and
- secondary payload bay supports, including communications relay payload (crp) and electronic warfare.

The support requirements for the RQ-21A are considerably less than those for the Shadow and clearly allow the Marines to work on their expeditionary support approach.

With regard to the RQ-21A, the squadron was working with industry to shape ways to enhance its capability. "We are looking at size, weight, power tradeoffs to enhance overall platform capability. Currently, we are at 135 pounds with the platform, and we could go as high as 165, which would give us more payload to carry onboard," said Faught. Throughout the discussion he emphasized the need to evolve the payloads along with other key aviation capabilities being shaped for the MAGTF. He especially thought that electronic warfare payloads would be increasingly of interest going forward.

And he thought that as the F-35B joined the force along with the Ospreys, the opportunity to rework evolving UAVs to operate with these more expensive combat systems would be significant.

VMU-2 Revisited (2015)

The use of UAS in Afghanistan was an important phase in the evolution of UAS use in the U.S. forces. But it was just one phase; it needs to be put into its historical place, and the services need to move on. In Afghanistan, UAS were used in a land operation with many years of infrastructure in place, and this infrastructure—wide ranging, expensive, and significant—is hardly going to be waiting for an expeditionary insertion force. And the concept of operations used in Afghanistan is a problem as well. As one VMU-2 member put it, "The UAS controllers were more part of the intelligence system in Afghanistan than [part] of the Marine Corps. They were an asset which plugged into the intelligence gathering system and did not operate as we do more generally with air assets in the USMC. . . . Normally, the airborne assets work with the ground element and share the intelligence picture in an operational context. This was the norm in Afghanistan: an external asset managed by the intelligence system rather than organic integration with the MAGTF."

As the operations officer bluntly put it, "We are trying to burn down the whole UAV structure which the Marine Corps created in Afghanistan and shaping a new approach, one in which it is integrated within MAGTF operations." According to the Marines interviewed, the intelligence community views UAVs as "their assets" because that is how the system evolved in Afghanistan. "UAV operations personnel would basically check in with the air officer who would then pass them over to intel and they would then work together." Rather than having UAVs as part of the fire support system, they became assets that were part of observation and evaluation, and the authorization of fires was handled separately. "This became a loop rather than a straight line, which is where we would like it be when we operate as a MAGTF."

The separation of Marine Corps UAV assets was the norm rather than the exception. "When I would fly in Afghanistan, I might look down and see a Shadow or ScanEagle below me, but I never once coordinated with these assets. I had no idea what they were looking at. I just knew that they were below me," noted the VMU-2 operations officer.

Lt Gen David A. Deptula, who in his last active-duty position oversaw the planning, policy, and development of Air Force UAVs and grew that force by over 500 percent, agreed with the Marine officers interviewed about the need for integration: "One of the biggest advantages of remotely piloted aircraft is that they allow for the condensation of the 'find, fix, and finish' kill chain onto one platform. To capitalize on this capability, these aircraft need to be integrated into the entire combat enterprise, not just one piece of it." In fact, integration of UAS in the Air Combat Element (ACE) of the MAGTF is the next phase of UAV development in the Marine Corps. According to Deptula, "The GCE should be requesting the capability, not the asset. If you need persistent IS [intelligence and surveillance] with full motion video, that will probably fall to UAS."

The UAS operator is a key part of the equation, and when the system works properly, the operator can work with the GCE and place the sensor on the target through shared situational awareness. The challenge is shaping ways to direct the information to the appropriate element in the MAGTF to make the GCE or ACE more effective.

A clear requirement in the future is to build swappable packages for the evolving USMC UAS as well so that missions can highlight command and control (C2), ISR, or electronic warfare needs.[9]

Shaping the Way Ahead: The Perspective of COL J. B. "Buss" Barranco

Appropriately, we will end this chapter by looking forward to the evolving path for the USMC with regard to UAS. On June 16, 2017, I had a chance to discuss that path with the person at Headquarters USMC charged with working that mission area. Colonel Barranco is a veteran Marine Corps aviator and graduate of the Naval Academy with several tours of duty in Iraq and Afghanistan. He approaches the question of the future of those systems in the USMC from this operational background and from a clear focus on how UAS serve the evolving USMC concepts of operations.

The current operation of Blackjacks at sea and on land is a key part of the learning curve for the systems' operation and their integration in evolving Marine Corps operations. As is Marine Corps practice, the Blackjack is in the force in advance of its being able to fully support the force. The Marines prefer to get capability to the force and to let the warfighter use that capability as it evolves and becomes fully operational. According to Colonel Barranco, Blackjacks are providing a significant learning experience that will affect later evolutions of UAS in the MAGTF. He said that the Blackjack experience was facilitating Marines' learning how to work unmanned systems along with manned systems on board ships, how to operate unmanned systems on board ships more generally, and how to use the various payloads in support of the Marine Corps afloat and ashore. Blackjacks are also influencing the design for future amphibious ships, which will be modeled on an enhanced *San Antonio*–class landing platform/dock ships (LPDs) and on the *America*-class landing helicopter assault ships (LHAs).

F-35s and UAS generate much larger volumes of data than traditional ISR platforms, and ships must significantly expand their capability to handle this volume of data. In this regard, the Navy–Marine

Corps team, not just the Marine Corps, is learning from Blackjack deployments. Colonel Barranco also noted that as a medium-range tactical UAS, Blackjack has replaced Shadow and will remain with the Marine Corps even as it works to add a new UAS to the force. For the Marines, the requirement to operate without a fixed runway is crucial. As Colonel Barranco noted, the Marines focus on force insertion in areas of interest and on the necessity of having organic capability carried with the force. Also, the Marines realize airfields are under threat from peer competitors and cannot be relied on. Allies are crucial, but if allied facilities are denied for political reasons, the Navy–Marine Corps team needs to be able to operate with organic sea-based assets.

The Marines are working to add a new, more robust UAS capability to the force by the mid-2020s. They are hoping that the U.S. Navy will buy in and so will allies who are building up their amphibious fleets. The Marines are looking for a platform that can fly with the Osprey, which means range and speed are essential. It may well be a tilt-rotor platform, although other platform variants might be feasible as well. This large, high-speed UAS will have an open architecture system allowing software to be upgraded to keep abreast of threats. Like the Royal Australian Air Force (RAAF), the Marines also want a platform with built-in software transient advantage.

The Marines are looking for the new platform to have several plug-and-play capabilities. They want to it to be an armed UAS with a variety of weapons that can be configured to the mission. The Marines are working to shape a digital interoperable MAGTF, and they want the UAS to be a key node in the network afloat and ashore. They are looking at the new UAS as a partner to the F-35, Osprey, and CH-53K, and the UAS may be a cargo carrier as well, dependent on the operation and the mission. As *Marine Aviation Plan 2016* put it about one of these requirements: "UAS are a planned critical component of the MAGTF EW [electronic warfare] concept. As such, EW expertise normally resident within the Marine tactical electronic warfare community began to transition to the VMU community in 2015. Airborne electronic attack (AEA) capabilities post-2019 will be provided by EW payloads such as the Intrepid Tiger II EW Pod, UAS EW payloads, and the EW capabilities inherent to F-35."[10] The new UAS will be short takeoff and vertical landing aircraft (STOVL) as that format fits both the shipboard and the no fixed airfield requirement. The MAGTF will rely on the F-35 and related systems for forcible entry so that the UAS as envisaged will operate largely in a noncontested air environment, although arming the UAS will be crucial for its self-defense in gray operating situations.

The Marine Corps aviation plan characterized the way ahead for UAS as follows:

> In the 2016–2029 timeframe, the family of unmanned aircraft systems (FoUAS) provides support to any sized MAGTF for influence of the electromagnetic spectrum, battlespace awareness, offensive air support, target acquisition, force protection, and digital communication backbone. Marine Corps UAS employment will continue to enhance and extend the lethal and non-lethal capabilities of MAGTF and joint force commanders, facilitating advancements in observation, understanding, and influence on the battlefield. The FoUAS will play a key role in all USMC missions across the range of military operations to include forward presence, security cooperation, counterterrorism, crisis response, forcible entry, prolonged operations, and counterinsurgency.[11]

The new UAS, labeled MUX, would leverage the operational experience of the Blackjack and combine with Blackjack in shaping a way ahead. Given the payload flexibility of the Blackjack, this system could well complement the new MUX as well.

But Colonel Barranco clearly underscored that UAS were *part of* the future of the MAGTF and Marine Corps aviation, not *the* future of Marine Corps aviation. Notably, he underscored that the need for forcible entry was crucial to the Navy–Marine Corps team and did not see the UAS on the horizon as the key enablers for that crucial mission. He also highlighted that both the Navy and the Marine Corps were working the manned and unmanned systems in an integrated manner and were clearly avoiding creating a UAS stovepipe.[12]

Conclusion

President Trump came to power at a time when a flexible force able to insert from the sea and rapidly return to the sea has emerged.

This Navy–Marine Corps capability has evolved beyond the classic ARG–MEU into a lethal amphibious task force. The evolving Marine Corps aviation assets, coupled with the reshaping of Marine Corps concepts of operations for conducting force insertion from the sea, are shaping a new capability, and within that capability unmanned aerial assets are playing a key role. Evolving the capability of the insertion forces rather than simply relying on putting "Walmarts" ashore and conducting combat support from forward operating bases and air bases in contested territory, the sea base provides its own integrated support and operational integrated capabilities. This force and support integration offshore provides capability for not only force protection but also surprise against enemies who wish to use agility to their advantage. And integrating unmanned with manned systems able to operate from the sea base or to move from the sea base for a limited duration operation can provide the American leadership with a very powerful tool set indeed.

Insertion forces are a key tool set, and with the changes in how amphibious task forces operate and with the coming of a whole new capability associated with USS *America*, the sea base is adding to its capability for force insertion in a vector of assault, destroy, and withdraw. For example, changing the nature of the force being used against the Islamic State in Iraq and Syria (ISIS) and reshaping the operational compass against a mobile force that likes to pop up across the region can meet its match—there is no place they can hide where the U.S. Marines cannot come, find, and kill them. And integrating the unmanned elements into this evolving force structure is the Marine Corps' approach and challenge.

Notes

1. "Shadow Company USA," SLDInfo, July 15, 2014, https://sldinfo.com/2014/07/shadow-company-uas/.
2. Robbin Laird and Ed Timperlake, "The GCE Drives USMC Aviation Innovation: Major Cuomo of the Infantry Officer Course Discusses the IOC's Team Perspective," *Second Line of Defense*, May 12, 2014, http://www.sldinfo.com/the-gce-drives-usmc-aviation-innovation-major-cuomo-of-the-infantry-officer-course-discusses-the-iocs-team-perspective.

3. ScanEagle Imagers, Insitu, https://insitu.com/information-delivery/unmanned-systems/scaneagle/imagers#2.
4. Marine Unmanned Aerial Vehicle Squadron, 3rd Marine Aircraft Wing, Marines, http://www.3rdmaw.marines.mil/Units/MAG-13/VMU-1/.
5. Marine Unmanned Aerial Vehicle Squadron 2, Marines, http://www.mag14.marines.mil/MAG-14-Units/VMU-2/.
6. Marine Unmanned Aerial Vehicle Squadron 3, Phantoms, Marines, http://www.1stmaw.marines.mil/Subordinate-Units/Marine-Aircraft-Group-24/VMU-3/.
7. 4th Marine Aircraft Wing, U.S. Marine Corps Forces Reserve, Marines, http://www.marforres.marines.mil/Major-Subordinate-Commands/4th-Marine-Aircraft-Wing/Marine-Aircraft-Group-41/Marine-Unmanned-Aerial-Vehicle-Squadron-4/.
8. Brytani Wheeler, "VMU-1 Receives New RQ-21A Blackjack," 3rd Marine Aircraft Wing (news), August 18, 2016, http://www.3rdmaw.marines.mil/News/News-Article-Display/Article/918857/vmu-1-receives-new-rq-21a-blackjack/.
9. Robbin Laird, "Visiting a USMC Unmanned Aerial Vehicle Squadron: The VMU-2 Discusses the Future," *Second Line of Defense*, July 14, 2015, http://www.sldinfo.com/visiting-a-usmc-unmanned-aerial-vehicle-squadron-the-vmu-2-discusses-the-future/.
10. U.S. Marine Corps, *Marine Aviation Plan 2016*, 2016, https://marinecorpsconceptsandprograms.com/sites/default/files/files/Marine%20Aviation%20Plan%202016%20FINAL.pdf.
11. Ibid.
12. For Colonel Barranco's discussion of future vertical lift technology, see John Grady, "Marines, Army Studying Vertical Lift Technology Advancements Ahead of New Programs," USNI News, December 12, 2016, https://news.usni.org/2016/12/12/pentagon-vertical-lift-technology; "Vertical Lift Aircraft," C-SPAN, December 9, 2016, video, 1:02:23, featuring John Barranco and Erskine Bentley, https://www.c-span.org/video/?419838-1/discussion-focuses-vertical-lift-aircraft.

07

Defeating the Threat of Small Unmanned Aerial Systems

Dillon R. Patterson

Unmanned aerial systems (UAS) offer new or improved military capability in many airpower applications. Contemporary UAS range in size from aircraft with wingspans exceeding 150 feet to vehicles that fit into the palm of an operator's hand. Medium-sized unmanned aircraft such as the MQ-1B Predator have become icons of American counterterrorism warfare, but small unmanned aerial systems (SUAS) have performed significant roles in militaries around the globe as well. SUAS provide game-changing potential for small militaries and non-state actors by enabling airpower capability that may have been previously out of reach. More advanced militaries can also leverage SUAS capability to enhance existing combat systems.

Innovative applications of SUAS by adversaries create new threats to U.S. joint forces. Defeating the threat posed by SUAS will require commanders to combine new technology and doctrine along with appropriate planning and policy to protect the joint force. Examining the proliferation, arming, and unique tactical advantages of SUAS is necessary to demonstrate the threat against a joint force. With the

This chapter was originally published in *Air and Space Power Journal*, Spring 2017, 15–25. U.S. government document, approved for public release, distribution unlimited.

threat to the force understood, methods for countering it can be identified and conclusions drawn to ensure joint force mission success.

Proliferation of Small Unmanned Aerial Systems

UAS have historically been the privilege of a few nations as technology limited to large aerospace companies was required to conduct remote or autonomous flight. Recent engineering achievement has led to commercially available unmanned flight control systems enabling the development or acquisition of UAS by much smaller entities, including individuals. Oxford University doctoral candidate Ulrike Esther Franke focused much of her research on the implications of increased military use of unmanned systems. Franke reported that in 2000 only seventeen countries possessed UAS for military application; by 2015 that number had risen to more than seventy-five.[1]

The spectrum of UAS military users spans the globe and has not been limited to sovereign countries. Non-state actors, such as the terrorist group Hezbollah, which has flown unarmed Iranian-built UAS over Lebanon and Syria, are operating UAS for military purposes.[2] As the development and export of UAS expand, the number of UAS users will no doubt increase to include more unstable or hostile governments as well as violent extremist organizations.

Smaller UAS present a substantial potential for armed groups that cannot afford or gain access to larger, more complex systems. For advanced militaries, SUAS provide a new opportunity to increase the quantity of military assets and introduce a new capability at significantly reduced cost compared to that of larger systems. The number of countries currently employing SUAS far exceeds those with medium and large systems. Ms. Franke's research notes that a multitude of European militaries have domestically developed SUAS programs. Additionally, many non-European countries are creating their SUAS systems.[3] It is hard to imagine a potential adversary, whether a state or non-state actor, that will not employ a form of SUAS during future armed conflict.

State-funded defense programs are not the only source of unmanned aircraft. Commercial production has exploded in recent years with low-cost aircraft offering advanced autonomy and sensor features.

Dà–Jiāng Innovation (DJI) Technology Company's Phantom 4 is an example of an SUAS available for purchase over the Internet. The Chinese-manufactured aircraft are capable of flight for almost thirty minutes, can reach altitudes over 18,000 feet, and come equipped with data-linked, high-definition cameras. The cost for this capability is a meager $1,400.[4]

In addition to cost savings and sensor capability, SUAS permit flexibility in employment. The systems are portable and do not require airfields or other support networks. Many small air vehicles are hand-launched or use some type of catapult for takeoff. Recovery is also relatively simple since most vehicles either land on short surfaces or employ a capture device to retrieve the aircraft in flight. Transportability allows SUAS to be used during maneuver warfare when one is operating in remote areas or when air cover and intelligence assets are otherwise unattainable. As identified in Franke's research, the proliferation of SUAS is proceeding at an alarming rate and will likely continue in the quantity of assets available and the armed groups that employ them. Combat capabilities will also expand through advancements in flight duration and autonomy, further enabling intelligence collection, communications, and strike missions.[5]

Arming Small Unarmed Aerial Systems

Many nations are rapidly acquiring UAS for military application. The ability to arm these aircraft has remained limited until recently. It is expected that armed UAS exports will grow swiftly to meet international market demand.

Evidence of armed UAS proliferation was provided in a January 2016 news story about Iraq operating armed unmanned aircraft manufactured in China. A deeper examination of Chinese exports showed that Saudi Arabia, the United Arab Emirates, and Egypt have also procured armed UAS from China. With more than seventy-five corporate and state organizations developing products for the UAS industry, China is postured to become a major supplier. The appeal of China as an armed UAS supplier comes from its export policy founded on "price, privacy, and product." China provides products at prices small governments can afford. Further, China's approach to privacy is highly attractive to many consumers who desire limited attention when procuring advanced weapons.[6]

Regardless of availability, the cost of medium to large aircraft can prohibit organizations from attaining armed UAS capability. The significantly lower cost of procurement and operation of SUAS has generated a new armed aircraft market. Although the current supply of armed SUAS is limited, the field is fast expanding. U.S.-based Textron Systems, which produces the RQ-7 Shadow fielded by the U.S. Army for intelligence collection, is one example of a new armed SUAS company. Bill Irby, senior vice president and general manager for Textron's unmanned systems, stated that Textron has successfully tested the RQ-7 with its lightweight, precision-guided weapons. Another example is the Chinese CH-3A.[7]

One challenge to armed SUAS development has been attaining weapons small enough to be employed from the air vehicles. Weapons like the AGM-114 Hellfire, carried on the MQ-1 and MQ-9, weigh about 100 pounds. Newer designs such as the AGM-176 Griffin missile are significantly smaller yet still too heavy for many air vehicles in development. To solve this problem, in 2010 the U.S. military released a request for proposals to develop precision weapons that weigh less than 11.3 kilograms (25 pounds).[8]

The industry responded to this request by designing a multitude of lightweight precision weapons. The Raytheon Pyros glide bomb weighs only 6 kilograms (13.2 pounds), while Lockheed Martin's Shadow Hawk weapon weighs only 5 kilograms (11 pounds).[9] Although attaining information on China's developments in small precision weapons is difficult, it is not a stretch to imagine that its corporations are steadfastly working on SUAS and their accompanying weapons for the Chinese military and the international marketplace.

Along with arming SUAS to provide strike capability, expendable miniature aircraft designed to be munitions in themselves are available. Small aircraft that have integrated sensor-warhead payloads offer an even lower cost and a highly flexible option to militaries of all sizes. AeroVironment's Switchblade SUAS is an example of a single-use vehicle with integrated warhead and sensors. The Switchblade comes in a portable package weighing just 2.5 kilograms

(5.5 pounds), including the weight of the vehicle and launcher. With a ten-minute flight time and a top speed of more than eighty-five miles per hour, the Switchblade offers individual warriors a weapon that can fly up to altitude, spot an enemy, and rapidly engage with precision, yielding lethal effects with limited collateral damage.[10]

Armed SUAS acquisition is not limited to organizations with access to defense contractors that might be subject to some degree of government oversight. For groups without a benefactor with access to military hardware, weapons may be attained through another method. Advanced SUAS for commercial purposes can be readily adapted for armed missions. By removing cameras or other commercial payloads on small air vehicles purchased through the Internet, small improvised explosive devices (IEDs) can be added, creating makeshift guided missiles. As an example, the DJI S1000 aircraft features a payload dock on the bottom of the vehicle. The system was designed to allow users to attach different camera equipment based on the mission. In the hands of an innovative user, the S1000 is a highly capable SUAS that can fly a 9.5 kilogram (20 pound) payload for fifteen minutes. This capability can enable a lone-wolf actor to perform precise kinetic strikes against targets in protected areas for less than $5,000.[11]

Whether purchasing SUAS that can carry precision-guided weapons, using aircraft that are weapons in themselves, or adapting drones ordered online to carry IEDs, the options for armed groups are rapidly expanding. The cost ranges from well above $500,000 to only a few thousand dollars, providing air-attack capability and quantity options never previously available.

Tactical Advantages of Small Unmanned Aerial Systems

The tactical applications of SUAS are numerous. Attempting to identify every potential military option would be virtually impossible, so it is perhaps more beneficial to focus on the tactical advantages unique to SUAS. These advantages can be understood by examining three properties of SUAS: size, speed, and swarm. Each of these properties provides a benefit in armed conflict. Combined, the properties generate combat potential that presents a significant threat to U.S. military forces.

The small size and relative speeds of the air vehicles create substantial defensive difficulties. Joint Publication (JP) 3-0, *Joint Operations*, states, "Unmanned aircraft are a new challenge to US air defenses, as many systems have smaller radar cross sections and fly at much slower speeds than manned aircraft making them much harder to detect."[12] This doctrinally stated weakness was demonstrated in January 2015, when a DJI Phantom—flown by an amateur operator in the Washington, DC, area—crashed on the lawn of the White House. While the event was an accident and had no apparent malicious intent, it highlighted how small, slow air vehicles could exploit a seam between robust air and ground defenses.[13] A few months later, on April 22, 2015, security personnel discovered another DJI Phantom on the roof of Japanese prime minister Shinzo Abe's office. Security personnel did not know when the aircraft landed on the building since the roof had not been accessed for a month and the approach and landing were not detected.[14]

SUAS have additional advantages beyond electronic and visual detection avoidance. Their small size makes them easily transportable; they can be moved with small vehicles and, in some instances, carried in a backpack. An adversary can move equipment and operators near joint force basing areas before deploying the air vehicle. Instead of trying to penetrate U.S. air defenses with fighter aircraft, adversaries could use passive detection measures to conceal the presence of armed SUAS and then launch them from a position inside U.S. fortifications.

Although slow moving compared to most aircraft, their mere ability to fly generates a speed advantage in bypassing obstacles from launch to engagement. With an operating speed of up to a hundred miles per hour in some systems, small air vehicles can close employment range very quickly. When combined with small size, the speed of SUAS can create attack options in which the first sign of an enemy presence would be weapon detonation. A profound benefit of speed and size is also the ability to operate inside the commander's decision loop. With the potential to attack repeatedly and to do so undetected, SUAS present a potentially devastating threat by creating a confusing environment for the unprepared operational commander. One's aircraft fleet size must be considered when analyzing the impact of SUAS.

The rapid growth of SUAS capability has led to a new reality in the application of airpower. Former secretary of defense Chuck Hagel alluded to this reality in a keynote speech to the Southeastern

New England Defense Industry Alliance in September 2014 when he stated, "Disruptive technologies and destructive weapons, once solely possessed by only advanced nations, have proliferated widely and are being sought or acquired by unsophisticated militaries and terrorist groups."[15] SUAS proliferation is adjusting the balance of airpower, which has for decades been dominated by a select few nations.

With the advent of armed SUAS, U.S. forces must change the way they have historically defended against enemy airpower. JP 3-0 identifies air and missile defense (AMD) as a key task of joint forces.[16] Historical assumptions in planning for AMD may no longer be valid owing to the SUAS threat. A joint base in a theater without a significant enemy air force may have few assets allocated for AMD. Through the employment of SUAS, an enemy could exploit this U.S. defense weakness or at least force operational commanders to allocate resources to air defense against the SUAS threat, removing offensive potential. Defense analyst Paul Scharre calls attention to the change in relative airpower capability created by SUAS. In a 2014 report, Scharre notes, "Overwhelming adversaries through greater numbers is a viable strategy for technology competition, and was used successfully by the United States in World War II. One of the chief advantages of this strategy is that it can be used to *impose costs* on adversaries because it forces one's adversary to counter large numbers of systems [emphasis in original]."[17] SUAS can impose air defense costs where none were previously necessary or drastically increase AMD costs against enemies with marginal air attack capabilities. The ability to acquire large quantities of SUAS further affects relative airpower by allowing an enemy the opportunity to mass tens or even hundreds of air assets in a coordinated attack instead of employing a few legacy aircraft. By attacking with overwhelming numbers, SUAS could require U.S. joint forces to engage numerous targets, imposing a significantly higher cost of defense compared to legacy airpower means. Although U.S. joint forces may enjoy a significant technology advantage, their defenses may not be sufficient against a swarm of small air vehicles.

In a separate 2014 report, Scharre evaluates superior quality against large quantities in military engagements using a principal called Lanchester's law. Scharre concludes, "A numerically inferior force can compensate with greater qualitative superiority, but a force that is out-numbered by its opponent 2-to-1 must, therefore, be *four times better* in quality in order to simply match its opponent [emphasis in original]. There is, in essence, a limit to how much qualitative superiority can compensate for smaller numbers."[18] The low cost of SUAS creates a possibility for a savvy adversary to simply overwhelm joint air defenses, adjusting the relative airpower for the attacker. Combining the advantages of size and speed of SUAS with the quantities available owing to low cost magnifies the change in the balance of airpower. Armed groups that previously had no option for successfully employing airpower can now challenge U.S. joint forces. By employing SUAS in swarms, adversaries can further tip the scale in their favor.

As defined by Scharre, "a swarm consists of disparate elements that coordinate and adapt their movements in order to give rise to an emergent, coherent whole." Swarming is much more than just coordinating an action with large masses. In a massed attack, the individual members use coordinated fire and maneuver to achieve a coherent objective. In swarming, coherency is within the mass itself. Scharre clarifies this distinction in noting that "a wolf pack is something quite different from a group of wolves."[19] The ability to swarm SUAS is restricted with current technology. Operators have limited capabilities to link SUAS together or, by using autonomy, to react in harmony to changes in the battle situation and within the swarm itself. However, with proper planning and coordination, an adversary can take advantage of some SUAS swarm capabilities. "Centralized coordination" is a basic model of swarm command and control that uses a designated leader to orchestrate mission plans and maneuvers and to assign tasks during the mission.[20] A team operating SUAS under a centralized coordination construct can impose greater levels of damage than can masses of SUAS operating alone.

The combination of speed, size, scale, and swarming allows SUAS tactical actions to extract operational gains. SUAS open a door for adversaries to counter joint force strengths through enabling their attack of critical vulnerabilities previously out of their reach. An example of an opportunity afforded through swarming is demonstrated by the role of mining in warfare. Dr. Milan Vego, a U.S. Naval War College professor of operations, suggests that mining is "in some cases almost the only means available to a weaker opponent at sea to challenge the control of a stronger navy."Vego adds that mines could be used to shape the battlespace by denying the free use of space and by forcing vessels out of protected waters where they may be vulnerable to attack by other means.[21] Like mines at sea or IEDs on land, large quantities of low-cost SUAS can be used to mine airspace in locations of high-density air traffic.[22] Airspace mining is just one illustration of how the unique advantages of SUAS can be used to challenge maneuver, sustainment, or protection measures. The threat posed by SUAS extends far beyond simple tactics. Adversary forces can use SUAS to impose costs on operational commanders by attacking personnel, infrastructure, and support systems. Delaying preparations to defend against the threat could end in disaster.

Defeating the Threat Created by Small Unmanned Aerial Systems

Averting disaster in joint operations will require commanders to address the SUAS threat. To be successful, commanders cannot wait and react to their enemy; rather, they must proactively work to achieve victory. Defeating the threat created by SUAS will require a combination of new technical solutions, updates to doctrine, incorporation of counter-SUAS efforts in planning for operations, and a new policy for fighting a new kind of enemy.

Technical solutions are intended to solve the problem of SUAS detection and provide an ability to destroy, disable, or neutralize the enemy aircraft. Leading the effort toward SUAS detection and defeat is the Joint Integrated Air and Missile Defense Organization (JIAMDO). JIAMDO is charged with planning, coordinating, and overseeing AMD and associated joint concepts, according to a defense budget justification report.[23] One of JIAMDO's efforts at technical solutions to counter the SUAS threat is the annual Black Dart exercise. In 2015 JIAMDO executed a $4.2 million budget for Black Dart. The event comprised a multiday series of experiments aimed at testing the detection and defeat of SUAS. Results from experiments at Black Dart revealed that a "system of systems" is necessary to identify and defend against SUAS. Detection involves a combination of radar, electro-optical, infrared, and acoustic technologies. Destruction or neutralization of the air vehicle requires a combination of kinetic and electronic solutions.[24] Attempting to counter the threat of SUAS by defending with technical solutions alone will not suffice. A solely technical effort applied to current force protection constructs may lead to unacceptable costs of defense at the expense of mission capability. Doctrine must be updated to consider the capabilities unique to SUAS. Although many sources of doctrine can be considered, *Countering Air and Missile Threats* (JP 3-01) offers a logically sound point of origin to assess current doctrinal suitability for defeating this new threat. Counter-AMD is typically led by the joint force air component commander. The counter-AMD construct is broken into two primary areas: offensive counter-air (OCA) and defensive counter-air (DCA). Each area must address the unique capabilities of SUAS.[25]

OCA is defined as "offensive operations to destroy, disrupt, or neutralize enemy aircraft, missiles, launch platforms, and their supporting structures and systems both before and after launch, and as close to their source as possible." Attack operations, as part of OCA, are aimed at striking these components of enemy airpower before they can be used against friendly forces. Airpower enablers, such as fuel storage and repair facilities, can also be targeted.[26]

The size and available quantity of SUAS make OCA missions against this threat difficult at best. Targeting the aircraft themselves can be an expensive and futile effort. Likewise, launch and support systems are easily concealable, transportable, and numerous. Because some SUAS use conventional fuel types, attacking fuel storage may yield some positive results. However, the low fuel volumes required enable adversaries to store sufficient quantities of fuel in small containers that are mobile and concealable. Also, many SUAS are electrically powered and can be charged from civil infrastructure that may be off-limits to attack. The unique characteristics of these systems reveal that current OCA doctrine is insufficient to provide an effective plan to counter enemy SUAS employment potential.

Deficiencies also exist in current DCA literature. The DCA mission is defined by JP 3-01 as "all defensive measures designed to detect, identify, intercept, and neutralize or destroy enemy forces attempting to penetrate or attack through friendly airspace."[27] Executing this role requires using a wide range of sensors and weapons based on land, sea, and air. The goal for DCA is to generate "defense in depth," allowing defensive systems an opportunity for multiple engagements against incoming air threats.[28] The unique attributes of SUAS allow for evasion of detection with current air defense technology, while developing adequate sensors to detect the full range of SUAS can be prohibitively expensive. The transportability of SUAS allows for penetration of outer defense layers on land and sea so employment can be initiated from close-in ranges that prohibit multiple engagements. When properly massed, swarms of SUAS can overwhelm inner defenses and create gaps for follow-on attacks to exploit.

Both OCA and DCA missions require significant study to generate doctrinal guidance to defeat the SUAS threat. However, a vector for solving this problem may come from the current doctrine itself: JP 3-01 identifies special operations forces (SOF) as a method of aiding the counter-air mission. SOF units can be used to locate and eliminate air and missile facilities, support systems, and command nodes.[29] Hunting enemy air systems that are mobile can be difficult. The size of SUAS makes this mission more difficult than it is for legacy missile systems by orders of magnitude because systems can be hidden virtually anywhere with ease. Although employing SOF units per current doctrine will likely yield insufficient results to counter the SUAS threat, it does illuminate a potential counter-SUAS technique. The attributes of the SUAS that afford an advantage in attack can also be used against it. Installation commanders may seek to clear larger perimeters around joint force facilities than are historically maintained. Eliminating havens from which to launch SUAS close-in against friendly operating areas could force enemy attacks from distances that enable detection and elimination and challenge the range of systems too small to detect. Using ground forces to clear and hold a perimeter can be viewed as a new means of OCA.

JP 3-01 states that ballistic missile defense is a different mission, unique from defense against aircraft and cruise missiles.[30] Countering the SUAS threat will also require a different emphasis from current air and missile defense literature. By providing adequate doctrine, commanders will be able to incorporate technical solutions within joint forces during the planning process to help defeat the SUAS threat.

Planning for this threat is essential in the current battlespace. The low cost of SUAS enables adversaries to increase their relative airpower in their favor. Intelligence assessments on the ability of an adversary to obtain and operate large masses of SUAS must be accounted for in a planner's time-space-force estimation. SUAS analysis must consider an adversary's increased force size, space covered by the air assets, and the short reaction times commanders may have when SUAS are discovered. In examining the force-time factor, planners must also determine how to replace their systems rapidly. When assessing how to protect one's center of gravity, a planner must weigh SUAS capabilities. In developing an operation idea, a planner must consider the SUAS's potential to disrupt, disable, or neutralize critical capabilities. The ability to collect intelligence and attack speedily against joint critical vulnerabilities must be evaluated.

Plans for sustaining forces and maintaining lines of communication (LOCs) need to be developed with the SUAS threat in mind. Long unprotected LOCs make ideal targets for highly mobile SUAS operations aimed at degrading resupply to forces in the field. As an operational axis is determined and operations are phased, planning for sustainment can be difficult against a capable adversary with masses of SUAS.

In addition to having a well-constructed plan that incorporates effective technological solutions and doctrinal practices, operational commanders must also enact appropriate policy. The most highly trained force operating under a perfect structure cannot be successful without adequate guidance, such as clearly delineated rules of engagement (ROEs). Applying a sound policy to the operating environment is a must if victory is to be achieved.

Since many operational bases, both land and maritime, exist in areas with significant populations, the use of SUAS for civil purposes can add a degree of complexity to the commander's mission. MAJ Scott Gregg, USAF, director of Black Dart, noticed this difficulty at the 2015 exercise. During an interview regarding the difficulty of detecting SUAS, Major Gregg questioned, "How do you differentiate between a 10-year-old kid who just doesn't know any better and is flying something from a hobby shop and somebody who's flying that identical something from a hobby shop but has nefarious intent? You can't tell that with a radar or an infrared sensor."[31] As technology and doctrine are developed to parry the threat generated by SUAS, a necessary policy such as ROEs must be identified during operational planning and enacted. Policy updates are needed not only in the operational sphere but also in the acquisition arena. SUAS advancements are largely driven by computer technology gains, so capabilities will likely continue to increase. The U.S. defense acquisition process is unfortunately at odds with this reality. New defense equipment takes years to design, test, and field. Under this framework, necessary hardware identified through Black Dart or other methods may be irrelevant by the time it is fielded if adversaries simply outpace U.S. technical solutions. A revised acquisition policy will facilitate timely technical solutions, allowing commanders to respond to the SUAS threat.

Conclusion

SUAS furnish an innovative adversary with new weapons that have substantial potential. The unique capabilities of SUAS—combined with their potentially large quantities—create the possibility of a completely new battlespace. Defense analyst Robert Martinage has studied the impending changes to battle brought on by advancements in technology. In *Toward a New Offset Strategy: Exploiting U.S. Long-Term Advantages to Restore U.S. Global Power Projection Capability*, Martinage observes, "The United States cannot afford to simply scale up the mix of joint power projection capabilities."[32] New systems with advanced technology are proliferating to enemies of the United States at an astounding pace. SUAS represent just one piece of the shift; the problem is a current and not solely a future threat. Scharre argues, "The history of revolutions in warfare has shown they are won by those who uncover the most effective ways of using new technologies, not necessarily those who invent the technology first or even have the best technology."[33] The views of Martinage and Scharre reveal the need to act on the threat of SUAS now. The technological advantage in unmanned systems, once wielded by an elite few, is disappearing rapidly. The gap is being filled in a manner that gives U.S. adversaries high-tech, effective means to attack joint forces worldwide. Successfully defeating groups armed with SUAS will require innovative solutions in technology, doctrine, planning, and policy.

Notes

1. Ulrike Esther Franke, "The Global Diffusion of Unmanned Aerial Vehicles (UAVs), or 'Drones,'" in *Precision Strike Warfare and International Intervention: Strategic, Ethico-legal, and Decisional Implications*, ed. Mike Aaronson et al. (New York: Routledge, 2015), 52.

2. Franke, 53–58.

3. Franke, 57–58.

4. DJI, "Phantom 4," accessed January 12, 2017, http://store.dji.com/product/ phantom-4?site =brandsite&from=buy_now_bottom.

5. Franke, "Global Diffusion," 56.

6. Adam Rawnsley, "Meet China's Killer Drones," *Foreign Policy*, January 14, 2016, http://foreignpolicy.com/2016/01/14/meet-chinas-killer-drones.

7. Grant Turnbull, "Small Bombs, Big Effect: Arming Small UAVs with Guided Weapons," December 17, 2014, Air Force Technology, http://www.airforce-technology.com/features/featuresmall-bombs-big-effect-arming-small-uavs-with-guided-weapons-4467893/.

8. Turnbull.

9. Turnbull.

10. AeroVironment, "Switchblade," fact sheet, accessed January 12, 2017, https:// www.avinc.com/uas/view/switchblade.

11. DJI, "Spreading Wings S1000+ Specifications," accessed January 12, 2017, http:// www.dji.com/product/spreading-wings-s1000-plus.

12. JP 3-0, *Joint Operations*, August 11, 2011, III-24.

13. Ryan J. Wallace and Jon M. Loffi, "Examining Unmanned Aerial System Threats and Defenses: A Conceptual Analysis," *International Journal of Aviation, Aeronautics, and Aerospace* 2, no. 4 (October 2015): 1, http://commons.erau.edu/cgi/ viewcontent.cgi?article=1084&context=ijaaa.

14. Pavel Alpeyev and Emi Urabe, "Japan Arrests Man for Landing Drone on Abe's Office Roof," Bloomberg, April 5, 2015, http://bloomberg.com/news/articles /2015–04–25/japan-arrests-man-for-landing-drone-on-abe-s-office-roof.

15. Robert Martinage, *Toward a New Offset Strategy: Exploiting U.S. Long-Term Advantages to Restore U.S. Global Power Projection Capability* (Washington, DC: Center for Strategic and Budgetary Assessments [CBSA], October 27, 2014), 2, http://csba-online.org/publications/2014/10/toward-a-new-offset-strategy-exploiting-u-s-long-term-advantages-to-restore-u-s-global-power-projection-capability.

16. JP 3-0, *Joint Operations*, III-29–III-30.

17. Paul Scharre, *The Coming Swarm: The Cost-Imposing Value of Mass* (Washington, DC: Center for a New American Security, 2014), 2, https://s3.amazonaws.com/ files.cnas.org/documents/CNAS_CostImposingValueofMass_Scharre.pdf.pdf.

18. Paul Scharre, *Robotics on the Battlefield Part II: The Coming Swarm* (Washington, DC: Center for a New American Security, October 2014), 18, https://s3.amazonaws .com/files.cnas.org/documents/CNAS_TheComingSwarm_Scharre.pdf.

19. Scharre.

20. Scharre.

21. Milan Vego, "Fundamentals of Mine Warfare" (Newport, RI: Naval War College, 2012), 1.

22. Scharre, *Robotics on the Battlefield*, 15.

23. Office of Management and Budget, "Exhibit R-2: RDT&E Budget Item Justification: PB 2013, The Joint Staff," in *President's FY 2013 Budget* (Washington, DC: Department of Defense, February 2012), 1, http://www.dtic.mil/descriptivesum/ Y2013/Other/stamped/0605126J_6_PB_2013.pdf.

24. Richard Whittle, "Uncle Sam Wants Your Ideas for Stopping Drones: Black Dart Tests," *Breaking Defense*, June 26, 2015, http://breakingdefense.com/2015/06/ uncle-sam-wants-your-ideas-for-stopping-drones-black-dart-tests/.

25. JP 3-01, *Countering Air and Missile Threats,* April 21, 2017, II-8.

26. JP 3-01.

27. JP 3-01.

28. JP 3-01.

29. JP 3-01.

30. JP 3-01.

31. Whittle, "Uncle Sam Wants Your Ideas."

32. Martinage, *Toward a New Offset Strategy*, 16.

33. Scharre, *Robotics on the Battlefield*, 12.

08

Narrowing the International Law Divide

The Drone Debate Matures | *Michael N. Schmitt*

Introduction

In late October 2013, two UN Special Rapporteurs presented their reports on drone warfare to the UN General Assembly.[1] Just days earlier, Amnesty International had published an investigation into drone strikes in Pakistan, and Human Rights Watch had issued its examination of such operations in Yemen.[2] The rapid-fire release of complementary investigations captured the attention of the media, blogosphere aficionados, and the international law community.

Commentators seized the opportunity to either pillory the U.S. drone program or leap to its defense. The existence of this divide is unsurprising, for international law is inherently ambiguous. After all, such law is the creation of states that are often unwilling to commit themselves to bright-line rules, especially with respect to armed force, lest they limit their scope of discretion. Room for interpretive maneuver results.

How this maneuver space is understood in the context of drone warfare depends on one's normative perspective. For instance, states facing terrorist activity will inevitably emphasize their right to self-defense;

This chapter was originally published by the *Yale Journal of International Law Online* (2014), 14 pages. Posted November 14, 2013, with permission of the author and the journal. The views expressed in this chapter are those of the author in his personal capacity.

states into which defensive operations may be mounted and those facing no serious threat will likely tout the impermeability of borders. Such conflicting standpoints contribute, as will become apparent, to a vibrant debate over the parameters of the *jus ad bellum* (the international law governing the resort to force by states).

Differences in normative perspective similarly plague the *jus in bello* (international humanitarian law [IHL]) debates surrounding drone strikes. Indeed, IHL is a particularly fertile environment for disparate views since each of its prescriptive norms represents a delicate compromise between a state's need to conduct military operations effectively ("military necessity") and its desire to protect its citizens, property, and activities from the ravages of war ("humanity"). Thus, for example, military officers and their civilian counterparts may draw conflicting conclusions as to where the balance lies.

Complicating matters is the fact that international human rights law (IHRL) coexists with IHL during armed conflict. IHRL is motivated by a desire to protect individuals from the prodigious power of states. Experts in IHRL might accordingly assess a situation involving harm to individuals differently than their IHL colleagues, who are likely to be more sensitive to the state's interests. Moreover, an ongoing debate over the geography of war, which determines the applicability of either IHL or IHRL use-of-force rules, animates the drone controversy.

The point is that how one evaluates the law governing drone strikes depends in great part on the legal construct within which one functions. What is striking about the four reports is the extent to which they appear to have narrowed the divide lying between the occupants of this multidimensional environment by adopting legal positions with which state lawyers and IHL experts will generally be familiar. It would appear that substantial agreement now exists between the key parties as to the legal framework for drone operations. Tellingly, although Human Rights Watch and Amnesty International offer drone attack case studies that they cite as legally questionable, most of their criticism revolves around questions of fact, not law. Shorn of the emotive trappings that had previously characterized the debate, the four reports, taken together, amount to a sea change in the nature of the debate over drones, one that will usher in a more sophisticated and constructive dialogue.

Informed by the reports, this article serves two purposes. First, it will set forth those aspects of international law regarding drone operations on which there now appears to be consensus. Second, it will highlight the residual disagreement and summarize the competing positions. The goal is to focus the dialogue on the issues that continue to require attention. The time is ripe to do so, for many states are now developing offensive drone capabilities.[3] Indeed, the United Kingdom has been conducting lethal Reaper drone strikes in Afghanistan for some time.[4] The drone debate is no longer a "U.S. issue."

Points of Agreement

Three international law regimes govern drone operations—sovereignty, IHL, and IHRL. The law of sovereignty, and the related area of the *jus ad bellum*, addresses the legality of crossing into another state's territory to conduct drone strikes. The latter two bodies of law determine the propriety of using lethal force against a target. Much of the confusion that has permeated the debate to date derives from conflation of these distinct legal regimes. All four of the reports, however, recognize the distinctions between them.

Sovereignty

Sending armed aircraft into another state's territory to conduct air strikes is a prima facie violation of that state's territorial integrity and, therefore, its sovereignty.[5] In most circumstances, such actions would equally amount to a use of force against the state as contemplated in Article 2(4) of the UN Charter and customary international law.[6] In only four situations do such operations not constitute a breach of sovereignty of the territorial state or a wrongful use of force.[7]

The least controversial is UN Security Council approval.[8] Drone strikes during North Atlantic Treaty Organization (NATO) operations against Libya were justified on this basis.[9] A second basis for cross-border use of force stems from the law of neutrality. In an international armed conflict (IAC) between states, belligerent forces may cross into a neutral state when the neutral state fails to ensure that its territory is not used by the enemy.[10] Neither situation is relevant to current drone operations.

As reflected in the two UN reports, agreement now exists on a third basis: consent.[11] Valid consent requires the satisfaction of two elements. First, the authority granted must be legitimate; there must be no manifest lack of authority on the part of the official concerned. Second, the action taken must fall within the scope of the consent. Any aspect of a drone strike that fails to fulfill these two criteria may only be justified based on self-defense (if at all).

Special Rapporteur Ben Emmerson has confirmed that Pakistan previously approved U.S. drones strikes.[12] However, its parliament has now prohibited the government from authorizing future attacks except pursuant to a special procedure. The parliament has also invalidated existing agreements regarding drones. Therefore, even if Pakistani military or intelligence officials authorize a strike, the consent justification no longer applies because their lack of authority has become manifest. This situation contrasts the situation in Yemen, which continues to consent to U.S. operations, thereby obviating the need to justify them on the basis of self-defense.[13]

A fourth legal ground for engaging in extraterritorial drone strikes is self-defense.[14] The United States relies on this ground for all strikes except those for which consent has been granted. As this stance is controversial, it will be dealt with in the following section.

International Humanitarian Law

Humanitarian law governs the conduct of drone strikes, irrespective of the legality of the border crossing. In particular, it addresses who may be attacked and sets forth the legal requirements and restrictions as to collateral damage that civilians and civilian objects might suffer. The lawfulness of a drone's presence in the territory where the operation is conducted has no bearing on the applicability of IHL norms.

Hostilities must be classified as an "armed conflict" before IHL applies; if they do not so qualify, IHRL is, as will be discussed, the applicable legal regime. All four reports illustrate the human rights community's acceptance of IHL as the prevailing legal regime for drone strikes during a conflict with an organized armed group, or "non-international armed conflict" (NIAC).[15] When one state uses force in support of another during a NIAC, IHL governs the operations of both states. Agreement has likewise coalesced around the

International Criminal Tribunal for the former Yugoslavia's Tadić criteria for NIACs—that the group be organized and that the hostilities reach a certain level of intensity.[16]

As noted in the UN reports, application of these criteria may preclude the possibility of a single global war against terrorism.[17] By the organization criterion, relationships between terrorist groups must be assessed to determine whether they can be considered a single entity or must be judged individually against the intensity and organization criteria. Merely sharing a common cause does not suffice; international law requires some cooperation before multiple groups may be treated as a single party to the conflict. This is the U.S. understanding of its phrase "al-Qaeda and its associated forces."[18]

Applying the rules on armed conflict classification can prove complex. Consider the U.S. conflict with al Qaeda, writ large, which the United States characterizes as non-international.[19] Special Rapporteur Emmerson has noted that success in disrupting the al Qaeda network paradoxically weakens compliance with the organization criterion.[20] Should it not be satisfied, only violence the individual groups direct against U.S. assets would be assessed against the intensity criterion. Whether the armed conflict is fading, or has faded, away is debatable, but this legal analysis is the correct one.

Even when the organization and intensity criteria are met for a particular group, it is necessary to be precise regarding the basis on which a state conducting drone operations is a party to the conflict. For instance, Amnesty International notes that U.S. drone strikes target three groups in Pakistan's tribal areas: the Afghan Taliban, the Pakistani Taliban, and al Qaeda.[21] Targeting the Afghan and Pakistani Taliban is considered assistance to Afghanistan and Pakistan in their respective NIACs with those groups. Targeting al Qaeda assets is an aspect of a separate NIAC between the United States and the organization. These are determinative distinctions because, for example, withdrawal of Pakistani or Afghan consent would deprive the United States of a legal basis for conducting operations in support of their NIACs and, therefore, for applying IHL rules of targeting instead of IHRL.

In Yemen, Human Rights Watch correctly acknowledges the ongoing NIAC between Yemen and al Qaeda in the Arabian Peninsula (AQAP). U.S. drone strikes could accordingly be justified as assistance to Yemen. However, Human Rights Watch has noted that the United States has not claimed it is conducting operations on behalf of Yemen. If it is not, the strikes have to be assessed against the requirements for a separate NIAC between the United States and AQAP (depending on the relationship between AQAP and al Qaeda). While there is little doubt that AQAP, if considered in isolation from the broader al Qaeda, would satisfy the organization criterion, it is less apparent that the intensity requirement would be fulfilled because only hostilities conducted between the United States and AQAP would factor into the equation. Should the conflict fail to qualify as a NIAC, restrictive IHRL standards would govern the U.S. attacks.[22]

Finally, each of the four reports adopts the "conduct of hostilities" approach typically employed by the IHL community. In this regard, the reports concur that drones are not unlawful per se under IHL.[23] Legal analysis of their use begins by determining whether the target qualifies as a member of the armed forces, including organized armed groups, or as an individual directly participating in the hostilities.[24] Those who so qualify may be attacked subject to the requirement to take precautions in attack and the rule of proportionality.[25] By the former, an attacker must take precautions to verify the target and use weapons and tactics designed to minimize civilian collateral damage. Even when everything has been done to minimize such harm, the latter rule will still prohibit an attack expected to cause collateral damage that is excessive relative to the anticipated military advantage.

These two IHL norms lie at the heart of some of the criticism leveled by Human Rights Watch and Amnesty International. Despite their reproach, both organizations have applied accepted IHL standards in a fashion that is consistent with state practice; censure derives from the organizations' understanding of the facts, not the law itself. Of particular note is the acceptance in all four reports of status-based targeting in qualifying cases and of the possibility that collateral damage may in some cases be lawful.

Human Rights Law

All parties to the debate agree that absent an armed conflict, IHRL rather than IHL applies. Under IHRL, "arbitrary" deprivation of life is prohibited.[26] In particular, IHRL does not permit targeting based solely on the status of the individual as is sometimes permissible under IHL (e.g., as a member of the regular armed forces or an organized armed group).[27] Any use of lethal force must be unavoidable to protect an individual's life or to preclude grievous bodily injury. It must also be proportionate to the circumstances. Application of this standard means, on the one hand, that capture is generally required in lieu of killing, although in limited circumstances a drone strike could comport with IHRL.[28]

Finally, the uncertainty about the applicability of IHRL during armed conflict appears to have been resolved, at least in part.[29] As illustrated in the four reports, the human rights community takes the position that IHRL applies alongside IHL. In 2011 the United States reversed its position and acknowledged the extension of IHRL into armed conflict, an important step in narrowing the divide.[30] It must be cautioned, though, that while IHRL applies, the arbitrariness of a lethal attack under that law is judged by reference to IHL standards.[31]

Surviving Points of Disagreement
Although the four reports suggest that the contretemps has paled, differences of opinion persist. As noted in the introduction, international law governing conflict is abstruse by nature, and thereby leads states and experts to adopt differing interpretations of the law based on their vantage points. It is especially commendable that the UN Special Rapporteurs sometimes acknowledge these differences without necessarily taking a particular position. In doing so, they open the door to constructive dialogue.

Self-Defense
The *jus ad bellum* right of self-defense lies at the heart of the current extraterritorial drone operations. This customary right is set forth in Article 51 of the UN Charter: "Nothing in the present Charter shall impair the inherent right of individual or collective self-defence if an armed attack occurs against a Member of the United Nations, until the Security Council has taken measures necessary to maintain international peace and security."[32] Absent such a right, the sole basis for the U.S. drone operations into another state's territory is consent.

Unfortunately, as noted by Special Rapporteur Emmerson, no consensus exists regarding extension of the right to self-defense against attacks by non-state actors.[33] Although the United States takes the position such a right exists, the International Court of Justice, seemingly ignoring state practice, has raised questions about this view.[34] The United States further asserts that such operations into another state's territory are lawful when the territorial state is either unwilling or unable to put an end to the activities of violent non-state groups from their territory.[35] Not all states accept this position.[36]

Additional disagreement surrounds anticipatory self-defense, that is, conducting drone strikes to preclude imminent attacks. As noted by both Special Rapporteurs, the traditional approach has been to apply the Caroline temporal standard.[37] By this standard, a state would have to possess intelligence that the terrorists were just about to attack before launching drone strikes against them.

This approach has struggled to survive in the face of potential attacks that can be mounted secretly and, in an era of weapons of mass destruction, catastrophically. Increasingly, the right of anticipatory self-defense is interpreted as permitting defensive actions once the "window of opportunity" to effectively defend oneself is on the point of closing.[38] For instance, if a state acquires actionable intelligence that key members of a terrorist group are at a particular location, and if it is unlikely to enjoy another chance to target them before future attacks occur, the imminence criterion is satisfied.

Geography of War
A significant ongoing debate highlighted in Special Rapporteur Emmerson's report surrounds the "geography of war."[39] It asks whether there are geographical boundaries to an armed conflict such that IHRL rather than IHL applies to drone operations conducted beyond the conflict's perimeters.

During an IAC, the law of neutrality sets out the permissible locations for military operations. However, no such established regime governs the geography of NIACs. As a result, extraterritorial drone operations ignited a dispute over whether a NIAC can extend beyond the borders of the state that is party to the conflict.

There are three approaches. The most restrictive confines NIACs to the territory of the state involved. This approach is based on Common Article 3 to the 1949 Geneva Conventions, which defines NIACs as those occurring "in the territory of one of the High Contracting Parties."[40] It would significantly limit drone operations against transnational terrorist groups by subjecting them to human rights standards except when the operations are in support of another state's NIAC on that state's territory.

The second approach is a variant of the first. It asserts that NIACs include hostilities that spillover into neighboring states.[41] Thus, for instance, drone operations against the Afghan Taliban in Pakistan's tribal areas could involve IHL status-based targeting, while those elsewhere would be bound to IHRL standards. Amnesty International adopts this position with respect to Afghan Taliban who "use North Waziristan as a staging ground for attacks on U.S. and Afghan government forces."[42]

A third approach, exemplified in the U.S. Supreme Court's Hamdan opinion, ignores geography and focuses on the parties to the conflict. It reasons that "the term 'conflict not of an international character' is used [in Common Article 3] in contradistinction to a conflict between nations."[43] By this interpretation, IHL follows participants in a conflict wherever they go. Lest the approach appear to spread the conflict globally, it must be remembered that before a state may conduct operations on another's territory, it must secure Security Council authorization or consent of the territorial state, or by the U.S. view, be exercising its right to self-defense after the territorial state has proved itself unwilling or unable to adequately police its territory.

Direct Participation in Hostilities

It is universally acknowledged that civilians who directly participate in hostilities may be targeted "for such time" as they participate.[44] In an important paper, the International Committee of the Red Cross (ICRC) has acknowledged that individuals who are members of an organized armed group and have a "continuous combat function" are targetable on the same basis as members of the regular armed forces.[45]

They are not treated as civilians subject to drone attacks only during the time in which they are taking a "direct part in hostilities." Disagreement surrounds the continuous combat function qualification. Those who oppose it, including the United States, argue that it creates battlefield disparity by allowing the targeting of members of the regular armed forces who do not engage in hostilities, while protecting similarly situated members of armed groups. For these critics, it seems incongruent and illogical to give the latter greater protection than the former.[46] It should be noted that the human rights community, as reflected in the Amnesty International and Human Rights Watch reports, almost universally adopts the ICRC position.[47] There is little likelihood that this debate will be resolved satisfactorily; both sides seem intransigent.

Capture-Kill

A related controversy exists over whether IHL imposes a duty to capture rather than kill individuals who qualify as lawful targets during an armed conflict. Clearly, this is the rule outside armed conflict. However, it has been suggested that during armed conflict, a drone strike would be unlawful if it were reasonably possible to capture the target.[48] Human Rights Watch criticized several drone strikes on this basis.[49]

These suggestions have met with significant resistance, particularly from IHL experts.[50] For them, targetability is only situational with respect to the possible harm to civilians, civilian objects, and other protected persons or places. Critics of the proposition hasten to add that it would usually be operationally insensible to conduct a lethal strike when capture is feasible because that target represents intelligence value. Nevertheless, they contend that such a kill operation, albeit ill-advised, would be lawful.

Investigations

Human rights law imposes stringent requirements to investigate possible human rights abuses and requires that such investigations be carried out in an impartial, independent, prompt, and effective manner. There is no doubt that these standards apply equally to investigation under IHL.[51]

However, not all experts or states agree on how they apply. Amnesty International's calls for an investigation into every strike causing civilian casualties go too far.[52] Some argue that an investigation is required only when there is reason to believe there may have been a violation of IHL.[53] For instance, a drone strike launched during an armed conflict with full knowledge that civilians will be killed would not necessitate an investigation so long as the requirement to take precautions in attack and the rule of proportionality were clearly satisfied. Those taking this position would, however, agree with Human Rights Watch that "where there is credible evidence that an attack has violated the laws of war, the responsible state party is obligated to investigate for possible war crimes and appropriately prosecute the perpetrators, or extradite them for prosecution elsewhere."[54]

Possible Errors of Law

Although the reports are refreshing in that they either reflect classic understandings of the applicable legal regimes or adopt positions that, while not universally accepted, are nonetheless the product of reasonable differences of opinion, on a limited number of occasions, they seem to err or mislead. The Human Rights Watch report, for instance, briefly discusses "signature strikes," noting that they expand "the notion of target beyond laws-of-war requirements."[55] The basis for this conclusion seems to be that these strikes violate the duty to "presume an individual is a civilian unless determined to be a valid military objective."[56] Amnesty International appears to have come to the same conclusion.[57]

In fact, the United States fully embraces the legal requirement to treat potential targets as civilians in cases of doubt; it trains its forces on the rule, which is reflected in U.S. rules of engagement and other use of force guidance.[58] A signature strike is simply one in which the identity of the target is unknown, but the individual's conduct reasonably leads to the conclusion that he or she is either a member of an organized armed group or a direct participant in hostilities. All IHL targeting rules apply to such strikes, including those regarding identification of the target.

In another example, Amnesty International asserts, "Reports that the USA targets individuals on a 'kill list' suggest the USA is not doing a case-by-case analysis of whether those persons are taking direct part in hostilities at the time they are targeted." It also states, "The extremely low civilian casualty numbers the U.S. government has given arguably imply that they do not presume unidentified individuals are civilians."[59] These statements are flawed on two levels. First, the claims are counternormative because individuals included on so-called kill lists are typically members of organized armed groups with a continuous combat function and therefore not subject to the rules on direct participation in hostilities. Second, the statements are counterfactual. The United States does not conduct drone strikes without some form of legal review to ensure that the individual qualifies as targetable at the time of the drone strike.

Concluding Thoughts

As demonstrated by these four reports, the debate over drone operations has matured. There is now substantial agreement among all parties involved on the applicable legal regimes and the application of most of the prescriptive norms making them up. The international law divide has narrowed measurably as consensus is reached on the terms of reference.

Yet optimism must be tempered by reality. The drone strike controversy will endure, for few topics are as emotive as terrorism and the response thereto, and few contemporary threats are as difficult to address effectively as transborder attacks by non-state actors. These and similar factors will continue to skew the objectivity of legal policy choice and assessment. Indeed, critics have alleged that the United States is even failing to observe the policy restrictions imposed by President Obama himself.[60] Moreover, the Human Rights Watch and Amnesty International reports illustrate that there will often be divergent views regarding the attendant facts, the legal regime that applies to specific strikes, and application of the relevant norms to particular cases.

Perhaps counterintuitively, such disagreement is healthy. Public scrutiny encourages governments to ensure their operations are lawful; there is no downside to careful fidelity to the law during military operations. Therefore, greater transparency and accountability, which each of the reports champion, is well advised. While it would be naive to suggest that all information regarding drone attacks must be publicly revealed, general information about the strikes should be released to the maximum extent reasonable in the circumstances. The legal basis for the drone program must also be publicly set forth in greater detail than has been the case to date. Failure to do so will continue to frustrate achievement of strategic and operational objectives.

Notes

1. Ben Emmerson, Report of the Special Rapporteur on the Promotion and Protection of Human Rights and Fundamental Freedoms While Countering Terrorism, A/68/389 (Sept. 18, 2013); Christof Heyns, Report of the Special Rapporteur on Extrajudicial, Summary or Arbitrary Executions, A/68/382 (Sept. 13, 2013).

2. Amnesty International (AI), "Will I Be Next?": US Drone Strikes in Pakistan (London: AI, 2013); Human Rights Watch (HRW), "Between a Drone and Al-Qaeda": The Civilian Cost of US Targeted Killings in Yemen (New York: HRW, 2013).

3. See, e.g., Edward Wong, "Hacking U.S. Secrets, China Pushes for Drones," New York Times, September 20, 2013, http://www.nytimes.com/2013/09/21/world/asia/hacking-us-secrets-china-pushesfor-drones.html.

4. Nick Hopkins, "UK Starts Controlling Drones in Afghanistan from British Soil," The Guardian, April 25, 2013, http://www.theguardian.com/world/2013/apr/25/uk-controllingdrones-afghanistan-britain.

5. On sovereignty, see Island of Palmas (Neth. v. U.S.), 2 R.I.A.A. 829, 83 (Perm. Ct. Arb. 1928).

6. UN Charter, art. 2, para. 4. The International Court of Justice has acknowledged the customary character of Article 2(4). Legal Consequences of the Construction of a Wall in the Occupied Palestinian Territory, Advisory Opinion, 2004 I.C.J. 136, 87 (July 9); Military and Paramilitary Activities in and against Nicaragua (Nicar. v. U.S.), 1986 I.C.J. 14, 186–91 (June 27).

7. See Michael N. Schmitt, "Extraterritorial Lethal Targeting: Deconstructing the Logic of International Law," Columbia Journal of Transnational Law 52, no. 1 (2013): 77–112.

8. UN Charter, arts. 39, 42.

9. See UN Security Council, Resolution 1973, S/RES/1973 (Mar. 17, 2011).

10. Hague Convention (V) Respecting the Rights and Duties of Neutral Powers and Persons in Case of War on Land, art. 5, Oct. 18, 1907, 36 Stat. 2310; see also U.S. Navy, U.S. Marine Corps, and U.S. Coast Guard, The Commander's Handbook on the Law of Naval Operations (Quantico and Washington, DC: Department of Navy and Department of Homeland Security, 2007), 7–2.

11. Paramilitary Activities, 1986 I.C.J. at 126, 246; Emmerson, Report, 51; Heyns, Report, 82–84; Special Rapporteur on Extrajudicial, Summary or Arbitrary Executions, Report of the Special Rapporteur on Extrajudicial, Summary or Arbitrary Executions, Human Rights Council, A/HRC/14/24/Add.6 (May 28,

2010) (by Philip Alston), 37–38. On consent by one state to the use of force by another, see Ashley S. Deeks, "Consent to the Use of Force and International Law Supremacy," *Harvard International Law Journal* 54, no. 1 (2013): 8–42.

12. Emmerson, Report, 53; see also AI, *Will I Be Next?*, 53–54; Greg Miller and Bob Woodward, "Secret Memos Reveal Explicit Nature of U.S., Pakistan Agreement on Drones," *Washington Post*, October 24, 2013, http://www.washingtonpost.com/world/nationalsecurity/top-pakistani-leaders-secretly-backed-cia-drone-campaign-secret-documentsshow/2013/10/23/15e6b0d8-3beb-11e3-b6a9-da62c264f40e_story.html.

13. Emmerson, Report, 52, 53–54.

14. UN Charter, art. 51; Oil Platforms (Iran v. U.S.), 2003 I.C.J. 161, 74 (Nov. 6); Legality of the Threat or Use of Nuclear Weapons, Advisory Opinion, 1996 I.C.J. 226, 38, 41 (July 8); Paramilitary Activities, 1986 I.C.J. at 94, 176.

15. Geneva Convention Relative to the Treatment of Prisons of War, art. 3, Aug. 12, 1949, 6 U.S.T. 3316, 75 U.N.T.S. 135 (hereafter cited as Common Article 3).

16. Prosecutor v. Tadić, Case No. IT-94-1-I, Decision on the Defence Motion for Interlocutory Appeal on Jurisdiction, 70 (Int'l Crim. Trib. for the Former Yugoslavia, Oct. 2, 1995).

17. Emmerson, Report, 66–68; Heyns, Report, 64–66; see also International Committee of the Red Cross (ICRC), *International Humanitarian Law and the Challenges of Contemporary Armed Conflicts* (Geneva: ICRC, 2011), 10–11.

18. See, e.g., Authorization for the Use of Military Force, S. Res. 23, 107th Cong. (2001); Barack Obama, Remarks by the President at National Defense University (May 23, 2013); Jeh C. Johnson, "National Security Law, Lawyers and Lawyering in the Obama Administration" (address at the Dean's Lecture, Yale Law School, February 22, 2012).

19. U.S. Department of Justice (DOJ), "Lawfulness of a Lethal Operation Directed against a U.S. Citizen Who Is a Senior Operational Leader of Al-Qa'ida or an Associated Force 3" (unpublished white paper, November 8, 2011), http://msnbcmedia.msn.com/i/msnbc/sections/news/020413_DOJ_White_Paper.pdf, (citing Hamdan v. Rumsfeld, 548 U.S. 557, 628–31 [2006]).

20. Emmerson, Report, 66; see also Heyns, Report, 59–63.

21. AI, *Will I Be Next?*, 14.

22. HRW, *Between a Drone*, 7.

23. See, e.g., Heyns, Report, 13.

24. Protocol Additional to the Geneva Conventions of 12 August 1949, and Relating to the Protection of Victims of International Armed Conflicts, art. 51(3), June 8, 1977, 1125 U.N.T.S. 3 (hereafter cited as Additional Protocol I); Nils Melzer, *Interpretive Guidance on the Notion of Direct Participation in Hostilities under International Humanitarian Law* (Geneva: ICRC, 2009), 21–22. See, generally, Jean-Marie Henckaerts and Louise Doswald-Beck, eds., *Customary International Humanitarian Law*, vol. 2, *Practice* (Cambridge: ICRC, 2005), 3–133 (collecting practice of states and international organizations on distinguishing civilians and combatants).

25. For the requirement to take precautions in an attack, see Additional Protocol I, art. 57; Henckaerts and Doswald-Beck, *Customary International Humanitarian Law*, vol. 2, ch. 5. For the rule of proportionality, see Additional Protocol I, arts. 51(5)

(b), 57(2)(a)(iii), and (b); Henckaerts and Doswald-Beck, *Customary International Humanitarian Law*, vol. 2, 297–335. Human Rights Watch questioned three strikes on the basis of proportionality. HRW, *Between a Drone*, 4–5, 61.

26. International Covenant on Civil and Political Rights, art. 6(1), Dec. 19, 1966, S. Exec. Doc. E, 95-2 (1978), 999 U.N.T.S. 171; Universal Declaration of Human Rights, art. 3, G.A. Res. 217 (III) A, U.N. Doc. A/RES/3/217(III) (Dec. 10, 1948); Heyns, Report, 7–8, 30–31.

27. Office of the High Commander for Human Rights, Basic Principles on the Use of Force and Firearms by Law Enforcement Officials, A/CONF.144/28/Rev.1 (Sept. 7, 1990), 118.

28. See McCann v. United Kingdom, App. No. 18984/91, 21 Eur. H.R. Rep. 97 203–14 (1995); Emmerson, Report, 35.

29. Legal Consequences of the Construction of a Wall in the Occupied Palestinian Territory, Advisory Opinion, 2004 I.C.J. 178, 106 (July 9); Legality of the Threat or Use of Nuclear Weapons, Advisory Opinion, 1996 I.C.J. 239–240, 24–25 (July 8). Disagreement about extraterritorial reach of human rights law persists. Heyns, Report, 42–51.

30. U.S. Department of State, *Fourth Periodic Report of the United States of America to the United Nations Committee on Human Rights Concerning the International Covenant on Civil and Political Rights* (Washington, DC: U.S. Department of State, 2011), 506–7, http://www.state.gov/j/drl/rls/179781.htm.

31. See Nuclear Weapons, 1996 I.C.J. at 240, 25.

32. UN Charter, art. 51.

33. Emmerson, Report, 55–56; see also Heyns, Report, 85–92.

34. DOJ, "Lawfulness of a Lethal Operation," 2; see also Harold H. Koh, "The Obama Administration and International Law" (address before the American Society of International Law, March 25, 2010), http://www.state.gov/s/l/releases/remarks/139119.htm; Legal Consequences of the Construction of a Wall in the Occupied Palestinian Territory, Advisory Opinion, 2004 I.C.J. 168, 146–47 (July 9).

35. Obama, Remarks by the President at National Defense University; White House, "Fact Sheet: U.S. Policy Standards and Procedures for the Use of Force in Counterterrorism Operations Outside the United States in Areas of Active Hostilities," press release, May 23, 2013, http://www.whitehouse.gov/the-press-office/2013/05/23/fact-sheet-us-policy-standards-andprocedures-use-force-counterterrorism; DOJ, "Lawfulness of a Lethal Operation," 1–2.

36. Emmerson, Report, 55–56.

37. Emmerson, Report, 57; Heyns, Report, 87. There must be a "necessity of self-defense [that] is instant, overwhelming, and leaving no choice of means, and no moment for deliberation." Daniel Webster, letter to Lord Ashburton, August 6, 1842, reprinted in *Moore Digest* 2, no. 217 (1907): 412.

38. DOJ, "Lawfulness of a Lethal Operation," 7; Michael N. Schmitt, "Counter-Terrorism and the Use of Force in International Law," *Israel Yearbook on Human Rights* 32 (2002).

39. Emmerson, Report, 60–65. The various approaches to the subject, as well as the views of the author, are set forth in Michael N. Schmitt, "Charting the Legal

Geography of Non-international Armed Conflict," *Military Law and Law of War Review* 90, no. 52 (2014): 93–102.

40. Common Article 3. IHL applies within a state irrespective of where hostilities are occurring. Prosecutor v. Tadić, Case No. IT-94-1-I, Decision on the Defence Motion for Interlocutory Appeal on Jurisdiction, 70 (Int'l Crim. Trib. for the Former Yugoslavia, Oct. 2, 1995), 70.

41. ICRC, *Contemporary Armed Conflicts*, 10.

42. AI, *Will I Be Next?*, 45.

43. Hamdan v. Rumsfeld, 548 U.S. 557, 562 (2006).

44. Additional Protocol I, art. 51(3); Protocol Additional to the Geneva Conventions of August 12 1949, and Relating to the Protection of Victims of Non-International Armed Conflicts, art. 13(3), June 8, 1977, 1125 U.N.T.S. 609; Henckaerts and Doswald-Beck, *Customary International Humanitarian Law*, vol. 2, 6.

45. Melzer, *Interpretive Guidance*, 27.

46. See, e.g., Michael N. Schmitt, "The Interpretive Guidance on the Notion of Direct Participation in Hostilities: A Critical Analysis," *Harvard National Security Journal* 1 (2010): 5–44.

47. AI, *Will I Be Next?*, 45; HRW, *Between a Drone*, 84–85. Note that AI confuses organized armed groups criteria with those applicable to civilians who directly participate. See also Heyns, Report, 68, 70, 72.

48. See, e.g., Ryan Goodman, "The Power to Kill or Capture Enemy Combatants," *European Journal of International Law* 24, no. 3 (2013): 819–53.

49. HRW, *Between a Drone*, 4.

50. See, e.g., Geoffrey S. Corn, Laurie R. Blank, Chris Jenks, and Eric Talbot Jensen, "Belligerent Targeting and the Invalidity of a Least Harmful Means Rule," *International Law Studies* 89 (2013): 536–626; Michael N. Schmitt, "Wound, Capture, or Kill: A Reply to Ryan Goodman's 'The Power to Kill or Capture Enemy Combatants,'" *European Journal of International Law* 24, no. 3 (2013): 855–61.

51. See, e.g., UN Human Rights Council, Human Rights in Palestine and Other Occupied Arab Territories: Report of the United Nations Fact Finding Mission on the Gaza Conflict, A/HRC/12/48 (Sept. 15, 2009), 1758.

52. AI, *Will I Be Next?*, 58.

53. As I have argued elsewhere, "There is no requirement to investigate particular categories of incidents, such as those involving civilian casualties or damage to civilian property. Such a requirement would be impractical during armed conflict. Only incidents based on a credible allegation of a war crime or other reason to suspect a violation necessitate investigation." Michael N. Schmitt, "Investigating Violations of International Law in Armed Conflict," *Harvard National Security Journal* 2 (2011): 31–84. But see Amichai Cohen and Yuval Shany, "Beyond the Grave Breaches Regime: The Duty to Investigate Alleged Violations of International Law Governing Armed Conflicts," *Yearbook of International Humanitarian Law* 14 (2011): 37–84.

54. HRW, *Between a Drone*, 88.

55. HRW, 87.

56. HRW. The requirement is set forth in Additional Protocol I, art. 50(1), and reflects customary law.

57. AI, *Will I Be Next?*, 46.
58. See, e.g., Richard P. Dimeglio et al., *Law of Armed Conflict Deskbook* (Charlottes-ville, VA: U.S. Army Judge Advocate General's Legal Center and School, 2012).
59. AI, *Will I Be Next?*, 46.
60. For an example of the criticism, see "Joint Letter from NGSs and Human Rights Groups to President Barack Obama on on Drone Program," https://www.justsecurity.org/4128/joint-letter-ngos-human-rights-groups-concerns-drone-program.

09

Autonomous Weapons and the Law

Christopher M. Ford

Introduction

Autonomous weapons—those weapons that can select and engage targets without human involvement—herald perhaps the most fundamental change in warfare in generations. The rise of autonomous weapons has sparked a robust debate in the legal community. Positions span the spectrum from a call for preemptive prohibition to arguments that current legal norms are adequate to regulate these future weapon systems.[1] An understanding of these issues is critical to ensuring the robust and legal development and application of various autonomy-enabled weapon (AEW) systems. It is well accepted that the law of armed conflict—including the requirement that attacks be discriminate, be proportional, and comply with requirements for precautions—applies to all weapon systems and, therefore, imposes restrictions on their use. However, the application of these concepts to autonomous weapons raises some questions. For example, can an autonomous system distinguish civilian from combatant? A civilian object from a military object? Can it do so in all environments? Or for proportionality, how does an autonomous system calculate and weigh anticipated military advantage and expected collateral damage?

This chapter was derived from a longer piece published in the *University of South Carolina Law Review* 69 (April 2017): 413 and is used with permission. The views expressed are the author's own and do not reflect the views of the Department of Defense or any other government agency.

Some commentators contend these issues are insoluble, arguing that autonomous weapons cannot comply with the requirements because doing so requires inherently human judgments, or the technology is not sufficiently sophisticated, or the current legal regime is insufficient to address autonomous weapons. This chapter concludes—as have others—that the law of armed conflict is adequate to regulate autonomous weapon systems that currently exist or will likely exist in the near future. That said, it is perilous to think of autonomous weapons as a homogenous category that is either compliant with the law or not. Certain components of given systems may be highly autonomous, while other elements may not have autonomous features at all. For this reason, this chapter uses the term "autonomy-enabled weapons" rather than the more common "lethal autonomous weapons."

Arguments concerning autonomy and the law of armed conflict tend to focus on a limited subset of potential engagements, specifically those engagements involving fully autonomous systems using deadly force against a person in cluttered and complex battlespaces. Unquestionably, conflicts will be fought in these environments and will raise significant issues regarding the employment of autonomous weapon systems. Conflicts will also, however, be fought in ways and in environments that will not raise issues in the law of armed conflict because of the way, the context, or the manner in which autonomy is used. For example, systems may employ autonomy in *technologies* that do not implicate the law of armed conflict. Many unmanned systems can autonomously refuel and navigate, functions that do not implicate the law of armed conflict.

It is also possible to employ AEWs in an *environment* that doesn't raise issues with some aspects of the law of armed conflict. For example, an AEW could be used in a very limited area (e.g., a remote desert battlefield) or in a very limited fashion (e.g., a weapon activates for a fraction of a second at a time when no civilians are present). In such circumstances, aspects of the law of armed conflict, such as proportionality, may not be implicated. Finally, highly autonomous AEWs could be employed but in a *manner* that does not implicate the law of armed conflict. For example, consider a hypothetical weapon that has been directed to attack a particular building. Before activation, the system is programmed to *de*activate when any civilians are present. Similarly, an artillery round could be programmed to turn itself off when civilians are detected. Here the autonomous feature of the system (i.e., the decision to deactivate) is being used in a manner that does not generate issues under the law of armed conflict and, in fact, can only cause enhanced compliance.

This chapter addresses the application of international law to autonomous weapons in two parts. The chapter first examines the requirement under international law to employ legal weapons and the process by which militaries ensure the lawfulness of their weapon systems. The second substantive section considers the various aspects of the law of armed conflict as applied to autonomous weapons.

Weapon Reviews

Before a commander uses any weapon in combat, he or she will (or should) demand assurances that the weapon will act in accordance with the specifications provided and in a lawful manner. The weapon review process generates this information. The legal lodestar for this obligation is Article 35 of Additional Protocol I, which reaffirms the long-standing proposition that the methods and means of warfare are not unlimited.[2] The weapon review process ensures weapons are not unlawful. Article 36 of Additional Protocol I imposes an obligation on states to review new weapons. Although the additional protocol does not mandate the form of the weapon review, it is widely accepted that a review should consider both the weapon itself and the planned and normal circumstances of the weapon's use.[3] While the United States is not a signatory to Additional Protocol I, it has long adopted, as a matter of policy, a requirement to review new weapons.[4]

The law of armed conflict prohibits two broad categories of weapons as unlawful per se: those that cause superfluous injury or unnecessary suffering and those that are inherently indiscriminate, including weapons that cannot be aimed or whose effects cannot be controlled.[5] Nothing inherent in an autonomous weapon system raises unique issues in this regard, as the technology of autonomy does not in and of itself create superfluous injury or unnecessary suffering. In the same way, the technology of autonomy does not create indistinction. Weapon reviews should, of course, consider these per se prohibitions, though they are unlikely to be violated by the autonomous aspect of the weapon. Determining the lawfulness of an autonomous weapon system in its normal and expected circumstances of use is more challenging.

While not unique to autonomous weapons, the implicit technological sophistication of autonomous systems demands increasingly sophisticated means of testing the systems. Addressing the issue of testing technologically complex weapons, Alan Backstrom and Ian Henderson write, "The use of a guided weapon with an autonomous firing option requires an understanding of the legal parameters; the engineering design, production, and testing (or validation) methods; and the way in which the weapon might be employed on the battlefield."[6] More than that, advancing technologies will require new approaches to test technologically sophisticated weapons.

The software that animates AEWs presents a particularly challenging area for testing. Many AEWs will rely on machine learning algorithms that enable the system to "iteratively learn from data" so that the system will "produce reliable, repeatable decisions and results."[7] Several methods are used to train machine learning algorithms, including supervised and unsupervised learning models.[8] The most common learning method, supervised learning, requires that the learning algorithm be fed training data to learn what the user desires the machine to learn. Thus, an algorithm designed to identify enemy tanks would be provided millions of images of tanks, and the system would self-adjust as it became more accurate.

In the context of AEWs, there are two broad concerns with machine learning. First, a machine learning algorithm is only as good as the training it receives. A supervised learning process for an AEW designed to identify and destroy enemy tanks might include feeding the algorithm images labeled as tanks and then later asking the weapon to identify a tank among a group of vehicle images. Corrupt data will lead to corrupt results. Thus, if the algorithm is provided pictures of a truck and told that it is a tank, the algorithm will have an impaired ability to identify tanks (and trucks). The second problem occurs when the training data does not fully replicate the environment in which the system is designed to operate. If that is the case, an algorithm is trained to identify tanks by being provided images of tanks taken in a wooded environment, the algorithm may come to define a tank as a tank-like object plus a wooded environment. In a desert or mountainous environment, the algorithm might be unable identify a tank. Where, as in these examples, the algorithm cannot identify its target, it is not malfunctioning; rather, it has been improperly or incorrectly trained.

The importance of testing weapons in the circumstances of their expected use also exists for conventional weapons, but this importance is particularly acute when considering autonomous weapons and other highly sophisticated weapons. A bullet, for instance, will perform the same in the daytime as in the nighttime. Where a weapon relies on a suite of sophisticated sensors, however, weather and time of day are critical. By way of example, consider the Israeli Harpy system. The Harpy is an unmanned aircraft that loiters above a battlefield until it detects enemy radar. Once it detects radar, it will engage the target in a kamikaze-style attack. Say, hypothetically, that during testing it was determined the Harpy could distinguish the military objective from civilian objects 98 percent of the time in dry, sunny weather. This conclusion is relevant to the use of the Harpy in dry, sunny weather but is irrelevant to other circumstances of use, for example, at night, in the rain, or in the fog.

The parallels to an armed conflict scenario using autonomous weapon systems are evident. Systems may be trained with incorrect data or data that is unconsciously biased. Weapon testing will only identify such issues where the training environment accurately reflects the context in which the system will be used. In all reviews, certain best practices should be considered. These include the following:

- Weapon reviews should either be multidisciplinary or include attorneys who have the technical expertise to understand the nature and results of the testing process.
- Reviews should delineate the circumstances of use for which the weapon was approved.
- Reviews should provide a clear delineation of human and system responsibilities. Who will do what in a given circumstance?

- Optimally, reviews should occur at three points in time: (1) when the proposal is made to transition a weapon from research to development, (2) before the weapon is fielded, and (3) periodically during deployment based on feedback on how the weapon is functioning. This suggestion necessitates the establishment of a clear feedback loop that provides information from the developer to the reviewer to the user and back again. This suggestion is perhaps not unique to AEWs, but it is of particular importance given the adaptability of autonomous weapon systems.
- Reviews should also address the learning capacity of the AEW. Are all sister systems trained exactly the same? Does the AEW learn in situ in the operational environment?

In short, there are certainly aspects of autonomous weapon reviews that need to be carefully considered. A robust weapon review is fundamental to ensuring autonomous weapon systems are used consistent with international humanitarian law.

The Law of Armed Conflict

The law of armed conflict imposes three fundamental requirements on the use of force: it must be discriminate, be proportional, and comply with requirements for precautions in attack. Distinction requires a person conducting the attack to distinguish between lawful targets (combatants, civilians taking direct part in the hostilities, and military objectives) from unlawful targets (civilians, those hors de combat, civilian objects, and other protected persons and objects).[9] There are aspects of distinction that may prove particularly challenging for an AEW. These issues, however, only arise in a very specific subset of engagements—attacks involving autonomous technologies selecting and engaging targets where civilians or civilian objects, or those who are hors de combat, are potentially present. Broadly, autonomy implicates two issues related to the principle of distinction. The first arises from the length of time the system is deployed, whereas the second derives from the inherent technological sophistication of autonomous systems.

Autonomy allows systems to potentially be deployed for extended periods. The longer the system operates, the greater the chance the environment will change. Changes can occur in the physical environment (e.g., atmospheric conditions, altitude, time of day, weather) and operational environment (e.g., the human element of the battlefield, including the persons and human-made structures). The interaction between environment and machine is critical as the ability of a system to distinguish is a function of the sophistication of the system and the complexity of the environment. An increasingly complex environment requires an increasingly sophisticated system.

Autonomy raises various issues with the rule of distinction in the context of attacks on persons. It is not inconceivable that a system could identify members of an armed force. They are, by law, required to take measures to ensure they are readily distinguishable from civilians.[10] An AEW could easily be programmed to identify a particular uniform or insignia. Participants in an armed conflict, however, are not always readily identified. Many attacks on U.S. forces in Iraq and Afghanistan were conducted by persons with no discernable affiliation with a military or organized armed group. In the law these individuals are classified as "directly participating in hostilities" and can be targeted for such time as they are directly participating.[11]

Determining the contours of "for such time" is difficult. Most agree that the direct participation in hostilities extends for some point in time before and after the participation in hostilities, but identifying the moment direct participation begins and ends has proved elusive.[12] The International Committee for the Red Cross holds that direct participation extends to preparatory measures and deployment to and from the location of the act.[13] An alternative view holds that "for such time" should be extended "as far before and after a hostile action as a causal connection existed."[14] The U.S. position is that persons taking direct part of hostilities are a legitimate target until "they have permanently ceased their participation" in hostilities.[15] AEWs will likely face significant difficulty in identifying a person immediately before the act constituting direct participation in hostilities. To be clear, this does not render "autonomous weapons" as a class of weapons indiscriminate; rather it limits the type and employment of weapon systems.

Another aspect of distinction that autonomy potentially disrupts is the targeting of objects. Article 52(1) of Additional Protocol I to the Geneva Conventions prohibits targeting civilian objects, which are defined as all objects which "are not military objectives."[16] The article provides a two-part test for military objectives. First, they must "by their nature, location, purpose or use make an effective contribution to military action," and second, their "total or partial destruction, capture or neutralization, in the circumstances ruling at the time, offers a definite military advantage."[17] Effective contribution is a broad concept that "does not require a direct connection with combat operation[s]."[18]

An object is a military objective by *nature* when its "intrinsic character" is military.[19] This includes weapons, military equipment, and military facilities. Autonomy likely does not have a significant impact on objects that are military by their nature since these objects are usually readily identifiable, can be programmed into an AEW, and are not likely to lose their status during the conflict. An object is a military objective by *location* when the location of the object provides an effective military contribution regardless of the use of the object.[20] A strategic bridge that affords the enemy forces freedom of movement would be a valid military object by location regardless of how the bridge is used at the time of the attack. Again, autonomy has little impact on objects that are military by their location. As with intrinsically military objects, objects that are military by location can be identified and programmed into an AEW. Depending on the scope of autonomy, the system could then select targets from among the potential targets. Changes to the operational environment do not change the status of such objects—changes may, however, affect the military advantage calculation discussed later.

The military *purpose* of an object speaks to its future use.[21] The *DOD Law of War Manual* provides runways at civilian airports as an example.[22] Designating an object a military objective by its purpose requires an understanding of the adversary's intent based on a knowledge of the enemy's tactics, techniques, and procedures (TTPs) and current intelligence showing enemy activity. This determination is more than supposition and must be supported with reasonable certainty that the object will be converted to military use. AEWs may have difficulty making determinations as to when an object qualifies as a military objective by its purpose. Such a determination would require a system that can sense enemy activity and make targeting determinations about the enemy's future actions. Take a hypothetical in which reliable intelligence indicates enemy forces are redirecting all aluminum to military purposes. Conceivably, an AEW could be sufficiently sophisticated to recognize all aluminum stock is being redirected to military installations. This level of sophistication is, however, unlikely given current technology. More likely, the system would have to be deployed with the information or provided an update regarding the status of the stocks. Absent such updates it is hard to conceive how an AEW could make sophisticated determinations regarding the future use of something.

An object is a valid military object by its *use* when the current function of a previously civilian object is now military in nature.[23] The object remains a valid military objective for such time as the object is used for military purposes. Measures would have to be taken to ensure objects are attacked only during the time they are military objectives. Determining the point in time when a civilian object becomes a military object, and when it regains it civilian status, may prove difficult depending on the circumstances. It is relatively clear, for instance, when a school is being used as a fighting position. Conversely, it is relatively *un*clear when a school is being used as a military headquarters. Whether an autonomous system can determine when an object is no longer being used for military purposes is a technical question. In some circumstances this determination might be simple and could be made with current technology. More complex scenarios would necessitate more sophisticated systems or programming to ensure the system is not permitted to make these determinations.

Systems displaying a large amount of autonomy are today employed in uncluttered environments (e.g., the open sea) against readily identified targets (e.g., an incoming missile). Difficulties arise when AEWs operate in dynamic circumstances or in situations that require contextual decisions. As other commentators have correctly noted, "It is conceivable that the battlefield situation might be too cluttered for the system to accurately distinguish between military objectives and civilian objects or between combatants and the civilian population. In those cases, an autonomous weapons system would be unlawful to use."[24]

Not only must the object of an attack be a legitimate object of attack, but the attack itself must comply with the rule of proportionality, which prohibits an "attack which may be expected to cause incidental loss of civilian life, injury to civilians, damage to civilian objects, or a combination thereof, which would be excessive in relation to the concrete and direct military advantage anticipated."[25] Determining anticipated military advantage and the expected collateral damage, and then weighing these unlike values against one another, is both subjective and contextual and therefore can be difficult for the most skilled humans, let alone computer systems.[26]

Proportionality operates only to protect civilians and civilian objects. Where there is no danger of collateral damage, the principle is not implicated. Similarly, proportionality is read to apply to loss of life, injury, and damage to civilian objects and would not thus extend to prohibit attacks that harass or inconvenience. It is equally important to consider the principle does not require an equitable balancing between military advantage and collateral damage; rather, an attack would violate this section only where the collateral damage is "excessive" relative to the "concrete and direct military advantage anticipated."[27]

In this context "concrete and direct" indicates the military advantage should be "substantial and relatively close" to the attack.[28] Computer systems (autonomous or conventional) are especially suited for this analysis as they can process large volumes of data relevant to a proportionality analysis, including the nature and destructive effects of various weapon systems, the composition and durability of buildings near the target, and the probability of civilian presence based on historical data. Thus, the collateral damage aspect is unlikely to cause significant issues for an AEW.

Determining military advantage, however, is particularly challenging for AEWs because the evaluation does not lend itself to a mathematically precise calculation. Military advantage must be calculated "in the circumstances ruling at the time."[29] This calculation requires an understanding of the military value of the target, including the contribution the item is making to the enemy in the circumstances of the time and the benefit that will accrue from its neutralization or damage.

Where the circumstances are dynamic, the challenges for an AEW becomes more acute. Consider a hypothetical battle involving three enemy tank battalions (A, B, and C), each with fifty-eight tanks. Before the engagement a friendly forces commander will develop an operational framework, which is a mechanism to frame their "concept of operations in time, space, purpose, and resources."[30] One operational framework methodology is to designate primary and secondary efforts.[31] In this example, the commander designates the destruction of Battalion A as the primary effort, and the destruction of Battalions B and C as supporting efforts. Target tanks in enemy Battalion A would then have a greater military advantage than tanks in B and C. The AEWs participating in the battle (AEW A, AEW B, and AEW C) would be programmed with the value of tanks in each battalion. This example assumes individual tanks in each battalion are fungible and would carry the same military advantage value as another tank but for the commander's designation to the contrary. Tanks will be destroyed as the battle progresses. Consequentially, the military advantage of a single tank would increase as the overall number of tanks decreases. How then, could AEW A, which is targeting Battalion A, know that the number of tanks in Battalion B have been decreased, thus increasing the relative value of each tank in Battalion A?

Proportionality is unquestionably a potential challenge for the lawful operation of autonomous weapons, particularly in uncertain environments or in cases where the systems are deployed for long periods during which the military advantage is likely to change. Lawful use of autonomous systems in such complex situations would require careful consideration of how systems would account for changes in the military advantage.

Persons conducting attacks with autonomous weapon systems must take feasible precautions to reduce the risk of harm to civilians and other protected persons and objects.[32] For states that are party to Additional Protocol I, this requirement appears in Article 57, which requires "constant care" to be taken to "spare the civilian population, civilians and civilian objects."[33] The additional protocol requirement applies to "those who plan or decide upon an attack," including commanders who make the decision to employ a weapon system on the battlefield and those staff officers "who plan the employment of the weapon system."[34]

"Constant care" is not defined, but by its plain meaning, it creates something more than a onetime obligation. That is to say, it would be insufficient to take constant care when the weapon is deployed but ignore the weapon as it loiters for months. Article 57(2) further requires that those who "plan or decide upon an attack . . . do everything feasible to verify that the objectives to be attacked are neither civilians nor civilian objects and are not subject to special protections but are military objectives."[35] Here, what is "feasible" should be a "matter of common sense and good faith."[36]

As discussed in the context of distinction and proportionality, autonomy has the potential to allow the activation of a weapon system long before targets are engaged. A prolonged engagement raises the question, When should precautions be taken in attack? When the system is deployed, when it is activated, when it is about to engage, or throughout the process? Precautions in attack are continuous in nature and run from the activation of the system to the engagement.[37] Technology has the potential to enhance these requirements. Thus, if a cruise missile has a video feed and the ability to abort, the operator would be obligated to monitor the feed and abort the missile should the proportionality calculation change significantly. Autonomy then raises the possibility that a system could be sophisticated enough to take continual precautions in attack. If AEWs possessed such a capability, a commander could rely on the system if he or she were confident the system could conduct the precautions analysis with reasonable certainty.

In sum, the requirements for precautions in attack are continuing obligations that affix to commanders and planners and all others who have the requisite information and ability to cancel or suspend an attack if necessary. Autonomy creates additional complexities in that the autonomous weapon system itself may possess the capability to conduct the feasibility analysis. There is nothing legally objectionable with this possibility, assuming the system is of sufficient sophistication that the commander employing the system is reasonably certain the system will comply with the obligations to take feasible precautions in the attack.

Conclusion

Autonomy will undoubtedly have an enormous impact on the conduct of hostilities. The newness and inherent complexity of the technology underlying autonomy creates a great deal of uncertainty about how the law of armed conflict applies to autonomy. As with any weapon system, the employment of autonomous weapon systems requires an understanding of the system and ability to control the system. The nature and reliability of the system's operation is informed through the weapon testing process. Effectively testing AEWs requires sophisticated, and possibly novel, means of testing. Tests must be designed to replicate the environment in which the system is sought to be used, and weapon reviews should reflect the scope of the testing protocols.

It is clear that the law of armed conflict applies and provides an effective normative framework to ensure the lawful employment of autonomous weapons. It is equally clear that not all autonomous weapons are the same. Some systems will be lawful and others will not. Indeed, a given system might be lawfully employed in one circumstance, but not another. Simply put, some systems employing autonomous technologies will be lawful in some circumstances, while others will not. In all circumstances, development and use of AEWs should carefully consider the uniqueness of the technology and the novel ways in which this technology affects the function of the weapon system.

Notes

1. For the argument for preemptive prohibition, see, e.g., Human Rights Watch, *Losing Humanity: The Case against Killer Robots* (New York: Human Rights Watch, 2012). For the argument that current legal norms are adequate, see, e.g., K. Anderson and M. Waxman, "Law and Ethics for Autonomous Weapon Systems: Why a Ban Won't Work and How the Laws of War Can" (Washington College of Law Research Paper No. 2013-11, American University, 2013).
2. Additional Protocol I to the Geneva Conventions (1977), art. 35. Hereafter cited as AP I.
3. Y. Sandoz, C. Swinarski, and B. Zimmermann, *Commentary on the Additional Protocols of 8 June 1977 to the Geneva Conventions of 12 August 1949* (Geneva: International Committee for the Red Cross, 1987), para. 1469. See also *U.S. Department of Defense Law of War Manual* (Washington, DC: Government Printing Office, 2016), para. 6.2.2.
4. *U.S. Department of Defense Law of War Manual*, chap. 6.

5. AP I, art. 35(2), 51(4)(b), 51(4)(c).
6. A. Backstrom and I. Henderson, "New Capabilities in Warfare: An Overview of Contemporary Technological Developments and the Associated Legal and Engineering Issues in Article 36 Weapons Reviews," *International Review of the Red Cross* 94 (2012): 484.
7. SAS, "Machine Learning: What It Is and Why It Matters," http://www.sas.com/it_it/insights/analytics/machine-learning.html.
8. J. Brownlee, "A Tour of Machine Learning Algorithms," *Machine Learning Mastery* (blog), November 25, 2013, http://machinelearningmastery.com/a-tour-of-machine-learning-algorithms/.
9. AP I, art. 57(2)(a)(1). The article requires the attacker to "do everything feasible to verify that the objectives to be attacked are neither civilian nor civilian objects and are not subject to special protection but are military objectives."
10. Geneva Convention No. IV Respecting the Laws and Customs of War on Land, art. 1, Oct. 18, 1907, 36 Stat. 2227, T.S. No. 539.
11. AP I, art. 51(3).
12. M. N. Schmitt, "The Interpretive Guidance on the Notion of Direct Participation in Hostilities: A Critical Analysis," *Harvard National Security Journal* 1 (2010): 36.
13. N. Melzer, *Interpretive Guidance on the Notion of Direct Participation in Hostilities* (Geneva: International Committee for the Red Cross, 2009), 65.
14. Schmitt, "Interpretive Guidance," 37, citing Y. Dinstein, "Distinction and the Loss of Civilian Protection in Armed Conflict," in *International Law Studies* 84 (2008): 189–90.
15. *U.S. Department of Defense Law of War Manual*, para. 5.9.4.
16. AP I, art. 52(1).
17. AP I, art. 52(2).
18. M. Bothe, K. J. Partsch, and W. A. Solf, *New Rules for Victims of Armed Conflicts* (Leiden: Brill, 1982), 324. See also *U.S. Department of Defense Law of War Manual*.
19. Y. Dinstein, *The Conduct of Hostilities under the Law of International Armed Conflict*, 2nd ed. (Cambridge: Cambridge University Press, 2010), 96.
20. Sandoz, Swinarski, and Zimmermann, *Commentary*, para. 2021. "Clearly, there are objects which by their nature have no military function but which, by virtue of their location, make an effective contribution to military action."
21. Sandoz, Swinarski, and Zimmermann, *Commentary*, para. 2022. "The criterion of 'purpose' is concerned with the intended future use of an object, while that of 'use' is concerned with its present function."
22. *U.S. Department of Defense Law of War Manual*, para. 5.7.6.1.
23. *U.S. Department of Defense Law of War Manual*, para. 5.7.6.1.
24. J. S. Thurnher, "Means and Methods of the Future: Autonomous Systems," in *Targeting: The Challenges of Modern Warfare*, ed. P. A. L. Ducheine, M. N. Schmitt, and F. P. B. Osinga (The Hague, Netherlands: Asser Press, 2016), 188. See also M. Sassóli, "Autonomous Weapons and International Humanitarian Law: Advantages, Open Technical Questions and Legal Issues to Be Clarified," *International Law Studies* 90 (2014): 320. "If it is technically not feasible to respect certain requirements of IHL [international humanitarian law] with autonomous weapons, this is not a sufficient reason for abandoning those requirements. The use of autonomous weapons in such cases is simply unlawful."

25. AP I, art. 57 2(a)(iii). See also art. 51(5)(b): "an attack which may be expected to cause incidental loss of civilian life, injury to civilians, damage to civilian objects, or a combination thereof, which would be excessive in relation to the concrete and direct military advantage anticipated."

26. Thurnher, "Means and Methods," 188.

27. AP I, art. 57 2(a)(iii).

28. Sandoz, Swinarski, and Zimmermann, *Commentary*, para. 2209.

29. AP I, art. 52(2).

30. Department of the Army, *Unified Land Operations*, Army Doctrine Publication 3-0 (Washington, DC: Department of the Army, October 2011), para. 47.

31. Department of the Army, paras. 58–60.

32. *U.S. Department of Defense Law of War Manual*, para. 5.1.1.

33. AP I, art. 57(1).

34. AP I, art. 57(2)(a)(1); Bothe, Partsch, and Solf, *New Rules for Victims*, 362. "[Article 57] imposes three distinct duties on commanders who decide upon attacks and staff officers who plan an attack."

35. AP I, art. 57(2)(a)(i).

36. Sandoz, Swinarski, and Zimmermann, *Commentary*, para. 2198.

37. Bothe, Partsch, and Solf, *New Rules for Victims*, 363.

10

Lethal Autonomous Systems and the Plight of the Noncombatant

Ron Arkin

It seems a safe assumption, unfortunately, that humanity will persist in conducting warfare, as evidenced over all recorded history. New technology has historically made killing more efficient, for example, with the invention of the longbow, artillery, armored vehicles, aircraft carriers, or nuclear weapons. Many think that each of these new technologies has produced a revolution in military affairs (RMA), as each has fundamentally changed the ways in which war is waged. Many now consider robotics technology a potentially new RMA, especially as we move toward more and more autonomous systems on the battlefield.[1]

Robotic systems are now widely present on the modern battlefield, providing intelligence gathering, surveillance, reconnaissance, target acquisition, designation, and engagement capabilities. Limited autonomy is also present or under development in many systems as well, ranging from the Phalanx system "capable of autonomously

Small portions of this essay appeared earlier in a Viewpoint article by the author appearing in the *Journal of Industrial Robots* 38, no. 5 (2011), and in a more comprehensive treatment of the subject in the author's book *Governing Lethal Behavior in Autonomous Robots* (Boca Raton, FL: CRC Press, 2009) and are included with permission. This article first appeared in *AISB Quarterly*, no. 137 (July 2013) and is reproduced with permission.

performing its own search, detect, evaluation, track, engage and kill assessment functions" to fire-and-forget munitions, loitering torpedoes, and intelligent antisubmarine or antitank mines, among numerous other examples.[2] Continued advances in autonomy will result in changes involving tactics and precision and perhaps, if done correctly, a reduction in atrocities as outlined in research conducted at the Georgia Tech Mobile Robot Laboratory (GT-MRL).[3] This chapter asserts that it may be possible to ultimately create intelligent autonomous robotic military systems that are capable of reducing civilian casualties and property damage when compared to the performance of human warfighters. Thus, some contend that calling for an outright ban on this technology, as groups are already doing, is premature.[4] Nonetheless, if this technology is to be deployed, then restricted, careful and graded introduction into the battlefield of lethal autonomous systems must be standard policy as opposed to haphazard deployments, which I believe is consistent with existing international humanitarian law (IHL).

Multiple potential benefits of intelligent war machines have already been declared by the military, including a reduction in friendly casualties, force multiplication, expansion of the battlespace, extension of the warfighter's reach, the ability to respond faster given the pressure of an ever-increasing battlefield tempo, and greater precision due to persistent stare (i.e., constant video surveillance that enables more time for decision making and more eyes on a target). These benefits indicate the inevitability of development and deployment of lethal autonomous systems from a military efficiency and economic standpoint, unless limited by IHL.

It must be noted that past and present trends in human behavior on the battlefield regarding adhering to legal and ethical requirements are questionable at best. Unfortunately, humanity has a rather dismal record in ethical behavior on the battlefield. Potential explanations for the persistence of war crimes include high friendly losses leading to a tendency to seek revenge; high turnover in the chain of command leading to weakened leadership; dehumanization of the enemy through the use of derogatory names and epithets; poorly trained or inexperienced troops; no clearly defined enemy; unclear orders that may be interpreted incorrectly as unlawful; youth and immaturity of troops; external pressure, for example, for a need to produce a high enemy body count; and pleasure from the power of killing or an overwhelming sense of frustration.[5] There is clear room for improvement, and autonomous systems may help address some of these problems.

Robotics technology, suitably deployed, may assist with the plight of the innocent noncombatant caught on the battlefield. If used without suitable precautions, however, it could potentially exacerbate the already existing violations by human soldiers. While I have the utmost respect for our young men and women warfighters, they are placed in conditions in modern warfare under which no human being was ever designed to function. In such a context, expecting a strict adherence to the laws of war (LOW) seems unreasonable and unattainable by a significant number of soldiers.[6] Battlefield atrocities have been present since the beginnings of warfare, and despite the introduction of IHL over the last 150 years or so, these tendencies persist and are well documented, even more so in the days of CNN and the Internet.[7] According to Slim, "Armies, armed groups, political and religious movements have been killing civilians since time immemorial."[8] Wrote Grossman, "Atrocity . . . is the most repulsive aspect of war, and that which resides within man and permits him to perform these acts is the most repulsive aspect of mankind."[9] The dangers of abuse of unmanned robotic systems, such as the Predator and Reaper drones, in war are well documented; abuse occurs even when a human operator is directly in charge.[10]

Given this, questions then arise regarding if and how these new robotic systems can conform as well as, or better than, our soldiers with respect to adherence to the existing IHL. If achievable, this adherence to existing law could result in a reduction in collateral damage (i.e., noncombatant casualties and damage to civilian property), which translates into saving innocent lives. If achievable, this could result in a moral requirement necessitating the use of these systems. Research conducted in our laboratory focuses on this issue directly from a design perspective.[11] No claim is made that our research provides a fieldable solution to the problem—far from it. Rather these are baby steps toward achieving such a goal, including the development of a prototype proof-of-concept system tested in simulation. Indeed, there may be far better approaches than the one we currently employ if the research community can focus on the plight of the noncombatant and the way technology may possibly ameliorate the situation.

As robots are already faster, stronger, and in certain cases (e.g., Deep Blue, Watson), smarter than humans, is it really that difficult to believe they will be able to ultimately treat us more humanely on the battlefield than we do each other, given the persistent existence of atrocious behaviors by a significant subset of human warfighters?[12]

Why Technology Can Lead to a
Reduction in Casualties on the Battlefield

Is there any cause for optimism that this form of technology can lead to a reduction in noncombatant deaths and casualties? I believe so, for the following reasons:

Robotic systems can act conservatively, that is, they do not need to protect themselves in cases of low certainty of target identification. Autonomous armed robotic vehicles do not need to have self-preservation as a foremost drive, if they need it at all. They can be used in a self-sacrificing manner if needed and appropriate without reservation by a commanding officer. There is no need for a "shoot first, ask questions later" approach, but rather a "first do no harm" strategy can be used instead. Robotic systems can truly assume risk on behalf of the noncombatant, something that soldiers are schooled in, but that some have difficulty achieving in practice.

Eventually, humans will develop and use a broad range of robotic sensors better equipped for battlefield observations than anything we currently possess. This technology includes ongoing advances in electro-optics, synthetic aperture or wall-penetrating radars, acoustics, and seismic sensing, to name but a few. There is reason to believe in the future that robotic systems will be able to pierce the fog of war more effectively than humans ever could.

Unmanned robotic systems can be designed without emotions that cloud judgment or result in anger and frustration with ongoing battlefield events. According to Walzer, "fear and hysteria are always

latent in combat, often real, and they press us toward fearful measures and criminal behavior."[13] Autonomous agents need not suffer
similarly.

Avoidance of the human psychological problem of "scenario ful-
filment" is possible. This phenomenon leads to distortion or neglect
of contradictory information in stressful situations, in which humans
use new incoming information in ways that only fit their preexisting
belief patterns. Robots need not be vulnerable to such patterns of
premature cognitive closure. Such failings are believed to have led to
the downing of an Iranian airliner by USS *Vincennes* in 1988.[14] Intelligent electronic systems can integrate more information from more
sources far faster before responding with lethal force than a human
possibly could in real time. These data can arise from multiple remote
sensors and intelligence (including human) sources, as part of the
Army's network-centric warfare concept and the concurrent development of the Global Information Grid. "Military systems (including weapons) now on the horizon will be too fast, too small, too
numerous and will create an environment too complex for humans
to direct," wrote Adams.[15]

A team of human soldiers and autonomous systems combined as an
organic asset has the potential to independently and objectively monitor ethical behavior on the battlefield by all parties, providing evidence
and reporting infractions that might be observed. This presence alone
might possibly lead to a reduction in human ethical infractions.

Addressing Some of the Counterarguments

But there are many counterarguments as well. These include the challenge of establishing responsibility for war crimes involving autonomous weaponry, the potential lowering of the threshold for entry into
war, the military's possible reluctance to give robots the right to refuse
an order, effects on squad cohesion, the winning of hearts and minds,
cybersecurity, proliferation, and mission creep.

I believe there are good answers to these concerns and discuss
them elsewhere in my writings.[16] If the baseline criterion becomes
outperforming humans on the battlefield with respect to adherence
to IHL (without mission performance erosion), I consider this to

be ultimately attainable, especially under situational conditions in which bounded morality (narrow, highly situation-specific conditions) applies, but not soon and not easily.[17] The full moral faculties of humans need not be reproduced to attain to this standard. Profound technological challenges, such as effective in situ target discrimination and recognition of the status of those otherwise hors de combat, among many others, have yet to be resolved. But if a warfighting robot can eventually exceed human performance with respect to IHL adherence, that then equates to a saving of noncombatant lives and thus is a humanitarian effort. Indeed if this is achievable, there may even exist a moral imperative for the robot's use, owing to a resulting reduction in collateral damage, similar to the moral imperative Human Rights Watch has stated with respect to the use of precision-guided munitions in urban settings.[18] This position seems contradictory to the organization's call for an outright ban on lethal autonomous robots, a call it made before it determined via research if indeed better protection for noncombatants could be afforded.[19]

Let us not stifle research in the area or accede to the fears that Hollywood and science fiction in general foist on us. Merely stating these systems cannot be created to perform properly and ethically does not make it true. If that were so, we would not have supersonic aircraft, space stations, submarines, self-driving cars, and the like. I see no fundamental scientific barriers to the creation of intelligent robotic systems that can outperform humans with respect to moral behavior. The use and deployment of ethical autonomous robotic systems is not a short-term goal for a current conflict, typically a counterinsurgency operation, but rather will take considerable time and effort to realize in the context of interstate warfare and situational context involving bounded morality.

A Plea for the Noncombatant

How can we meaningfully reduce human atrocities on the modern battlefield? Why is there persistent failure and perennial commission of war crimes despite efforts to eliminate them through legislation and advances in training? Can technology help solve this problem?

I believe that simply being human is the weakest point in the kill chain, that is, our biology works against us in complying with IHL. Also the oft-repeated statement that "war is an inherently human endeavor" misses the point. Then atrocities are also an inherently human endeavor, and to eliminate them, we need to perhaps look to other forms of intelligent autonomous decision making in the conduct of war. Battlefield tempo is now outpacing the warfighter's ability to make sound rational decisions in the heat of combat. Nonetheless, I must state the obvious: peace is unequivocally preferable to warfare in all cases, so this argument applies only when human restraint fails once again, leading us back to the battlefield.

While we must not let fear and ignorance rule our decisions regarding policy toward these new weapons systems, we nonetheless must proceed cautiously and judiciously. It is true that this emerging technology can lead us into many different futures, some dystopian. It is crucially important that we not rush headlong into the design, development, and deployment of these systems without thoroughly examining their consequences on all parties: friendly forces, enemy combatants, civilians, and society in general. This can be done only through reasoned discussion of the issues associated with this new technology. Toward that end, I support the call for a moratorium to ensure that such technology meets international standards before being considered for deployment as exemplified by the 2013 report from the United Nations Special Rapporteur on Extrajudicial, Summary or Arbitrary Executions.[20] In addition, the U.S. Department of Defense has recently issued a directive restricting the development and deployment of certain classes of lethal robots, which appears tantamount to a quasi-moratorium.[21]

Is it not our responsibility as scientists and citizens to look for effective ways to reduce man's inhumanity to man through technology? Where is this more evident than on the battlefield? Research in ethical military robotics can and should be applied toward achieving this end. The advent of these systems, if done properly, could possibly yield a greater adherence to the laws of war by robotic systems than from using soldiers of flesh and blood alone. While I am not averse to the outright banning of lethal autonomous systems on the battlefield, if these systems were properly inculcated with a moral ability to adhere to the laws of war and rules of engagement, while ensuring that they are used in narrow bounded military situations as adjuncts to human warfighters, I believe they could outperform human soldiers with respect to conformance to IHL. The end product then could be, even though these systems could not ever be expected to be perfectly ethical, a saving of noncombatant lives and property when compared to human warfighters' behavior.

This is obviously a controversial assertion, and I have often stated that the discussion my research engenders on this subject is as important as the research itself. We must continue to examine the development and deployment of lethal autonomous systems in forums such as the United Nations and the International Committee of the Red Cross to ensure that the internationally agreed on standards regarding the way in which war is waged are adhered to as this technology proceeds forward. If we ignore this, we do so at our own peril.

The Way Forward?

It clearly appears that the use of lethality by autonomous systems is inevitable, perhaps unless outlawed by international law—but even then enforcement seems challenging. But as stated earlier, these systems already exist: the Patriot missile system, the Phalanx system on Aegis class cruisers, antitank mines, and fire-and-forget loitering munitions all serve as examples. A call for a ban on these autonomous systems may have as much success as trying to ban artillery, cruise missiles, or aircraft bombing and other forms of standoff weaponry (even the crossbow was banned by Pope Innocent II in 1139).[22] A better strategy perhaps is to try and control their uses and deployments, which existing IHL appears at least at first glance to adequately cover, rather than a call for an outright ban, which seems unenforceable even if enacted.

The horse is out of the barn. Under current IHL, these systems cannot be developed or used until they can demonstrate the capability of adequate distinction and proportionality and show that they do not produce unnecessary suffering, and they must only be used given military necessity. Outside those bounds any individuals responsible should be held accountable for violations of IHL, whether they are scientists, industrialists, policymakers, commanders, or soldiers. As these systems do not possess moral agency, the question of responsibility becomes equated to other classes of weapon systems, and a human must always ultimately bear responsibility for their use.[23] Until it can be shown that the existing IHL is inadequate to cover this RMA, only then should such action be taken to restructure or expand the law. This may be the case, but unfounded pathos-driven arguments based on horror and Hollywood in the face of potential reductions of civilian casualties seem at best counterproductive. These systems counterintuitively could make warfare safer in the long run to the innocents in the battlespace if coupled with the use of bounded morality, narrow situational use, and careful graded introduction.

Let it be restated that I am not opposed to the removal of lethal autonomous systems from the battlefield if international society so deems it fit, but I think that this technology can actually foster humanitarian treatment of noncombatants if done correctly. I have argued to those that call for a ban, they would be better served by a call for a moratorium, but that is even hard to envision unless these systems can be shown to be in clear violation of the LOW. It is not clear how one can bring the necessary people to the table for discussion starting from a position for a ban derived from pure fear and pathos.

For those familiar with the Martens clause in IHL, a case could be made that these robotic systems potentially "violate the dictates of the public conscience."[24] But until IHL lawyers agree on what that means, this seems a difficult course. I do believe, however, that we can aid the plight of noncombatants through the judicious deployment of these robotic systems, if done carefully and thoughtfully, particularly in those combat situations where warfighters have a greater tendency or opportunity to stray outside IHL. But a careful examination of the use of these systems must be undertaken now to guide their development and deployment, which many of us believe is inevitable given the ever-increasing tempo of the battlefield as a result of ongoing technological advances. It is unacceptable to be "one war behind" in the formulation of law and policy regarding this RMA that is already well under way. The status quo with respect to human battlefield atrocities is unacceptable and emerging technology in its manifold forms must be used to ameliorate the plight of the noncombatant.

Notes

1. We do not use autonomy in the sense that a philosopher does, i.e., possessing free will and moral agency. Rather we use in this context a roboticist's definition: the ability to designate and engage a target without additional human intervention after having been tasked to do so.
2. U.S. Navy, "MK 15 Phalanx Close-in Weapons Systems," U.S. Navy Fact File, accessed July 23, 2013, http://www.navy.mil/navydata/fact_display.asp?cid=2100& tid=487&ct=2.
3. R. C. Arkin, *Governing Lethal Behavior in Autonomous Robots* (Boca Raton, FL: CRC Press, 2009).
4. Notably, Human Rights Watch, International Committee on Robot Arms Control (ICRAC), and Article 36 of 1977 Additional Protocol I to the Geneva Conventions of 1949.
5. B. Bill, ed., *Law of War Workshop Deskbook* (Charlottesville, VA: International and Operational Law Department, Judge Advocate General's School, June 2000); S. Danyluk, "Preventing Atrocities," *Marine Corps Gazette* 8, no. 4 (June 2000): 36–38; W. H. Parks, "Crimes in Hostilities: Part I," *Marine Corps Gazette* 60, no. 8 (August 1976): 56–81; W. H. Parks, "Crimes in Hostilities: Conclusion," *Marine Corps Gazette* 60, no. 9 (September 1976): 121–30; H. Slim, *Killing Civilians: Method, Madness, and Morality in War* (New York: Columbia University Press, 2008).
6. Surgeon General's Office, Mental Health Advisory Team (MHAT) IV Operation Iraqi Freedom 05-07, Final Report, November 17, 2006.
7. For a more detailed description of these abhorrent tendencies of humanity discussed in this context, see R. C. Arkin, "The Case for Ethical Autonomy in Unmanned Systems," *Journal of Military Ethics* 9, no. 4 (2010): 332–41.
8. Slim, *Killing Civilians*, 3.
9. D. Grossman, *On Killing: The Psychological Cost of Learning to Kill in War and Society* (Boston: Little, Brown, 1995), 229.
10. J. Adams, "US Defends Unmanned Drone Attacks after Harsh UN Report," *Christian Science Monitor*, June 5, 2010; D. Filkins, "Operators of Drones Are Faulted in Afghan Deaths," *New York Times*, May 29, 2010; R. Sullivan, "Drone Crew Blamed in Afghan Civilian Deaths," Associated Press, May 5, 2010.
11. For more information see Arkin, *Governing Lethal Behavior*.
12. IBM Research, https://www.research.ibm.com/deepqa/deepblue.shtml.
13. M. Walzer, *Just and Unjust Wars: A Moral Argument with Historical Illustrations*, 4th ed. (New York: Basic Books, 2006).
14. S. Sagan, "Rules of Engagement," in *Avoiding War: Problems of Crisis Management*, ed. A. George (Boulder, CO: Westview Press, 1991).
15. T. Adams, "Future Warfare and the Decline of Human Decisionmaking," *Parameters*, Winter 2001–2, 57–71.

16. E.g., Arkin, *Governing Lethal Behavior.*

17. W. Wallach and C. Allen, *Moral Machines: Teaching Robots Right from Wrong* (Oxford: Oxford University Press, 2010).

18. Human Rights Watch, "International Humanitarian Law Issues in the Possible U.S. Invasion of Iraq," *Lancet*, February 20, 2003.

19. Human Rights Watch, *Losing Humanity: The Case against Killer Robots* (New York: Human Rights Watch, 2012).

20. Christof Heyns, Report of the Special Rapporteur on Extrajudicial, Summary or Arbitrary Executions, UN Human Rights Council, 23rd Session, April 9, 2013.

21. U.S. Department of Defense, "Autonomy in Weapons Systems," Directive Number 3000.09, November 21, 2012.

22. Royal United Services Institute for Defence and Security Studies, "The Ethics and Legal Implications of Unmanned Vehicles for Defence and Security Purposes" (workshop, February 27, 2008), accessed May 12, 2013, http://www.rusi.org/events/ref:E47385996DA7D3.

23. R. C. Arkin, "The Robot Didn't Do It" (position paper for the Workshop on Anticipatory Ethics, Responsibility, and Artificial Agents, Charlottesville, VA, January 2013).

24. The clause reads, "Until a more complete code of the laws of war is issued, the High Contracting Parties think it right to declare that in cases not included in the Regulations adopted by them, populations and belligerents remain under the protection and empire of the principles of international law, as they result from the usages established between civilized nations, from the laws of humanity and the requirements of the public conscience." (Available at the ICRC website, https://www.icrc.org/eng/resources/documents/article/other/57jnhy.htm).

11

The Ethics of Remote Weapons

Reapers, Red Herrings, and a Real Problem | *Joe Chapa*

Introduction

Finding the right answers begins with asking the right questions. The debate over the ethics of drones rages on, but few of its participants are actually discussing the ethics of drones at all. We should begin with the age-old (in fact, Aristotelian) taxonomy of genus, species, and differentia.[1] If we are to know about a set of things (a species), we must know to what group that set belongs (its genus) and what characteristic or characteristics separate that set of things from the other sets within the genus (its differentia). To have a meaningful discussion about precision-guided munitions, for example, we would have to recognize that precision-guided munitions (species) are munitions (genus) that are precision-guided (differentia). Likewise, if we are to say anything meaningful at all about these drones, we are going to have to say something about what kind of thing they are and what makes them different.

Colloquially, we use the word "drone" to refer to unmanned or remotely piloted *aircraft*. I once entertained a question from a naive student who asked, "Is there any interest in developing drones in space?" I responded (more sarcastically than I had intended), "You mean . . . satellites?" Unmanned technological systems have been around for almost a century and in space for half of one, and until recently, no one seemed all that bothered by it. So, when people discuss the ethics of drones, I must assume that they are talking, at least primarily, about airplanes. But they must not be talking about *all* airplanes. They must be talking about the species "drone," which is a member of the genus "airplane," whose differentia is "unmanned" or "remotely piloted." All this is to say, if we are to have a meaningful discussion on this topic, we must begin by recognizing that we have but two options: Either we must talk about things that are unique to this species of aircraft, or if we talk about something else, we must recognize that, whatever we might want to call them, our discussion is not about drones at all, but probably about the whole genus of airplanes. This may seem obvious in principle, but the admonition I offer here is violated over and over again in print. These faulty arguments distract from genuine discussions about the ethics of remote and autonomous weapon systems and ought to be identified and dismissed as red herrings. The following paragraphs intend to do just that.

Before looking at particular specious arguments, a note about the term "drones" may be of some use. The U.S. Air Force and some of its sister services have long held that the term "drone" is inadequate to describe the weapon systems in question (the Air Force's MQ-1 Predator and MQ-9 Reaper, the Navy's X-47 and MQ-8 Fire Scout, and the Army's MQ-1C Gray Eagle, to name a few). Though it has become the standard term outside the Department of Defense, we can quickly see that filtered through the structure of genus, species, and differentia, "drone" is unhelpful. If what is meant by "drone" is "an aircraft that does not have a pilot in it," then the term "drone" indeed describes these weapon systems. But so does "airplane." So does "system." So does "thing." The problem with these terms is that they represent genera to which the species belongs but not the species itself. They are simply too broad to refer only to those systems to which we want to refer. The drone category includes everything from the $100 million RQ-4 Global Hawk to the $30 toy quad-copter. The term is so broad that it is unclear what "the ethics of drones" can even mean.

Solving this problem is not simple as has been demonstrated by the ongoing name game that led the U.S. Air Force from "unmanned aerial vehicle" (which failed to incorporate the satellite architecture) to "unmanned aircraft system" (which failed to include the pilot and crew) to "remotely piloted aircraft" (which failed to distinguish between kinetic and nonkinetic capable systems) to "persistent attack aircraft" (which failed to acknowledge the intelligence, surveillance, and reconnaissance missions sets) and finally to "persistent attack and reconnaissance aircraft" (which, though appropriately descriptive, evades a helpful acronym).[2] In this chapter I will refer to the armed, remotely piloted aircraft on which the ethical debate seems to focus as persistent attack and reconnaissance (PAR) aircraft.

One may recognize that "persistent attack and reconnaissance aircraft" makes no reference to "remoteness." This is intentional. LTC Dave Blair has made the case that remotely piloted aircraft are the only set of aircraft in the Department of Defense that are categorized by control mechanism.[3] No one suggests that an F-16 pilot and a C-17 pilot have a great deal in common simply because both aircraft have fly-by-wire control mechanisms. Instead, we group aircraft by mission type (e.g., F-fighter, B-bomber, E-electronic). The move to the term "persistent attack and reconnaissance aircraft" is intended to group aircraft by operational mission sets and as a result is inclusive not only of remote PAR aircraft like the MQ-1 and MQ-9, but also the AC-130 and possible future long-endurance, traditionally piloted weapon systems.

With these distinctions in view, we turn to the red herrings.

Red Herrings
Questions of Precision
Some arguments begin by asserting that the problem with drones is that they are imprecise.[4] There are a number of problems with this claim, not least among them that the claim is nearly always bolstered by poor analysis of available data.[5] One such problem is that the U.S. Air Force's remotely piloted aircraft that have received the lion's share of the attention in print (the MQ-1 Predator and MQ-9 Reaper) carry the same munitions and deliver them in the same ways as aircraft that precede them by decades. The Predator carries the AGM-114 Hellfire laser-guided missile.[6] The Reaper carries the same Hellfire as well as a series of precision-guided 500-pound bombs, including

the GBU-12 laser-guided bomb and the GBU-38 Global Positioning System / inertial navigation system (GPS/INS) guided joint direct attack munition (JDAM),[7] and it may perhaps soon include the best-of-both-worlds GBU-54 laser JDAM.[8] All of these weapons have been tested, developed, and carried operationally by manned weapon systems (including, for example, the Army's AH-64 Apache and the Air Force's F-15E Strike Eagle[9]) long before they were carried by Predator and Reaper aircraft. These are members of the most precise family of munitions in the hundred-year history of aerial bombardment. But even if they were not, if one has an ethical problem with the precision of these weapon systems, one has not successfully identified the differentia of remote PAR aircraft. One's ethical problem is not with the Predator, Reaper, or Fire Scout, but with precision-guided munitions in general. Thus, the conversation over the ethical implications of this purported absence of precision is a discussion about modern airpower broadly speaking and is not about remote or autonomous weapons.

There is, however, a more nuanced concern over precision that turns on what is meant by "precise." If one means by "precision" the degree to which a weapon hits where it is intended to hit, then the weapons are undoubtedly precise. There are, however, two other possible uses. One might mean by "precision" the degree to which the pilot knows that the person or object under her crosshairs is, in fact, the person or object that she intends to strike. In my view, this use of "precision" does some considerable injustice to the English language. Nevertheless, the concern is a legitimate one.[10] Our brief discussion here must be limited to the following response: If there is a problem with PAR aircraft in terms of this definition of precision, it is not a concern over PAR aircraft but over the intelligence on which PAR aircraft strikes are conducted. The concern would equally apply to an MQ-9 using a GBU-12 and an F-16 using a GBU-12. As a result, it is not a concern over PAR aircraft, but over rules of engagement and airpower policy.

There may be a third definition of "precision" at play that refers to the degree of collateral damage or civilian casualties (CIVCAS) resulting from the weapons' employment. This is another imprecise use of the word "precision." Here too, because the weapons are the same on both traditional and remote PAR aircraft, a concern about CIVCAS is a concern about airpower policy, counterinsurgency, counterterror, U.S. foreign policy, and numerous other conceptual areas. But it is not, strictly speaking, about PAR aircraft.

"Riskless" Warfare

Another common argument suggests that the real problem with remote PAR aircraft is that the crews do not face risk. This argument also fails to isolate the remoteness of the remote pilot. While some see traditionally manned fighter and bomber aircraft as a return to the chivalric days of old in which, as a coauthor of mine has put it, the pilot is "a technical wizard who triumphs over faceless masses of conscript forces through verve and swagger," this romantic vision has not captured the operational realities of twenty-first-century aerial warfare.[11] There have been periods in the history of U.S. airpower in which the casualty rate was higher in aircraft than on the ground, but so far as we can tell, those days have come and gone.[12] In sixteen years of U.S. combat airpower in Afghanistan, Iraq, Libya, and Syria, not a single fighter or bomber pilot has been shot down over enemy territory. One is forced to wonder, if we really must establish a risk-requisite threshold between the "real warriors" and those imposters who fight from a distance, where should we draw that line? In this century it is the infantry soldiers on the ground who absorb the physical risk to self, not the fighter or bomber pilot. Once again we must ensure that we are asking the right questions. Before assuming that there is something wrong with killing at a distance of 7,000 miles, we must first ask whether there is a problem with doing so from an altitude of 20,000 feet. Statistically and historically speaking, the absence of risk criteria applies equally in both cases. In this war even ground support personnel have faced greater physical risk to themselves than have aerial warriors in fighter and bomber aircraft.

Furthermore, many wish to claim that "riskless" pilots of remote PAR aircraft represent a revolution in military affairs (RMA), but this is a shortsighted view. Remote killers were present in the ranks of the U.S. military long before the advent of the Predator and Reaper. There is an argument to be made (indeed many have already made it) that, rather than a revolution, remote PAR aircraft represent merely the next evolution in the distance military technology imposes between oneself and one's enemy.[13] Though the examples throughout military history abound, one particularly interesting evolution took place in the English use of longbows at Agincourt in 1415 to engage the enemy from outside the enemy's effective range. This new weapon allowed peasant archers to engage swashbuckling knights without risk to themselves and shortly thereafter, allowed "groups of peasants [to] triumph over knights [in general], ending the age of feudalism."[14]

This *evolution* in military affairs, in addition to changing the class landscape in fifteenth-century Europe, also generated one of the more ironic turns in military colloquy. The (at the time) improved "D" model of the U.S. Army's AH-64 Apache attack helicopters featured a fire control radar mounted above the rotor; this allowed the helicopter pilots to hide behind tree lines and terrain features exposing just the radar so that they could see without being seen. Like the longbowmen of Agincourt, they could hold the enemy at risk without facing risk themselves.[15] So proud of the system's newfound ability to identify targets without exposing itself to risk, the U.S. Army dubbed this new Apache the "Longbow." The irony continues in that the Apache Longbows carried the Hellfire missile years before the Predator inherited it.[16]

Though the nomenclature was undoubtedly intended to conjure images of death and inferno, the Hellfire's explicit etymology is fairly tame. The weapon has come to be almost universally associated with the Predator and Reaper, but it was originally the *heli*copter-launched *fire*-and-forget weapon—the "Hellfire." Though expedited after September 11, 2001, the decision to arm the Predator with the Hellfire was made earlier that year to provide strategic leaders with a means of striking Osama bin Laden in Afghanistan six months before the al Qaeda attacks on the World Trade Center and Pentagon. But President Bush was not the first to recognize the bin Laden threat. In fact, in December 1998, President Clinton ordered cruise missile strikes against bin Laden's presumed location in Afghanistan and his training camp in Sudan. This attempt on bin Laden's life, though it predated the armed Predator by three years, was carried out by remote warriors of the previous century, firing cruise missiles from offshore naval vessels. Thus, the criticism that remote PAR aircraft are unethical because they fight from a distance cannot gain much ground without implicating cruise missiles, attack helicopters, antitank Hellfire missiles, and Henry V's longbowmen of Agincourt.

As early as World War II, the U.S. Army Air Forces (USAAF) and U.S. Navy experimented with B-17s and B-24s packed with boxes of explosive powder, flown by a single pilot and radio operator who would bail out of the aircraft and remotely control the flying powder kegs into their targets. Though it receives little fanfare in the discussion of remote weapons, this experiment may have had significant, even if unintended, implications for American political developments. President John F. Kennedy's older brother Joseph was killed in one such operation when his aircraft prematurely detonated. The USAAF operation, though wildly unsuccessful, was likely the impetus for GEN Henry "Hap" Arnold's prescient quote, "We have just won a war with a lot of heroes flying around in planes. The next war may be fought by airplanes with no men in them at all. . . . [Tomorrow's aviation] will be different from anything the world has ever seen."[17]

Since the end of World War II, the U.S. military has employed cruise missiles, standoff bombs and missiles, intercontinental ballistic missiles, naval guns, and long-range artillery pieces. Once again, if the claim is that the ethical problem with remote PAR aircraft is that their crews are at some great distance from their weapons' effects, then the criticism is not focused on the right differentia. Such critiques ought not to focus on PAR aircraft in particular, but on standoff weapons in general. I am aware of no such critique in the recent literature.

"Remoteness" and "Autonomy"

Another common criticism regards autonomy. This deserves close attention not because it is a valid concern but because it is grounded in a common misunderstanding and that misunderstanding warrants careful correction. It is unwise to consider autonomy as a binary feature. Rather than saying that one system is autonomous while another is not, it is much more accurate to say that one system is more or less autonomous than another. One would be right to say that twenty-first-century commercial airliners are more autonomous than were their twentieth-century predecessors. But it would be odd to call them simply "autonomous" because, after all, a pilot and copilot sit in the cockpit on every flight. Modern military aircraft, like their civilian counterparts, are equipped with flight management systems that can fly the aircraft throughout the route of flight (e.g., the C-17 Globe-master III) and some even have auto-land capabilities (e.g., the RQ-4 Global Hawk).[18] The U.S. Navy has pushed this technology even further with its X-47B unmanned aircraft system. Not only is the X-47B capable of auto takeoff and land and of preprogrammed flight profiles, but it can also conduct autonomous aerial refueling from a tanker aircraft, a traditionally challenging task among U.S. Air Force and Navy pilots.[19] In the discussion of military ethics, autonomy of the kind common to C-17s, RQ-4s, and X-47Bs is set quite apart from autonomous weapons employment; enter the common misunderstanding.

Perhaps in part owing to less than careful uses of the word "drone," many interested observers believe that the Predator and Reaper not only fly from one point to another on a preprogrammed mission, but also employ weapons autonomously. This is not the case. Every weapon that leaves the rail of an MQ-1 Predator or MQ-9 Reaper does so at the consent to release of the pilot. In fact, unlike for some other semiautonomous weapon systems, for Predator and Reaper missions, the pilot can not only abort the computer's decision to release a weapon, but must initiate the decision to release a weapon. Though space does not permit a thorough investigation, suffice it to say here that we ought to keep remote weapons and autonomous weapons apart as two conceptually distinct categories.[20]

The Psychology of Remote Killing

There is an increasing body of literature that focuses, not on the external or objective ethical analysis of remote PAR strikes, but on the aircraft crews themselves. There are, broadly speaking, two avenues on which to address these questions. The first is grounded in psychology and the second in virtue theory. The psychological questions remain largely unanswered, but there is significant ongoing research in this area. Some of the relevant topics include the causes of post-traumatic stress disorder (PTSD) beyond perceived physical risk to self, operational burnout among remote crews due to shiftwork and other demands, increases in emotional stress resulting from facing hard moral dilemmas, and the psychological distancing (or lack thereof) imposed by physical distance and technological mediation.[21] These are related to the ethical questions in the following ways.

Some arguments against remote weapons suggest that there is something wrong with killing in war while one faces no risk to self.[22] If there are causes for PTSD other than personal *physical* risk to self (and given that there have been PTSD cases resulting from remote PAR operations, there must be), then it may be the case that remote PAR pilots do in fact face some risk—even if that risk is of a different kind (psychological or emotional) than the risks faced by traditional warfighters (physical). In fact, it may be the case that even though traditional warfighters face some psychological risk by killing, the psychological risk (or emotional stress) faced by PAR crews is increased because they are phenomenologically removed from the physical risks of war. Their motivations for killing must be something other than personal self-defense, and therefore, the probability of moral injury may be higher.[23]

Psychological distancing plays a role in the ethical debate insofar as the ethics of killing in war is at least partially grounded in one's approach to one's enemy. If, as many have asserted (without providing evidence for the assertion), remote PAR crews treat their work as a video game,[24] it may render their lethal actions unethical. There has been significant qualitative psychological work to suggest that the premise is false, that is, that PAR aircraft crews are anything but detached.[25] The unfounded accusation nevertheless persists in the literature.

The Martial Virtues

A second line of inquiry into the crews themselves takes a virtue ethics approach. Some have argued that remote warfighters are unable to cultivate long-standing martial virtues such as courage, loyalty, honor, and mercy.[26] On the surface this argument seems compelling: how can a warfighter who is not exposed to risk cultivate courage? On further analysis, though, it is subject to the same set of concerns as some of the psychological arguments. Traditional conceptions of military ethics rely heavily on an Aristotelian virtues-based approach. This view suggests that as soldiers gain experience and grow in their careers, they will face opportunities to cultivate virtue, including the virtue of practical wisdom (or *phronesis*). Having cultivated these virtues, when faced with difficult ethical dilemmas, *phronesis* alongside the other character virtues will be sufficient to guide the soldier to the morally right (or a morally right) decision.

Any argument against remote PAR crews cultivating these kinds of virtues would seem to indict the vast majority of military members. What makes a finance officer able to cultivate martial virtues, or a fighter pilot tens of thousands of feet outside the enemy's weapon engagement zone? Most military members will spend a small percentage of their time engaged in combat operations. The same is true for MQ-1/9 pilots who still deploy to the theater of operations to conduct launch-and-recover (LR) operations.[27] Indeed, may Predator and Reaper crews have conducted base defense operations from a ground control station at Kandahar Air Base, Afghanistan, or Balad Air Base, Iraq, searching for the indirect fire teams lobbing mortars into the base. While other base personnel seek shelter in concrete bunkers, the PAR aircraft crews remain exposed in their ground-based cockpits. Such actions would seem at least as courageous as those of the fighter or bomber pilot in uncontested airspace. Aristotelian virtue cultivation is concerned primarily with the habit patterns of agents, not with discrete actions.

Some have accepted the claim that remote warfighters cannot cultivate the traditionally martial virtues and have responded by proposing that militaries should move away from a virtues-based conception of military ethics. Marcus Schulzke has recently argued that this system is not viable for remote PAR aircraft crews and that because they will not have the opportunities to cultivate these important virtues, the militaries that employ them should transition to a rules-based (or "deontic") system that emphasizes rule following rather than virtue.[28]

This may seem like a viable alternative on paper, but it may make matters worse in practice. The difficulty with such a system is that it assumes the possibility (or plausibility) of generating rules in advance of ethical dilemmas. The fact that warfighters face ethical dilemmas at all suggests an alternative conclusion. Ethical dilemmas ("di" meaning "two") are cases in which there are at least two choices and neither is obviously right (or best). War takes place at the fringes of permissible human activity. War is an activity in which we empower soldiers, not only to take life in self- and other-defense as we do with law enforcement officers, but to go out *intending* to kill other human beings. In day-to-day life, legal requirements often conform to ethical ones. It is wrong to steal a car, and it is illegal to steal a car; wrong to murder and illegal to murder; wrong to commit sexual assault and illegal to commit sexual assault. But because war creates an environment in which intentionally killing one's fellow human is morally permissible, the law is often insufficient to capture the ethical nuances. One can imagine situations in which the morally right thing to do is illegal and in which the legally permissible option is immoral.

I have written elsewhere of a real-world remote PAR aircraft case in which the pilot was directed to carry out a strike against a high-value individual (HVI) while the target's two children were in the field of view and would likely have been killed in the strike.[29] This strike was deemed legal in accordance with discrimination, proportionality, and necessity requirements, but its legality would not have made it any less tragic. The pilot chose, on his own authority, to delay the strike and wait until he could take the shot without holding the children at physical risk. One wonders, what if, rather than using his *phronesis* as an officer and pilot, he was instead asked only to follow a list of rules. Presumably those rules would have been similar to those codified in the laws of war, suggesting that the strike was permissible—even though he knew the children would likely be killed. Would that pilot have worked so hard to reduce risk to the children? Or would he instead have consulted his rulebook, found that the shot was permissible, and engaged the enemy with the children in the field of view without giving it a second thought? Despite arguments to the contrary, remote PAR aircraft crews in particular and warfighters in general are subjected to difficult moral dilemmas with the most severe of consequences. Thus, military commanders, to include aircraft commanders, should be endowed with greater freedom to cultivate and rely on character virtues like *phronesis*, not less.

The Real Problem: Collapsing the Strategic and the Tactical
So is there a problem? If the majority of recent books and articles on the ethics of these weapon systems are consumed by red herrings, is there anything about PAR aircraft we should be wary of? There is at least

one potential problem.[30] The U.S. military has developed a trend over the recent decades in which it buys only two kinds of systems: really cheap and really expensive. The MQ-1 Predator costs $4 million per airplane, and the MQ-9, initially operationally capable (IOC) in 2007, costs $14 million. The F-22 Raptor, which was IOC just two years before, costs $143 million per airplane and the F-35 is $148 million— more than ten times the Reaper cost and more than thirty times the Predator cost.[31] An unintended consequence of this order of magnitude reduction in unit costs has been the massive production and implementation rate of MQ-1s and MQ-9s. While the U.S. Air Force owns only 183 Raptor tails (individual aircraft), it owns 370 Reapers and 600 Predator tails (almost 1,000 in total).[32] It should come as no surprise that an order of magnitude reduction in cost has resulted in an increase of nearly an order of magnitude in quantity.

This acquisitions phenomenon comes into contact with ethical concerns when one recognizes that the Air Force has already produced an unprecedented network of strike-capable intelligence, surveillance, and reconnaissance (ISR) air assets (the nearly 1,000 Predator and Reaper aircraft) and it plans to grow rather than shrink that enterprise.[33] Combatant commanders continue to demand more PAR aircraft, capable of conducting the entire kill chain (find, fix, track, target, engage, and assess) using a single aircraft.[34] To a higher degree than ever before, combatant commanders and strategic leaders have the ability to find a single person in some far off place, track him, target him, and kill him. There may be cause for concern here.

Imagine a Department of Defense with no retention problems, no source selection concerns over the next PAR system, and no attrition concerns over the aircraft we have today. If the PAR enterprise *could* grow unbounded, that is precisely what decision makers would have it do. What does the end state look like? Some ethicists are concerned that such growth would generate a set of circumstances in which the U.S. government could kill anyone it wanted at any time. This is not science fiction, nor is it a doomsday call about falling skies. Instead, it is a recognition that over the last seventeen years, what U.S. strategic decision makers have come to expect is that they can put a terrorist leader's name on a list and he will subsequently be killed in a Hellfire strike.

The ethical concern in a counterterrorism fight like the one the United States has been engaged in, prosecuted by a massive network of PAR aircraft, is that the tactical concerns and the strategic concerns will naturally become conflated. In a traditional war, strategic leaders, including the president, the secretary of defense, and combatant commanders, would craft "a prudent idea or set of ideas for employing the instruments of national power in a synchronized and integrated fashion to achieve theater and multi-national objectives." The subordinate operational-level commanders would "link strategy and tactics by establishing operational objectives needed to achieve the military end states and strategic objectives." Then at the tactical level, commanders and operators would "focus on the ordered arrangement and maneuver of combat elements in relation to each other and enemy to achieve combat objectives."[35] In current U.S. counterterrorism operations, these three levels of war may be flatter than they have ever been.

This ability to discretely target one individual while sparing the rest has profound and unintended consequences on the levels of war. Strategic leaders are sucked into the soda straw view of the tactical. Policymakers who ought to be in the business of managing forests become preoccupied with the felling of individual trees. The picture of President Barack Obama watching the Osama bin Laden raid in real time has become the stuff of history books. Many would have said, and perhaps many still do, that killing Osama bin Laden was a strategic, rather than a tactical goal; but what strategic implications did it bring about in the battlespace? Al Qaeda outlived its founder.

The just war tradition, all the way back to Aristotle (fourth century BC), who allowed for state-sponsored lethality in the name of the better peace, justifies the ugly things combatants do—namely, killing other human beings—because these things are done in the pursuit of the greater good. Just war brings death for the sake of peace. But in the present case, we are left wondering what that greater good might be. The tactical-level trigger puller in the ground control station might have as her objective the targeted killing of a particular terror network operational commander. And if we are to believe the reports that the president and secretary of defense build the "kill lists" on "Terror Tuesdays," then those at the most strategic level of the warfighting and war-planning structure likewise have as their objective the targeted killing of a particular terror network operational commander.[36] The strategic and the tactical have collapsed.

The ethical question that results is grounded in the doctrinal demand that tactical killing serves strategic ends and the just war demand that soldiers kill for the sake of lasting peace. Just warriors, regardless of their domain and their physical distance from their weapons' effects, kill not because they can and certainly not because they want to, but because they *must* in order to achieve higher order objectives. The difficult ethical question that remains is whether any warfighting at all can be justified without a strategic framework that can tie death at the tactical level to the better peace at the strategic level.

There may be good reasons to doubt that twenty-first-century U.S. counterterrorism operations will produce the better peace. If one considers President Bush's Global War on Terror and President Obama's overseas contingency operations to be the same conflict under two different names, then the United States has been fighting the same war since 2001, making this war on interstate terror organizations the longest in U.S. history, spanning nearly seventeen years, two U.S. presidents, and four U.S. presidential terms.[37] *If* a targeted killing campaign against terrorist leaders and fighters can produce the better peace, then the conflation of tactical and strategic aims may be justifiable, but given the decades-long duration of the fight against these enemies, this is a dubious conditional.

Or perhaps this war offers no better peace. Perhaps we face instead perpetual war. If this is the case, then it may also be the case that strategic leaders are morally unjustified in asking tactical-level operators to kill enemy combatants, not because those tactical-level operators have violated individuated principles of just war or the laws of war, but because the precondition for ethically justifiable war in the first place—the pursuit of peace—is absent at the strategic level. Put another way, the just war tradition requirement that military actions be "necessary" forces us to ask: Necessary for what?[38] If they must be necessary to achieve the better peace and U.S. strategy promises no such peace, then it may be the case that *no* military operations—

including everything from the infantry soldier to the Reaper pilot—
can be deemed necessary under such a strategy.

One final possibility is that we are not at war at all. Instead we have
been conducting discrete acts of violence in self-defense against discrete threats. Such acts may be justified, but they also promise unend-
ing violence. This may be our best hope if we have given up hope of
a viable strategy.

This is a deeply troubling proposition, and the solution is not a
simple one. The best solution demands a sound strategy for achieving
lasting peace. For this, we must look not to trigger pullers but to strategic leaders and policymakers. We must look outside the Department
of Defense and the nation's intelligence agencies. If we have learned
anything in the last seventeen years, it is that killing terrorists, though
a necessary condition, is not a sufficient condition for ending terrorism. It is here that questions of ethics and questions of wisdom over-
lap. It may be the case that killing in the absence of a sound strategy
for lasting peace at best only begets more killing and at worst lacks the
moral justification of a traditional war. It may be the case that killing
in war is only morally justified if the strategy is wise. Have we such a
strategy? I do not begin to claim that I have found it. I do not claim to
know how to vanquish cross-border terror networks and achieve the
lasting peace. I only claim that finding the right answers begins with
asking the right questions.

Notes

1. Aristotle, *Nicomachean Ethics*, trans. Terence Irwin (Indianapolis: Hacket, 1999), 23–24.
2. The other branches of service did not follow all the Air Force iterations and continue to use "unmanned aircraft systems."
3. Dave Blair, "A Categorical Error: Rethinking 'Drones' as an Analytical Category
for Security Policy," *Lawfare* (blog), April 24, 2016, https://www.lawfareblog.com/
categorical-error-rethinking-drones-analytical-category-security-policy.
4. C.f., John Kaag and Sarah Kreps, *Drone Warfare* (Cambridge: Polity, 2014), 12;
Matt Schiavenza, "Drones and the Myth of Precision," *The Atlantic*, April 24,
2015, http://www.theatlantic.com/international/archive/2015/04/drones-and-
the-myth-of-precision/391445/; Micah Zenko and Amelia Mae Wolfe, "Drones
Kill More Civilians Than Pilots Do," *Foreign Policy*, April 25, 2016, http://for
eignpolicy.com/2016/04/25/drones-kill-more-civilians-than-pilots-do/; Scott
Shane, "Drone Strikes Statistics Answer Few Questions, and Raise Many," *New*

York Times, July 3, 2016, https://www.nytimes.com/2016/07/04/world/mid dleeast/drone-strike-statistics-answer-few-questions-and-raise-many.html?_r=0; Greg Miller, "Why the White House Claims on Drone Casualties Remain in Doubt," *Washington Post*, July 1, 2016, https://www.washingtonpost.com/world/ national-security/why-the-white-house-claims-on-drone-casualties-remain-in-doubt/2016/07/01/7eb968e8-3c70-11e6-a66f-aa6c1883b6b1_story.html?utm_ term=.d97eba87f595.

5. Steven J. Barela and Avery Plaw, "The Precision of Drones: Problems with the New Data and New Claims," *E-International Relations*, August 23, 2016, http:// www.e-ir.info/2016/08/23/the-precision-of-drones-problems-with-the-new-data-and-new-claims/.

6. U.S. Air Force, "MQ-1B Predator," fact sheet, September 2015, http://www.af.mil/ AboutUs/FactSheets/Display/tabid/224/Article/104469/mq-1b-predator.aspx.

7. U.S. Air Force, "MQ-9 Reaper," fact sheet, September 2015, http://www.af.mil/ AboutUs/FactSheets/Display/tabid/224/Article/104470/mq-9-reaper.aspx.

8. The U.S. State Department recently approved the sale of armed MQ-9 Reapers to the government of Italy. That approval included 156 Hellfire missiles, 30 GBU-12s, and 30 GBU-54s, suggesting a connection between the MQ-9 Reaper and the GBU-54 laser JDAM. Defense Security Cooperation Agency, "Italy—Weaponization of MQ-9s," news release, November 4, 2015, http://www.dsca.mil/ major-arms-sales/italy-weaponization-mq-9s.

9. U.S. Army, "AH-64E Apache Attack Helicopter," November 2014, https://www .army.mil/article/137579; U.S. Air Force, "F-15E Strike Eagle," fact sheet, April 2005, http://www.af.mil/AboutUs/FactSheets/Display/tabid/224/Article/104499/ f-15e-strike-eagle.aspx.

10. John Kaag and Sarah Kreps recognize the danger in conflating factual claims about "precision" (the degree to which the weapon strikes the desired point of impact) and value-laden claims about who ought to be targeted. Though not identical, their distinction is similar to the one I have proposed here, and their discussion may be of value to interested readers. Kaag and Kreps, *Drone Warfare*, 132–35.

11. Joe Chapa and Dave Blair, "The Just Warrior Ethos: A Response to Colonel Riza," *Journal of Military Ethics* 15, no. 3 (December 2016): 170–86.

12. Donald L. Miller, *Masters of the Air: America's Bomber Boys Who Fought the Air War against Nazi Germany* (New York: Simon & Schuster, 2006), 130.

13. C.f., Charles J. Dunlap Jr., "Does Lawfare Need an Apologia?," *Case Western Reserve Journal of International Law* 43, no. 121 (2010): 121–43.

14. David Hastings Dunn, "Drones: Disembodied Aerial Warfare and the Unarticulated Threat," *International Affairs* 89, no. 5 (2013): 1237–46; P. W. Singer, "War of the Machines," *Scientific American* 303, no. 1 (2010): 56–63.

15. Hugh M. Dimmery, "The AH-64D Apache Longbow, Affordable Evolution," Defense Technical Information Center, April 1999, http://www.dtic.mil/dtic/ tr/fulltext/u2/p010314.pdf.

16. Department of Defense, "Army Aviation—Apache Longbow Weight and Communication Issues," NSIAD-98-203, September 1998, https://www.gpo .gov/fdsys/pkg/GAOREPORTS-NSIAD-98-203/html/GAOREPORTS-NSIAD-98-203.htm.

17. Brian T. Stahl, *Blunting the Spear: Why Good People Get Out* (Montgomery, AL: Air University Press, 2015), 75.

18. U.S. Air Force, Instruction 11-2C-17, vol. 3, "C-17 Operations Procedures," November 16, 2011 (incorporating Change 1, March 20, 2015), 73, http://static.e-publishing.af.mil/production/1/af_a3_5/publication/afi11-2c-17v3/afi11-2c-17v3.pdf; Office of the Secretary of Defense, *Unmanned Aerial Vehicles Roadmap: 2000–2025* (Washington, DC: Department of Defense, April 2001), 54.

19. Northrop Grumman, "X-47B UCAS Makes Aviation History . . . Again!" press release, http://www.northropgrumman.com/Capabilities/X47BUCAS/Pages/default.aspx.

20. Examples of existing autonomous weapons include Israel's Iron Dome missile defense system, the Navy's Mk-15 close-in weapon system (CIWS), and South Korea's SGR-1 system, which patrols the demilitarized zone. C.f., Lazar Berman, "Israel's Iron Dome: Why America Is Investing Hundreds of Millions of Dollars," *National Security Outlook*, no. 2 (September 24, 2012), http://www.aei.org/publication/israels-iron-dome-why-america-is-investing-hundreds-of-millions-of-dollars/; Raytheon, "Phalanx Close-In Weapons System," http://www.raytheon.com/capabilities/products/phalanx/; Mark Prigg, "Who Goes There? Samsung Unveils Robot Sentry That Can Kill from Two Miles Away," *Daily Mail Online*, September 15, 2014, accessed January 11, 2017, http://www.dailymail.co.uk/sciencetech/article-2756847/Who-goes-Samsung-reveals-robot-sentry-set-eye-North-Korea.html.

21. Scott Fitzsimmons and Karina Sangha, "Killing in High Definition: Combat Stress among Operators of Remotely Piloted Aircraft" (paper presented at International Studies Association Annual Meeting, San Francisco, April 3–6, 2013); Wayne Chappelle, Kent McDonald, Billy Thompson, and Julie Searengen, "Prevalence of High Emotional Distress and Symptoms of Post-Traumatic Stress Disorder in U.S. Air Force Active Duty Remotely Piloted Aircraft Operators: 2010 USA-FAM Survey Results" (Wright-Patterson AFB, OH: Air Force Research Laboratory, 2012); Markus Christen, Michael Villano, Darcia Narvaez, Jesús Serrano, and Charles R. Crowell, "Measuring the Moral Impact of Operating 'Drones' on Pilots in Combat, Disaster Management and Surveillance," in *Proceedings of the European Conference on Information Systems* (Tel Aviv: European Conference on Information Systems, 2014).

22. C.f., John Kaag and Sarah Kreps, "The Moral Hazard of RPAs," *New York Times*, July 2012; Paul W. Kahn, "The Paradox of Riskless Warfare," *Yale Law School Legal Scholarship Repository* 1, no. 1 (2002): 1–8; Suzy Killmister, "Remote Weaponry: The Ethical Implications," *Journal of Applied Philosophy* 25, no. 2 (2008): 121–33.

23. C.f., Joe Chapa, "Remotely Piloted Aircraft, Risk, and Killing as Sacrifice: The Cost of Remote Warfare," *Journal of Military Ethics* 16, no. 3-4 (2017): 256–71.

24. Philip Alston, Report of the Special Rapporteur on Extrajudicial, Summary or Arbitrary Executions, UN Human Rights Council, May 28, 2010.

25. Christen et al., "Measuring the Moral Impact," 1; Chappelle et al., "Prevalence of High Emotional Distress," 1; Dan Gettinger, "Burdens of War: PTSD and Drone Crews," Center for the Study of the Drone, April 21, 2014, http://dronecenter.bard.edu/burdens-war-crews-drone-aircraft/; Joseph Campo, "From a Distance:

The Psychology of Killing with Remotely Piloted Aircraft" (PhD diss., Air University, Maxwell Air Force Base, 2015).

26. Rob Sparrow, "War without Virtue?," in *Killing by Remote Control*, ed. Bradley Jay Strawser (Oxford: Oxford University Press, 2013).

27. Renni Thornton, "62nd ERS Reaches 250K Flying Hours in AOR," *Kandahar Chronicle: 451st Air Expeditionary Wing*, June 14, 2010, 1.

28. Marcus Schulzke, "Rethinking Military Virtue Ethics in an Age of Unmanned Weapons," *Journal of Military Ethics* 15, no. 3 (2016): 187–204.

29. Joe Chapa and Brad DeWees, "Developing Character at the Frontier of Human Knowledge," *Journal of Character and Leadership Integration* 3, no. 2 (Winter 2016): 74–85.

30. There are really at least two. Though space does not permit a thorough explanation here, an additional strategic-level concern of remote PAR aircraft is what John Kaag and Sarah Kreps call the "moral hazard" problem. They argue that because strategic leaders can use these weapons systems without risk to friendly forces, the normal democratic resistance to war—grounded in concerns over risks to American sons and daughters in combat—is diminished. The result of a weapon system that keeps our own forces safe generates a perverse incentive to employ lethal force where lethal force would have been otherwise unavailable based on the concerns of heavily invested voters. C.f., Kaag and Kreps, *Drone Warfare*, 105–36.

31. U.S. Air Force, "F-22 Raptor," fact sheet, September 2015, http://www.af.mil/AboutUs/FactSheets/Display/tabid/224/Article/104506/f-22-raptor.aspx; David Francis, "How DOD's $1.5 Trillion F-35 Broke the Air Force," *CNBC: The Fiscal Times*, July 31, 2014, http://www.cnbc.com/2014/07/31/how-dods-15-trillion-f-35-broke-the-air-force.html.

32. U.S. Air Force, "MQ-1 Predator"; U.S. Air Force, "MQ-9 Reaper"; U.S. Air Force, "F-22 Raptor."

33. Secretary of the Air Force Public Affairs, "Air Force Senior Leadership Addresses Need to Stabilize RPA Enterprise," January 2015, accessed February 9, 2016, http://www.af.mil/News/ArticleDisplay/tabid/223/Article/560282/air-force-senior-leadership-addresses-need-to-stabilize-rpa-enterprise.aspx.

34. U.S. Air Force, *Air Force Doctrine Annex 3-60: Targeting* (Maxwell AFB, AL: Curtis E. LeMay Doctrine Center, 2017), 2.

35. Department of Defense, *Joint Publication 1: Doctrine of the Armed Forces of the United States* (Washington, DC: Joint Staff, March 2013), I-7, I-8.

36. Rosa Brooks, *How Everything Became War and the Military Became Everything: Tales from the Pentagon* (New York: Simon & Schuster, 2016), 115; Jo Becker and Scott Shane, "Secret 'Kill List' Proves a Test of Obama's Principles and Will," *New York Times*, May 29, 2012, http://www.nytimes.com/2012/05/29/world/obamas-leadership-in-war-on-al-qaeda.html?_r=0.

37. Scott Wilson and Al Kamen, " 'Global War on Terror' Is Given New Name," *Washington Post*, March 25, 2009, http://www.washingtonpost.com/wp-dyn/content/article/2009/03/24/AR2009032402818.html.

38. Seth Lazar, "War," in *Stanford Encyclopedia of Philosophy*, ed. Edward N. Zalta (Metaphysics Research Lab, 2016), https://plato.stanford.edu/cgi-bin/encyclopedia/archinfo.cgi?entry=war.

12

Techno-Partners All Around Us

Civilian Applications for Drones | *Brian Wynne*

On May 9, 2017, Brian Krzanich, Intel chief executive officer (CEO), took the stage at the Association for Unmanned Vehicle Systems International (AUVSI) annual conference and exhibition, XPONENTIAL, and demonstrated how unmanned systems and robotics will change commerce and the way many of us live in the future. Intel was already famous for its drone light shows, including at the 2017 Super Bowl, but at XPONENTIAL Krzanich highlighted the various commercial uses for unmanned systems. He rode to the stage astride the Loomo robot, which Intel builds with Segway, and then he dispatched the Loomo backstage to bring him a cool drink. He had "forgotten" his remote control, so a drone flew it out to him. Then, another of the company's small unmanned aircraft, the Falcon 8+, flew a more complicated mission: it inspected a mock bridge that Intel had built next to the stage for the occasion. Using Intel's Mission Control software and the Falcon 8+'s flexible camera, the unmanned aerial system (UAS) was able to quickly find cracks in the bridge, flying its mission autonomously end to end, sending images and positioning information along the way. Those are just a few examples of the commercial uses for unmanned systems, whether in the air, on the ground, or in the water. As we have seen over the past few years, the list is nearly endless for government, humanitarian purposes, and the burgeoning commercial sector.

To help first responders and government and humanitarian workers do their jobs, unmanned systems can be used for the following tasks:

- Protecting first responders. Unmanned aircraft can minimize the risks facing firefighters, while helping them to act faster and with the best information available to save lives. Able to fly through smoke-filled skies too dangerous for manned flights, UAS give firefighters a better understanding of the circumstances they will encounter at incident scenes, such as the size and scope of a wildfire or hotspots in a burning building, before putting a firefighter in harm's way. For instance, firefighters in the western United States have used UAS for fighting wildfires; UAS have assisted first responders with water drops, supply deliveries, and aerial surveying. The New York City Fire Department is planning to use UAS to provide firefighters with real-time aerial views of fires, enhancing situational awareness. Ground robots can also be used to set small fires to control the movement of larger ones.

- Supporting law enforcement. Drones can help pursue a fugitive or offer a critical vantage point when responding to a hostage situation. For example, in 2013 law enforcement officials in Alabama deployed a UAS in response to a hostage situation. The U.S. Customs and Border Protection Agency has flown UAS to patrol the U.S.-Mexican border, helping prevent drug smuggling and illegal immigration. Drones can monitor remote areas that would take agents days to reach on the ground. UAS also help reduce costs. The purchase price of a UAS is also significantly less than that of a manned aircraft. The average cost of a well-equipped small UAS is comparable to the price of a patrol car with standard police gear. Ground robots have also proved to be a critical tool in the law enforcement kit, helping study and, if needed, dispose of potential bombs or map rooms where armed suspects may be hiding. It is always better to have a robot be the first thing through the door in a high-stakes hostage situation.

- Aiding search and rescue. Drones can reach higher vantage points to survey a large search grid for a missing child, land consumed by wildfires, or water where a boat might be adrift. Bad weather and difficult terrain can prolong search-and-rescue efforts, lowering chances for a victim's survival while raising the financial cost. However, UAS make searching for lost hikers and missing persons cheaper, faster, and safer than manned aircraft. A three-year-old boy in Wisconsin who went missing in an eighty-acre cornfield was found with the help of UAS. During a flood in North Carolina, a UAS operator's Instagram posts led the Federal Emergency Management Agency (FEMA) to a successful rescue of a man trapped in his attic who was unable to contact local emergency services.

- Responding to natural disasters. Drones can enter hazardous areas for long periods in a way that humans simply never could. UAS have been used to survey flooding in the Upper Midwest, assessing damage and providing responders and engineers with live video and radar. UAS were used in search-and-rescue efforts along the Gulf Coast following Hurricane Katrina. And they can give responders visual access to areas devastated by tornadoes, tsunamis, or earthquakes, such as at the 2011 nuclear plant accident in Fukushima, Japan, or in remote areas of Nepal after the 2015 earthquake.

- Advancing scientific research. UAS have been used to help research pathogens, wildlife, volcanoes, climate change, extreme weather, and more. UAS are a cost-effective tool for budget-conscious research institutions such as public universities. They can offer researchers perspectives that are difficult to obtain otherwise: flying into the eye of a hurricane, analyzing the plume of a volcano, and even hovering above whales to collect samples of their spray to study whale health. The National Aeronautics and Space Administration (NASA) has conducted a five-year mission to research changes in hurricane formation and intensity over the Atlantic Ocean by using high-flying Global Hawk aircraft, which can reach from the East Coast of the United States to the shores of Africa. Recently, UAS have also been used to map areas of melting ice in Greenland, survey the spread of avocado fungus, and track endangered wildlife.

- Providing humanitarian assistance. Drones have been deployed to safely deliver provisions to remote or hard-to-reach areas that emergency crews have difficulty reaching because of a disaster, such as an earthquake, flood, or blizzard. After flooding in India in 2013, UAS were used to locate survivors and drop off supplies. Also, the international humanitarian organization Doctors Without Borders is experimenting with UAS to deliver supplies to treat and prevent tuberculosis in remote areas of Papua New Guinea, and Zipline has partnered with Rwanda to deliver medical supplies as well.

The commercial market affords even more opportunities. According to an AUVSI report, "The Economic Impact of Unmanned Aircraft Systems Integration in the United States," the unmanned aircraft industry is poised to create more than 70,000 new American jobs in the first three years following the integration of UAS into the national airspace and 103,776 new jobs in the first decade. Of the 70,000 jobs created in the first three years, 34,000 would be manufacturing jobs. The total economic impact stemming from the integration in the first three years is projected to surpass $13.6 billion and will grow sustainably for the foreseeable future, cumulating in more than $82.1 billion in impact in the first decade following UAS integration.[1]

Some commercial uses include the following:

- Agriculture. Drones can provide farmers with a cost-efficient way to spray for pests and diseases, manage crops, and check for signs of drought and disease. Yamaha uses its RMAX UAS to spray vineyards in California and has been working with the University of California–Davis to research its effectiveness. In addition, researchers at Florida International University have been using UAS equipped with infrared and multispectral cameras to monitor crop health and even predict crop yield or diseases. Ground robots can pluck weeds, distribute fertilizer, and transport workers.

- Oil and gas infrastructure. Oil and gas companies see tremendous value in using UAS to inspect and monitor infrastructure such as hard-to-reach offshore oil rigs or miles of pipeline. General Electric (GE) has developed a UAS that can conduct high-quality pipeline inspections for leaks faster and cheaper than current methods can. UAS have also helped emergency responders in Alaska monitor oil spills and wildlife over the Beaufort Sea.

- Filmmaking. The sports and movie industries see value in using drones to gain new vantage points and conduct aerial filming at a lower cost. For example, Southern California–based Aerial Mob, an innovator in UAS cinematography and technology, is considered a pioneer in the development of UAS safety standards by the Motion Picture Association of America and the Federal Aviation Administration (FAA). The company has filmed Super Bowl promos for NBC, a promo for a new show on Amazon Prime, and a commercial for Apple. The National Football League has expressed interest in replacing Goodyear blimps with UAS, and the Professional Golf Association wants to use UAS for major tournaments. In fact, *In the Robot Skies*, a science fiction movie filmed entirely by UAS, premiered at the London Film Festival in October 2016. Drones also pursued agent 007 across the rooftops of Istanbul for the James Bond movie *Skyfall*, and 500 of them helped Lady Gaga create a memorable spectacle at the 2017 Super Bowl. More than 1,200 Intel Corporation Shooting Star drones flew over the 2018 PyeongChang Winter Olympics.

- Real estate. Real estate professionals have used drones to produce relatively inexpensive aerial photographs and videos of high-end homes for sale. Douglas Trudeau of Tucson, Arizona, was the first realtor to receive approval from the FAA to fly UAS to capture unique aerial perspectives for his listings—images that he could not obtain from the ground. According to an AUVSI analysis, the FAA has granted more than 3,400 exemptions for real estate use. Many real estate professionals now consider UAS to be a standard part of real estate marketing and believe that not hiring UAS operators puts you at a disadvantage in the market.

- Insurance. According to the National Association of Mutual Insurance Companies, insurers are using UAS in risk assessments, especially in dangerous places like high-pitched roofs, and to speed up claims adjudication after disasters, when time is most important in helping victims recover from their losses. In addition, using UAS for simple claims assessment cases has been saving time, effort, and money for employees of Travelers and other insurance companies. AIG, State Farm, and USAA are among other insurance companies that have been approved to fly UAS commercially.
- Materials transport and package deliveries. Ever since Amazon caught the eye of the public with its announcement of its planned Prime Air delivery service on *60 Minutes*, companies have been racing to bring goods to consumers faster than ever before. Many industries have expressed interest in using UAS to transport goods such as household items, gifts, books, and other products. Amazon, Google, Walmart, and China's Alibaba are among the major players that hope to eventually launch UAS delivery services and that are currently testing the concept. Walmart is also planning on using UAS at its factories and warehouses to track inventory efficiently and cheaply.

All of these uses are possible or are even being done. We got a big window into industry's plans for unmanned systems, particularly aircraft, when the FAA created the Section 333 program, which exempted unmanned aircraft from certification requirements (but still required the operator to have a pilot's license). Those exemptions, as they are known, were eagerly sought by commercial enterprises who wanted to use drones. Although they were later mostly superseded by another rule—the FAA's small UAS rule—we learned a lot about industry demand from tracking them. More than 5,500 exemptions were granted, with California leading the way at 639. Florida was second at 571, and Texas came in third with 468. Companies in all fifty states and Puerto Rico received exemptions. Aside from the numbers, one of the most interesting things about exemptions were what they were for. Aerial photography led the way, with 4,789 exemptions. Following closely behind was real estate with 3,434. Other top uses included aerial inspection, aerial survey, construction, infrastructure, agriculture, filmmaking, search and rescue, and emergency management. The bulk of them were granted to small, rotary-wing UAS, most built by DJI Innovations Co. Ltd., the world's largest builder of consumer drones, some models of which have commercial uses as well.[2]

AUVSI monitors the many commercial uses of unmanned systems, and the following examples come from the association's reports, website, or monthly magazine. The actual uses of drones are fascinating. The pulse-quickening sequence *Skyfall*, which was shot in Istanbul, Turkey, is one often-cited example of effective aerial cinematography using a small UAS. Daniel Craig as 007 is shown from above and many other angles as he rides a motorcycle in a wild chase on the roofs of buildings, battles with a bad guy atop a speeding train, plunges off a cliff, and is swept over a roaring waterfall. "While we have already seen movies filmed with SUAS [small unmanned aerial systems] from overseas productions—take for example the roof sequence of 'Skyfall'—the sky is literally the limit in imagining what new angles and views filmmakers will thrill us with next," Lauren Reamy, director of government affairs for the Motion Picture Association of America, told AUVSI.[3] "Every day, moviemakers are increasingly leveraging the latest technologies to advance their craft. Using SUAS is an example of that, one in which audiences will continue to see scenes and shots we could only have imagined a few years ago. . . . Small unmanned aircraft systems are a safer, more efficient and a more flexible alternative in many cases," Reamy continued. "For example, SUAS run on electricity, while manned helicopters require thousands of gallons of gasoline."[4]

"Independent filmmakers and other producers whose budgets don't allow for manned helicopters could save money and broaden their creative possibilities by using drones," said Richard Crudo, president of the American Society of Cinematographers. "The independents will embrace the cheapness of it, and the studios will embrace the trendiness of it."[5]

Real estate professionals working with residential, commercial, and land parcels are also benefitting from the images and information obtained from using UAS technology. This imagery is an incredible tool for potential homeowners moving to a different city, buying a second home, or trying to streamline the research process necessary to buy a new home. Many commercial properties or large parcels of land do not lend themselves well to traditional photography. Capturing the entirety of the plot will give a better representation of the property at hand. Easily viewing images obtained through the use of unmanned aerial vehicle (UAV) technology will help better inform the consumer. Just as digital photography made it easier to create high-quality, affordable images, real estate practitioners look forward to using UAS technology to take their listings to the next level in technical creativity and quality. Many real estate professionals want to hire a professional who offers UAS photography services, while some others obtained FAA waivers and used the machines themselves.

Inspection is another key area of commercial drone use, one that can pose hazards for the people doing the work. One example of a hazardous site to inspect is a flare stack, a device that burns off unusable oil and natural gas at drilling rigs and refineries. Inspecting this flame-tipped tower for damage has traditionally been dangerous and difficult. UAS could make such inspections far safer and easier. Flare stacks can stand several hundred feet tall and emit two-thousand-degree Fahrenheit heat. Having inspectors climb flare stacks or nearby structures or elevating inspectors with sky lifts is risky, and using manned helicopters can be cost prohibitive. Small UAS offer a better option, according to operators and manufacturers. The unmanned vehicles keep people out of harm's way and are relatively inexpensive and simple to operate. Their agility and compact size allow them to easily fly above and around flare stacks, potentially providing better views than other means. And flare stacks do not have to be shut down for UAS inspections.

"Drone technology improves safety, reduces liability, increases accuracy, and saves time and money for our customers while allowing them to continue work as usual during the inspection process," Houston-based Total Safety U.S. Inc., one of several companies that plan to participate in the American UAS flare stack inspection market, told AUVSI.[6]

"The risk to an onboard pilot and crew during an incident or accident is eliminated with the use of a UA [unmanned aircraft] for the inspection operation," the FAA wrote in its approval document for

Total Safety. "In addition, utilizing UAS to conduct flare stack inspections will reduce the need for inspection personnel to perform this hazardous activity."[7] "There are potentially 3,500 inspection sites just in the Gulf of Mexico," said Brian Whiteside, founder and president of VDOS Global, the first company approved for flare stack inspections. "There are something like 60,000 cell phone towers throughout the U.S., one-third of which have to be inspected every year. All the refineries throughout the U.S." are inspection candidates, as are the pipelines and windmills.[8]

The oil and gas industry is also moving to incorporate unmanned systems in other ways. In 2014 British Petroleum (BP) became the first company to be granted permission by the FAA to use UAS during its operations. Once granted this permission, BP began using AeroVironment's Puma AE UAV to conduct flyovers of its Prudhoe Bay oil field on Alaska's North Slope. At the time that BP was granted permission to use UAS, U.S. Secretary of Transportation Anthony Foxx said, "These surveys on Alaska's North Slope are another important step toward broader commercial use of unmanned aircraft. The technology is quickly changing, and the opportunities are growing."[9] He wasn't kidding. In 2016 Silent Falcon UAS were used to conduct inspections and monitor oil and gas production and distribution assets in northwestern New Mexico on behalf of an international oil and gas company. The inspections, which took place over the course of two days, were completed using two different payloads; one to provide aerial visual inspection, the other to detect leaks and inspect liquid levels in tank batteries. The flights were conducted with two goals in mind. The first was to simply provide a visual inspection of numerous wells, compressors, tank batteries, and pipelines, while the second was to detect leaks known as "fugitive hydrocarbon emissions."

During the flights, video evidence and associated metadata collected were live-streamed to the Silent Falcon's ground control station, further confirming the effectiveness of the system during these operations. "Our ability to stay aloft for extended long range missions, quickly change payloads, and provide both live-streaming video and data as well as post flight processing, analysis, exploitation and dissemination of the data collected underscores the effectiveness of the entire

Silent Falcon system in both flight operations and post flight data analysis," Silent Falcon CEO John W. Brown told AUVSI.[10]

Peoples Gas, which distributes gas in Pennsylvania, West Virginia, and Kentucky, also began using UAS in 2016. In this case, the company used UAS to find methane gas leaks along 14,000 miles of natural gas pipelines in the region. "We're flying a drone to get a visual inspection of the pipeline that crosses the bridge," says Peoples Gas spokesman Barry Kukovich, speaking to Pittsburgh's KDKA news. He noted how effective UAS could be when conducting these inspections, especially depending on the location of a leak.[11]

"You can imagine some of the elevations that we have to go up and down. This drone could be much safer for our employees as well."[12] GE one-upped Peoples Gas in 2016, when it developed its own UAS capable of sniffing methane at its brand-new oil and gas technology center in Oklahoma City. The UAS, known as Raven, proved capable of handling its objective, successfully finding gas leaking from two oil well sites in Arkansas during its initial trial run. John Westerheide, the technology leader at GE's Oil and Gas Technology Center in Oklahoma City, told AUVSI that GE designed Raven as a customizable "productivity tool" to augment or replace the current methods used to conduct inspections, while also reducing the costs for inspections.

Agriculture uses shouldn't be ignored either. In AUVSI's market report, we predicted that agriculture would be a major user of these systems, and evidence is mounting that this is the case. For instance, Yamaha is using its RMAX unmanned helicopter to spray grape vines in California's famous Napa Valley. Some of the vines are on hillsides, which are dangerous and tedious for people to spray manually. Many vintners in the valley don't use manned aircraft for spraying, instead relying on ground tractors. Spraying crops with those can take much longer—tractors can travel only about three miles per hour, while the RMAX can move along at twelve to fifteen miles per hour. Even if manned aircraft were used in Napa, the RMAX would have some advantages. It can fly very low over the grapes, thereby minimizing fertilizer waste and runoff, and it is more nimble and able to steer away from the houses and other structures that share the space with the vineyards.

In 2016 the FAA exemptions process was largely replaced by the Part 107 rule, also known as the small UAS rule. This kept some provisions present in the exemptions—no flights over four hundred feet, aircraft must remain in the line of sight of the operator, no flights over people—but did away with the requirement of a pilot's license, instead requiring a knowledge-based test. Thousands upon thousands of operators could now take to the sky and make money with their aircraft and have done so. Federal Aviation Administrator Michael Huerta said in mid-2017 that about 60,000 commercial operators had registered their aircraft with the FAA, and the agency had issued more than 43,000 remote pilot certificates, both numbers that have only continued to grow. In fact, the FAA expects that more than 400,000 UAS could be flying for commercial purposes over the next five years—a more than sixfold increase from today. "It wasn't that long ago that we were talking about how drones might be used for aerial photography or package delivery," Huerta said in his last appearance as administrator at AVUSI's XPONENTIAL in May 2017.

> Now, we're having very intense and very real conversations about a day in the not-that-distant future when a drone taxi might lift you above the rush-hour traffic in a dense metropolitan area and make sure you get to that meeting across town on time. Now, clearly there's a lot to be done between here and there. But it's a "there" that has only come on to the horizon recently. This pace of this development is something that we talk about a lot. It's something that inspires a great deal of awe. In the traditional aircraft industry, new jetliners are introduced maybe once every 10 or 15 years. In the world of unmanned aircraft, 10 or 15 new products might be introduced every year.[13]

Indeed, numerous challenges remain, and we have only scratched the surface of what can be accomplished with unmanned systems. Many companies and individual operators obviously want to go beyond what the FAA currently allows. As part of the Part 107 process, the FAA also set up a waiver provision that would allow operators to fly in ways not otherwise permitted. The number one petition for these new waivers? To be able to fly at night. One of the first companies to get such a waiver was Intel, which has made such a splash with its nighttime drone shows—really a form of advanced fireworks. The second most popular request was to fly multiple drones at once, and the third was to fly beyond line of sight. Those two provisions will be critical in enabling what could be one of the most pervasive uses of drones, for package delivery. Imagine ordering something from Amazon and getting it within half an hour, straight to your door; that is the promise of Amazon Prime Air, and Google, UPS, China's Alibaba, and others are also investigating this service. The state of Virginia has even demonstrated the delivery of Chipotle burritos to hungry college students.

At a hearing before Congress in 2017, I told members of the House Appropriations Committee's Subcommittee on Transportation, Housing, and Urban Development that the FAA needs more funding to facilitate the full integration of UAS into the national airspace and to make some of these commercial uses viable. "The UAS industry is primed for incredible growth, thanks to industry representatives and government regulators nurturing innovation that helps more businesses be more competitive in the marketplace than ever before," I told committee members. "We hope that these efforts can be sustained and that we continue to reach new historic milestones in integrating this technology into the national airspace. Vital to these efforts, however, is an FAA that is appropriately funded and empowered to engage meaningfully in the process, alongside industry stakeholders."[14] To help pave the way for a true, holistic plan for full UAS integration that includes beyond line of sight operations, flights over people, and access to higher altitudes and platforms above fifty-five pounds and to safely manage the hundreds of thousands of UAS anticipated to operate in American skies, the FAA needs to automate its UAS processes. Many of those processes are done manually today, leading to sometimes lengthy delays, although the FAA has tried to speed them up. The FAA needs more employees dedicated to developing UAS rules for more complex operations beyond Part 107; those additional resources are necessary to advance UAS regulations that will help enhance the safety and security of the national airspace.

Notes

1. The Association for Unmanned Vehicle Systems International, "The Economic Impact of Unmanned Aircraft Systems Integration in the United States," AUVSI, March 2013, http://www.auvsi.org/our-impact/economic-report.

2. The Association for Unmanned Vehicle Systems International, "Waivers under Part 107: Interactive Report," http://www.auvsi.org/our-impact/waivers-under-part-107-interactive-report.

3. The Association for Unmanned Vehicle Systems International, "Motion Picture: How Hollywood Says the Sky's the Limit for Unmanned Aerial Cinematography," AUVSI News, February 4, 2015, http://www.auvsi.org/motion-picture-hollywood-says-sky%E2%80%99s-limit-unmanned-aerial-cinematography.

4. Ibid.

5. Ibid.

6. The Association for Unmanned Vehicle Systems International, "The First 1,000 Commercial UAS Exemptions," AUVSI, https://higherlogicdownload.s3.amazonaws.com/AUVSI/b657da80-1a58-4f8f-9971-7877b707e5c8/UploadedFiles/ZAvlB-nqWSeSYXPsnKkoc_Section333Report_online022516.pdf, p. 9.

7. Ibid.

8. Ibid.

9. W. J. Hennigan, "FAA Allows First Commercial Drone Flights over Land," *LA Times*, June 10, 2014, http://www.latimes.com/business/la-fi-0611-faa-bp-drone-20140611-story.html.

10. Silent Falcon, "Silent Falcon UAS Inspects Oil and Gas Operations in New Mexico," http://www.silentfalconuas.com/post/silent-falcon-uas-inspects-oil-and-gas-operations-in-new-mexico.

11. Jon Delano, "Peoples Gas Experimenting with Drones to Detect Gas Leaks," CBS News, November 18, 2016, https://pittsburgh.cbslocal.com/2016/11/18/peoples-gas-experimenting-with-drones-to-detect-gas-leaks/.

12. Ibid.

13. Michael Huerta, "AUVSI Xponential," (lecture, Dallas, TX, May 10, 2017), https://www.faa.gov/news/speeches/news_story.cfm?newsId=21654.

14. Association for Unmanned Vehicle Systems International, "AUVSI Describes Vision for UAS Integration in Senate Testimony," May 8, 2018, http://www.auvsi.org/auvsi-describes-vision-uas-integration-senate-testimony.

13

The View Downrange

The Decades Ahead | *John Edward Jackson*

Whatever they are called—drones, robots, or unmanned systems—these "digital assistants" will have a profound impact on the way people live and the way combat is conducted in the future. Experts such as P. W. Singer and others believe that today's drones are at the developmental stage analogous to where the Model-T Ford was in the early days of the automobile and where personal computers were in the early 1980s. As impressive as current capabilities may be, they pale in comparison with where they will be in ten, fifteen, or twenty years.

The exponential increase in the capabilities of intelligent machines has at its base some simple laws of physics and the growth of micro-miniature manufacturing. What is commonly referred to as Moore's law is not a law in the legal or scientific sense. Instead, it is a prediction made in 1965 by Gordon Moore, the cofounder of Intel Corporation, that the number of transistors on a microchip would double every two years. This prediction held true for four decades and then accelerated until we now see such growth about every eighteen months. These incredibly small and complex microchips enable unimaginable levels of computing power. For example, in 2016 Intel's Xeon Broadwell chip contained 7.2 billion transistors on a single chip. Better microchips (and other factors) lead to faster, more powerful, and cheaper computers for virtually every application. The cofounder of Sun Microsystems, Bill Joy, has predicted that by 2030 we will have computers a million times more powerful than today's personal computers. One must wonder about the astounding computerized world that could exist in a few short decades.

The Campaign to Stop Killer Robots

Countless stories have been written, and movies produced, about intelligent and malevolent robots who turn on their human masters. Whether the threat comes from all-powerful Skynet in the *Terminator* movies or from the Cylons in television's *Battlestar Galactica*, the drama is derived from humanity's struggle to defeat mechanical super machines. Flesh-and-blood *Homo sapien* is portrayed as slower, weaker, and less intelligent than its artificial opponents. The tipping point in the narrative usually occurs when the robots reach a level of self-awareness (or sentience) that makes them question the master-servant or master-slave relationship. The previous chapters have looked in some detail at the meaning of "One Nation under Drones." It is fair to ask who will be in charge: man or machine. While the question may seem ridiculous on the surface, many critics with impressive credentials believe action must be taken now to forestall a future that does not bode well for humanity.

A sentient or conscious machine would have a capacity to feel, perceive, and exercise a need for self-preservation. It would have a level of intelligence equal to or greater than a human being and would also be able to display desire, ambition, will, ethics, personality, and other human qualities. Turning again to science fiction, the character Data, an android or artificial human, appears in the television series *Star Trek: The Next Generation* and several movie spin-offs. He is shown in a permanent quest to become more humanlike and even tries to understand and use humor in his actions with other crew members. The fictional story line of *Star Trek: The Next Generation* takes place more than three centuries into the future, in the year 2338. But a growing movement of critics sees a dangerous future much closer to today.

In July 2015 more than a thousand scientists, engineers, and experts in the area of artificial intelligence (AI) signed a public letter warning of the threat represented by further research into military-focused intelligent machines and calling for a ban on developing autonomous weapons. Released at the Twenty-Fourth International Joint Conference on

Artificial Intelligence in Buenos Aires, the letter included noted inventors and scholars among its signatories: astrophysicist Stephen Hawking, Tesla founder Elon Musk, Apple cofounder Steve Wozniak, cognitive scientist Noam Chomsky, and others. The participation of such luminaries demonstrates that the concerns are not coming from some neo-Luddite fringe element, but rather from some of the most highly regarded minds of our time. Stephen Hawking was quoted by the BBC as saying, "The development of full artificial intelligence could spell the end of the human race. It would take off on its own, and re-design itself at an ever increasing rate. Humans, who are limited by slow biological evolution, couldn't compete, and would be superseded."[1] Elon Musk has called AI "our biggest existential threat."[2] A less-alarmist group of researchers suggests that such threats could be mitigated by the manner in which artificial "brains" are designed and built.

Continuing with the notion expressed throughout this book that concepts developed by science fiction writers can be useful when one considers possible future events, it is informative to review how human control over AI-based systems was handled by award-winning author Isaac Asimov. He solved the problem by imprinting on the "positronic" brains of high-order robots what he referred to as the "Three Laws of Robotics." Writing in 1942, he quotes from the fictitious *Handbook of Robotics*, 56th edition, 2058 AD, which defined the three laws as follows:

> First Law: A robot may not harm a human being, or through inaction allow a human being to come to harm.
>
> Second Law: A robot must obey the orders given to it by human beings except when such orders would conflict with the First Law.
>
> Third Law: A robot must protect its own existence as long as such protection does not conflict with the First or Second Law.[3]

In Asimov's stories, whenever robots encountered situations that violated any of the laws, the circuitry in their "positronic brains" would be damaged beyond repair, and the robot would become inert. Robots following these three laws appeared in more than four dozen of Asimov's novels and short stories. After his death in 1992, his estate authorized medical doctor Mickey Zucker Reichert to publish a trilogy of books that tell how the "positronic brain" was developed in the earliest years of Asimov's robotic universe. Asimov's original books and Reichert's prequels are recommended reading for those interested in "future history."

Robots programmed to follow something like Asimov's three laws could be an answer to humanity's present-day, real-world concerns, and a number of top-ranked computer scientists and engineers are working on versions of these laws today. First among them is Georgia Tech's Ron Arkin, whose ideas on how autonomous systems might lessen the risk to noncombatants in a warzone were detailed in chapter 10 of this book. If robots could be programmed to follow the laws of war rather than the fictitious Laws of Robotics, they could truly become trusted partners on the battlefield.

Where Are We Today?

Putting aside the existential questions embedded in some possible man versus machine contest, we find ourselves at some point along a developmental and operational continuum that ranges from dumb machines controlled 100 percent of the time by human operators to robotic soldiers given a set of targets and released to exterminate them in any manner they see fit. In 2018 military systems fall clearly on the "dumb machines" side of the scale, although trends are moving inexorably toward the right. Virtually all military unmanned systems used today are controlled by a remote operator, and decisions to kill are firmly in the hands of a unit commander. The policy of the U.S. Department of Defense as codified in Instruction 3000.09 of November 21, 2012, is "autonomous and semi–autonomous weapons systems shall be designed to allow commanders and operators to exercise appropriate levels of human judgement over the use of force."[4] This directive addresses autonomous systems that can perform a limited set of actions and activities without direct human supervision. It is a substantial (if not impossible) leap from task-based autonomy to generalized artificial intelligence, but autonomous machines are a reality today and constitute the first steps down a path that could result in artificially intelligent "thinking machines." This path is filled with the potential for both good and evil, and it is up to us to determine how we follow this path into the future. Examples of drones being used for evil purposes are not hard to find. It was widely reported in the international press on September 15, 2013, when a quadrotor drone crash-landed mere feet from German chancellor Angela Merkel during a campaign rally in Dresden, Germany. Investigators ultimately determined that the unarmed drone had been flown by members of the Pirate Party to protest the use of drones by countries in the European Union.

A much more serious incident occurred on August 4, 2018, in Caracas, Venezuela, when two explosive-laden hexacopters (6-bladed drones) were used in an apparent assassination attempt on President Nicholas Maduro, who was interrupted while speaking at a military parade and hustled to safety. The Maduro incident was the first such armed attack on a national leader, but potentially not the last. Security forces must, in the future, be concerned with both ground-level attack and possible danger from above.

Taken together, the writers of each of the preceding chapters (and your humble editor) envision a future in which robotic and unmanned systems continue to be refined as powerful tools. They will be used to improve the human condition by freeing many workers from the drudgery of repetitious manual labor; to increase agricultural production through the use of precision agricultural methods; and to take men and women out of jobs that are dull, dirty, and dangerous. Our hope is that this future world will be more peaceful, but if that is not the case, robotic and unmanned weapons will be used to fight more efficiently, more humanely, and with greater precision. They will shift conflict away from the potential need to use weapons of mass destruction to a more focused application of force when and where it is necessary.

This is what it will mean to live in "One Nation under Drones"!

Notes

1. Rory Cellan-Jones, "Stephen Hawking Warns Artificial Intelligence Could End Mankind," BBC News, December 2, 2014, https://www.bbc.com/news/technology-30290540.
2. Ibid.
3. Quoted in "Asimov's Laws of Robotics," Razor Robotics, February 6, 2017, https://www.razorrobotics.com/laws-of-robotics/.
4. Department of Defense Directive, "Autonomy in Weapon Systems," November 21, 2012, Number 3000.09, http://www.esd.whs.mil/Portals/54/Documents/DD/issuances/dodd/300009p.pdf.

Contributors

Dr. Ron Arkin

Ron Arkin is Regents' Professor, director of the Mobile Robot Laboratory, and associate dean for research in the College of Computing at the Georgia Institute of Technology. He has earned a PhD from the University of Massachusetts, an MS from Stevens Institute of Technology, and a BS from the University of Michigan. The thematic umbrella for his research is multiagent control and perception in the context of robotics and computer vision. A primary thrust is the use of models of existing biological motor and perceptual systems, as developed by neuroscientists and cognitive scientists, within intelligent robotic systems. The emphasis is on generalizable, flexible methods for intelligent robotic control. A high-level goal is to produce survivable robotic systems capable of fitting into a particular ecological niche and successfully competing and cooperating with other environmental agents.

Maj Joe Chapa, USAF

Joseph Chapa is a major in the U.S. Air Force and an instructor of philosophy at the U.S. Air Force Academy. He holds an MA in philosophy from Boston College, an MA in theological studies from Liberty Baptist Theological Seminary, and a BA in philosophy from Boston University. His areas of expertise include the just war tradition, military ethics, and especially the ethics of remote weapons. He is also an Air Force senior pilot with more than a thousand flight and instructor hours in support of major U.S. combat and humanitarian operations.

LTC Christopher M. Ford, USA

Christopher Ford attended Furman University in Greenville, South Carolina, and received a BA in 1999. He then graduated from the University of South Carolina School of Law in 2002. Entering active-duty service in 2003, he attended the Judge Advocate General's Corps Officer Basic Course in Fort Lee, Virginia, and Charlottesville, Virginia. He later served as an assistant professor at the U.S. Military Academy (West Point) and as the executive officer for the Department of Law. In 2010 he earned a Master of Law degree in military law, with an international and operational law specialty, from the U.S. Army Judge Advocate General's Legal Center and School, Charlottesville, Virginia.

Dan Gettinger

Dan Gettinger is a writer and photographer covering national security and technology. He is a founder and the codirector of the Center for the Study of the Drone at Bard College. Gettinger has written for *Drone360* and *Motherboard* and has been quoted or cited by the BBC, NBC News, *Wired, The Verge, Forbes,* WAMC, *The Intercept,* and *TakePart,* among others. He is the coauthor of *The Drone Primer: A Compendium of the Key Issues.* Gettinger holds a BA in political studies from Bard College. He served as photo editor in preparation of this book.

CAPT John Edward Jackson, USN (Ret.)

John Edward Jackson is a senior professor at the U.S. Naval War College, Newport, Rhode Island, where he holds the E. A. Sperry Chair of Unmanned and Robotic Systems. He also teaches in the area of national security affairs and concurrently serves as program manager for the Chief of Naval Operations Professional Reading Program. A longtime proponent of emerging technology, he has taught one of the college's most popular elective courses, Unmanned Systems and Conflict in the Twenty-First Century, since the 2009 academic year. Retiring as a Navy captain in 1998 after twenty-seven years of service in the logistics and graduate education fields, he holds a bachelor's degree in speech and communications from the University of New Mexico, a master's degree in education from Providence College, a master's degree in management from Salve Regina University, a Certificate of Advanced Graduate Studies from Salve Regina University, and a diploma from the Naval War College. He has been listed in *Who's Who in America* since 1997.

Konstantin Kakaes

Konstantin Kakaes was a fellow at New America. He is the author of *The Pioneer Detectives*, an e-book about space exploration. Before coming to New America, Kakaes was a Knight Science Journalism Fellow at the Massachusetts Institute of Technology. He was the *Economist*'s bureau chief in Mexico City from 2005 to 2009, and before that he covered science and technology for the *Economist* from London. He has a BA in physics from Harvard.

Dr. Robbin Laird

Robbin Laird received his PhD from Columbia University in 1974 and has worked in several major think tanks. He has been associated with the Research Institute of International Change at Columbia University, worked as special assistant for the director of the Defense Intelligence Agency, was a research staff member at the Center of Naval Analyses, and served as a senior staff member of the Institute for Defense Analysis, where he worked on issues for the Joint Chiefs of Staff and Office of the Secretary of Defense. Over the past two decades, he has been affiliated with several research institutions while running his consulting firm. He served as senior adviser to Michael Wynne during Wynne's tenure as secretary of the U.S. Air Force and as head and deputy of the Office of Acquisition, Technology, and Logistics. Laird is a senior adviser to the U.S. Marine Corps Aviation Command and to the chief of staff of the U.S. Coast Guard on a variety of strategic issues.

Dr. George R. Lucas Jr.

George R. Lucas Jr. is an internationally recognized authority in the field of military and applied ethics, focusing in particular on ethics and emerging military technologies. He has written and lectured extensively on policy and ethics pertaining to cyber conflict and unmanned systems. He has served as the Distinguished Chair in Ethics in the Vice Admiral James B. Stockdale Center for Ethical Leadership at the U.S. Naval Academy, as professor of ethics and public policy at the Graduate School of Public Policy at the Naval Postgraduate School, and as a visiting professor at the U.S. Naval War College. Professor Lucas is the author of seven books, of over sixty peer-reviewed articles and book chapters, and of translations, book reviews, and essays in public media.

Arthur Holland Michel

Arthur Holland Michel is an author, researcher, and the codirector of the Center for the Study of the Drone at Bard College, an interdisciplinary research and education institute that examines the challenges and opportunities associated with the proliferation of unmanned systems technology in military and civilian spheres. Holland Michel is particularly interested in how stakeholders can leverage innovative research and inquiry-driven resources to get ahead of the adoption curve of emerging technologies and effectively anticipate the potential social, economic, legal, and ethical implications of these systems. He has written extensively about drones, robots, and defense for a variety of publications. He is author of several research reports, including *The Drone Primer: A Compendium of the Key Issues*, *Drone Sightings and Close Encounters: An Analysis*, *Local and State Drone Laws*, and *The Drone Revolution Revisited: An Assessment of Military Unmanned Systems in 2016*. He is the author of the forthcoming book about airborne surveillance, *Eyes in the Sky*, to be published by Houghton Mifflin Harcourt in spring 2019.

Maj Dillon R. Patterson, USAF

Dillon Patterson holds a BS from Embry-Riddle Aeronautical University and an MA from the U.S. Naval War College. He formerly served in the Director's Action Group, Office of the Director of the Air National Guard. He now serves as the commander, 214th Operations Support Squadron. He is a remotely piloted aircraft pilot with more than three thousand hours of flight operations over Afghanistan, Iraq, and East Africa. He served as a mission pilot in the RQ-170 Sentinel and as an evaluator pilot in the MQ-1B Predator. Patterson has deployed as a liaison officer to joint task forces in Afghanistan and Iraq.

Dr. Michael N. Schmitt

Michael Schmitt is professor of public international law at Exeter Law School. Additionally, he serves as the Charles H. Stockton Professor at the U.S. Naval War College and Francis Lieber Distinguished

Scholar at the Lieber Institute of the U.S. Military Academy at West Point. Schmitt is a senior fellow at the NATO Cyber Defence Centre of Excellence, senior research associate at Hebrew University, affiliate at Harvard's Program on International Law and Armed Conflict, and general editor of both *International Law Studies* and the Lieber Studies series. He served twenty years in the U.S. Air Force as a judge advocate specializing in operational and international law. The author of over 150 scholarly publications, he has several academic degrees, including a D.Litt (Durham University), JD (University of Texas), LL.M (Yale University), and two MAs (Naval War College and Texas State University). He is a life member of the Council on Foreign Relations and a fellow of the Royal Society of the Arts. In 2017 he was awarded the Order of the Cross of Terra Mariana by the president of Estonia for his work in promoting cyber defense.

Dr. P. W. Singer

P. W. Singer is strategist at New America and an editor at *Popular Science* magazine. He has been named by the Smithsonian as one of the nation's hundred leading innovators, by Defense News as one of the hundred most influential people in defense issues, by *Foreign Policy* to their Top 100 Global Thinkers List, as an official "Mad Scientist" for the U.S. Army's Training and Doctrine Command, and by Onalytica social media data analysis as one of the ten most influential voices in the world on cybersecurity and twenty-fifth most influential in the field of robotics. Singer's award-winning books include *Corporate Warriors: The Rise of the Privatized Military Industry*, *Children at War*, *Wired for War: The Robotics Revolution and Conflict in the 21st Century*, and *Cybersecurity and Cyberwar: What Everyone Needs to Know*. His latest is *Ghost Fleet: A Novel of the Next World War*, a techno thriller crossed with nonfiction research, which has been endorsed by people who range from the chairman of the Joint Chiefs to the co-inventor of the Internet to the writer of HBO's *Game of Thrones*. His past work includes serving as coordinator of the Obama-08 campaign's defense policy task force, in the Office of the Secretary of Defense, and as the founding director of the Center for 21st Century Security and Intelligence at Brookings, where he was the youngest person named senior fellow in its hundred-year history.

Dr. Robert Sparrow

Robert Sparrow is an Australian Research Council Future Fellow in the Philosophy Program and a professor in the Centre for Human Bioethics at Monash University, where he works on ethical issues raised by new technologies. He was previously employed in the Philosophy Department at the University of Wollongong and at the Centre for Applied Philosophy and Public Ethics at the University of Melbourne. His current research interests include the ethics of pre-implantation genetic diagnosis, technologies of human enhancement, stem cell technologies, artificial organs, and the ethics of robotics. He also has published on xenotransplantation, human cloning, and the ethics of nanotechnology. He is cochair of the IEEE Technical Committee on Robot Ethics.

Brian Wynne

Brian Wynne is the president and CEO of the Association for Unmanned Vehicle Systems International (AUVSI), the largest association representing the unmanned systems and robotics industries. He previously held a senior leadership role at the Intelligent Transportation Society of America and was CEO of the Association for Automatic Identification and Mobility. He holds a bachelor's degree from the University of Scranton and a master's degree from the School of Advanced International Studies at Johns Hopkins University, and he was a Fulbright Scholar at the University of Cologne in Germany.

Index

Names beginning with al and al- are alphabetized under the main element of the name. For example, al Qaeda is alphabetized under Q.